THE WORLD OF PELÉ

THE WORLD OF PELÉ

BY JOE MARCUS

MASON/CHARTER

NEW YORK 1976

1 2 3 4 5 6 7 8 9 10

Library of Congress Cataloging in Publication Data

Marcus, Joe, 1933–
The world of Pelé.
1. Nascimento, Edson Arantes do, 1940– I. Title.
GV942.7.N3M36 796.33′4′0924 [B] 76–14214
ISBN 0–88405–366–0

This book is dedicated to my two sons, Bruce and Arthur, and to all the youngsters, both male and female, who are sure to benefit in their soccer upbringing because of Pelé's decision to play in the United States.

ACKNOWLEDGMENTS

The author would like to thank all who made this book possible. Special thanks go to Webb McKinley, the World Service editor of the Associated Press; to Professor Julio Mazzei, who helped recount some of Pelé's experiences; to Bob Beyer, Pelé's long-time friend in the United States, who helped with the clarification of various details; to Reid Boates, my editor; and especially to Pelé, whose decision to end his retirement and play for the New York Cosmos not only propelled my interest in writing this book but also—I feel—gave soccer in the United States and Canada the shot in the arm it so desperately needed.

CONTENTS

FOREWORD

Ever since I first became involved in soccer, two names have meant the most to me. One was Pelé, the name of the finest player the game has ever produced. I longed for a chance to play goal against him. I had that chance in 1975, while I was a member of the Boston Minutemen. I will always remember the games in which I matched skills against him.

The other name was that of Joe Marcus, an outstanding soccer writer with a long and fruitful career in the sport not only as a reporter but as a coach and manager. A typical Saturday might well see Joe up early in the morning to coach a team of youngsters, then on his way to a college game, going directly from there to a professional game. Unlike many other reporters, Joe doesn't simply report who scored the goals; he goes deep into the game, explaining how a goal was set up and scored. I have been reading reports from Joe for many years; his reporting in papers and magazines around the world and his colorful commentary on such outstanding events as the World Cup are among the best in the history of the sport.

Joe's book on Pelé is an outstanding job not only of writing but of reporting the many and often distorted stories we have heard. The way Joe describes the scene in Boston the night Pelé was mobbed and injured by overeager fans is a perfect example of his reporting ability. I was there when Pelé was thrown to the ground; even though Joe was in the press box, which itself was a wild scene, he was able to get the facts accurately and report back to his readers. His account of the way Pelé lives is something I am sure fans all over will get a kick out of reading.

Pelé's name will live in the history of soccer, and I feel this book will be one of the best accounts both of Pelé's life and of the sport of soccer since he arrived on the scene. Joe Marcus deserves a great deal of credit for the story of Pelé, truly the man who is the king of soccer.

SHEP MESSING
Goalie
Boston Minutemen, U.S. Olympic Team and Pan-American Games;
Member, U.S. team to the Maccabiah Games in Israel

INTRODUCTION

The name Pelé has no literal translation in Portuguese, but to soccer fans all over the world it has come to mean the best man ever to don a pair of soccer boots. Even those Americans who had never seen a soccer game knew that by the acquisition of Pelé the New York Cosmos of the North American Soccer League had signed the top team athlete in the world. The cost was high. It is estimated that Warner Communications, the group which owns the Cosmos, spent between $4,000,000 and $7,000,000 for Pelé's services over a three-year period.

The great success Pelé has enjoyed since breaking into the headlines as a sixteen-year-old performer for Santos of Brazil when he was selected to play for the Brazilian National Team has not made him aloof. His nature is unique among other top athletes; unlike them, he does recognize that the average man, whether a youngster or some disabled person, has the right to stop him and talk about soccer. After many weary hours running clinics in some small African country or in the United States, he takes more time to sign autographs and ask the youngsters how they enjoy playing soccer. Some might call him a simple man, but he's simple only in the way he expresses kindness for the average man. If that's simple then we need more of his kind. But put Pelé together with a group of businessmen who are trying to get him to endorse a product or join them in a venture, and Pelé turns into a cold, calculating, shrewd business executive.

Pelé is a typical proud father and the love he expresses for his son as he carries the youngster to Randalls Island, where the Cosmos play their home games, is carried over to his concern about the well-being of children who have come to see him play. His concern on one occasion in Dallas was that his security guards should not step over the hundreds of youngsters who lined Texas Stadium bowing to him, the undisputed king of soccer. During his first season Pelé was injured, but again his concern for those less fortunate than he was evident as he trotted over to a group of disabled persons who were sitting in their wheelchairs and personally greeted each of them.

Pelé is not always strictly business either on or off the field. There was the time when Joe Namath, one of the most popular players in the National Football League, got together with Pelé to endorse a commercial product. Pelé was intrigued by the American football Joe was holding and started bouncing it off his own head. After the meeting and the signing of the contract, Joe went back to the field where his Jets were practicing, while Pelé talked to about 100 youngsters who had come to witness the two great stars in action. Those who saw the two, Joe and Pelé, together also got the opportunity to witness Pelé's concern for his fellow man. He was concerned that Namath had such bad knees.

Pelé's concern for people, especially those who are ailing, is evident as he spends a great deal of time visiting children's hospitals both in his native Brazil as well as in foreign countries where he might be. Sometimes his concern causes his team some worry: once the entire Cosmo delegation almost missed a plane because Pelé was taking too long to sign autographs for a group of Japanese businessmen who happened to be at the airport in Vancouver at the same time the Cosmos were departing for New York.

Throughout his long career, Pelé has had many meetings with royalty as well as heads of state and even the Pope, but give him a group of youngsters to talk to and he's much more at ease. Often he has bewildered his security guards by insisting on stopping and watching a group of youngsters play in a preliminary game—just as he did before he held a press conference with the Cosmos prior to joining them. And many a youngster has been thrilled as Pelé, even after being seriously injured, stopped and talked to them despite the warnings of his coach, his teammates and even his bodyguards. Emotions are certainly strong with Pelé; he still takes a defeat as hard today as he did when he first started playing street soccer with his friends in his youthful days in Brazil.

Pelé hasn't always had a rich carpet to walk on. His life as a youngster was a hard one, and he had to fight his way to the top. He fought when his friends gave him the name Pelé because he didn't like it. He fought with opponents to demonstrate to them, not by using his fists, but by using his skill that he is the best ever in soccer.

Pelé didn't like going to school. He'd much rather play hooky and practice soccer. Finally he quit school and went to work for about $2 a month as a cobbler's apprentice. He still shows a lot of skill today in fixing his soccer boots.

Working many hours a day and practicing soccer in his spare time, young Pelé built up quite a reputation around his area before former Brazilian star player Waldemir de Brito discovered him. De Brito knew when he first saw Pelé play that he was indeed more than just another youngster playing the world's most popular sport. In the following pages, you'll relive those early days and the hard work that went into starting Pelé on the road to what he is today.

From those early days of training Pelé recalls some of the incidents that led him eventually into a Santos uniform and on the road to stardom. From the time he was named to the National Team of Brazil until he was a firm fixture on the Brazilian World Cup team there were anxious moments when even a man like Pelé felt disappointment.

During the first two games of the 1958 World Cup, held in Sweden, he sat on the bench with an injury. Then he finally got a chance to show his talent: after scoring what has to be the most incredible goal ever scored in World Cup competition, he was hailed like no other soccer player had ever been before. But four years later injuries prevented him from playing an active role in Brazil's second straight World Cup win, and four years after that in England he paid dearly for his fame and talent as he was butchered by Bulgarian defenders. Pelé, he said then, was through with World Cup competition.

So loved and respected was Pelé that when he was injured, the people of Brazil turned out in force to pray for the recovery of "Our Savior." Pelé didn't recover sufficiently to help the Brazilian cause, and the team was eliminated. Since to many in Brazil soccer is more a religion than a sport, police were kept busy preventing suicide attempts. Some of their efforts failed: numerous persons jumped to their deaths from bridges.

Pelé was so disgusted that he swore never to play another World

Cup. Of course he later changed his mind, and the Brazilian people were grateful—especially after his efforts helped Brazil retire the Jules Rimet Trophy.

Following the 1966 World Cup, Pelé was called on to face a challenge for his title of king of soccer, and how convincingly he managed to emerge again as the top player of all time showed once more that Il Re, The King, as the Italians call him, is at his best when the pressure mounts.

Meanwhile, playing was not the only thing that kept Pelé busy. He was becoming involved in various business activities, and love—in the form of an attractive Caucasian girl, Rosemarie—entered into his life. How he handled the secret courtship is just another one of the things Pelé does so well.

Santos, meanwhile, was busy booking games around the world, and the fans were coming to see Pelé perform his magic, doing things no other player in the long history of the sport has ever been able to do and, many feel, will never be done again. For Pelé is one of a kind.

The courtship led to marriage, and here again Pelé showed tact as he took his wedding vows. It could well have been the largest wedding ceremony ever held in Brazil, but instead it was a simple, dignified affair.

Marriage didn't slow Pelé down, as he agreed to play for Brazil in the 1970 World Cup in Mexico. Before the final game, Pelé was again with children, youngsters from a Mexican orphanage. He made them a promise and later did everything to make sure that he kept it.

The celebrated salute Pelé gives the crowd every time he scores a goal came early in that 1970 final game against Italy as Brazil humiliated the Italians and Pelé was indeed super. Now it was time for him to devote more of his efforts to his business interests, but still wherever he went with the Santos team the fans were there. And as always Pelé dealt humanely with the people in the street.

There was the happiness of being a new father and of building for the future. Then there was one of the greatest moments in sports when Pelé notched his 1000th goal, a feat once never believed to be possible.

Pelé and Rosie got settled in their $600,000 mansion, a home fit for a king but actually designed by the couple strictly as their home and not a showplace. Read Pelé's long-time friend Bob Beyer's description of the house, and you'll see that indeed it is the home of the Nascimentos.

Then came time for Pelé to think about retiring from the sport he had given so much to and taken so much from, not only in money but in the means of enjoying the pleasures of life—a far cry from his early days.

He hit the Brazilian people hard when he announced that he would quit the National Team. Politicians as well as average fans begged him to change his mind, but Pelé turned them down. He felt that if Brazil was to win the 1974 World Cup it would have to be without him. The people, who had rooted so hard so often for him, now were angry at him. They even booed him on occasion and tried to persuade him to alter his mind. But it was once said that when Pelé makes up his mind, he usually sticks to his decision, no matter what the consequences.

Finally it was time for him to play an exhibition game for Brazil against Yugoslavia. The fans, more than 150,000 of them, turned out for the encounter. Everyone was there, including the president of Brazil, who made a futile personal plea to Pelé to reconsider. The day of the game arrived and at the end of the first half Pelé wound up his Brazilian National Team career. The emotion on the part of Pelé and on the part of the fans brought shivers to many who were there that day and millions of others who watched the finale of his National Team career on closed-circuit television. As he trotted around the field, the crowd, to a man, woman and child, stood and begged him to stay, yelling *Fica! Fica!* time and again. But Pelé had made up his mind and he joined the Brazilian president in the special box of honor to watch his teammates play the second half.

There were hopes on the part of some, although they later proved to be unfounded, that Pelé would once again play for Brazil. But as it came time for Brazil to select their team for the 1974 World Cup, Pelé stood firm in his decision despite the fact that it brought to his ears insults and to his house gunshots.

Although he was finished with the National Team, there was still a great deal of soccer left in Pelé and he demonstrated it whenever he played with Santos. The Santos tours took him all over the globe and even to Nigeria where his crowd appeal caused a three-day ceasefire in the war between Nigeria and Biafra.

In 1974 he made his decision to end his playing career. The stadium at Santos was a carnival as everyone turned out to see the king end his playing days . . . or so they thought. Pelé was drained of emotion at the end of the game and headed for the seclusion of his private ranch. But Pelé the businessman was denied that peace of mind, as his brother and financial adviser were forced to meet with him to solve a business problem only he could decide.

Shortly afterward rumors started flowing about Pelé's changing his mind and ending his brief retirement. At first the chances of his coming to the United States to play for the Cosmos seemed a publicity man's dream. But the groundwork had already been laid and, in a series of negotiations, some held in strange surroundings, the Cosmos had made Pelé an offer.

Pelé, knowing how the Brazilian people would feel regarding his return to soccer in a foreign land and not with his own people, expected them to be resentful when the story about the Cosmos seeking him reached them. He even used one of his rare ploys, announcing that he would not play for the Cosmos. But the Cosmos kept trying. Finally, in a historic moment, they made the announcement: Pelé would play for them.

The Brazilian people started hurling insults, saying that the only reason Pelé was returning to soccer was because he was near bankruptcy. Of course, Pelé rejected their claim and explained that money was not the main reason he was returning to soccer.

He was returning to the game as a missionary, to fulfill a dream that the United States would one day become a soccer power.

Someone said that the day Pelé agreed to play soccer for the Cosmos, the sport in the United States jumped from the stone age right into the jet age. Pelé was the one man who could build the sport here.

Pelé showed his emotion and nervousness as he appeared with his teammates in practice. He wanted to make a good showing, just as he had done eighteen years earlier when he joined Santos.

He knew that reporters from all over the world would be on hand to see him play his first game in a Cosmo uniform. He was greeted by a near-capacity crowd as he took to the field. Many oldtimers were on hand, feeling that all their hopes of past years to see the sport emerge here would now be fulfilled. There was an impressive flag-changing ceremony before the game, with Pelé receiving an American flag and in return giving Kyle Rote, Jr., the son of a former great with the New York football Giants, the Brazilian flag.

Once the whistle sounded to start the game, Pelé was all business —not only performing his magic but also acting the role of a traffic cop as he helped his new teammates, many of them young, to do things and go in directions they had rarely ventured before.

He was like a general directing the battle, and he gave a performance worthy of himself.

The following few months were hectic as Pelé and the Cosmos traveled throughout the country and in Canada playing league games and exhibition games. No matter where he went, even to the White House to visit with President Ford, Pelé was a big hit.

Pelé tried to be just one of the guys to his teammates, helping the trainer unpack the luggage from the bus carrying the team from an airport to a hotel. He also showed his love of being able to relax, and even hooked two sharks from the second story of a motel in Seattle. But there were some players, just like those players from the Bulgarian World Cup Team nine years earlier, who didn't want the king to embarrass them, and they fouled him to stop him. There were also the overeager fans in Boston who mobbed him after he scored an apparent goal. Only quick action on the part of his security guards and the Boston goalie saved him from further injury.

After the season came a tour of Europe, where in Sweden he was introduced to a tow-headed boy named Pelé in his honor because the youngster's father had seen Pelé play in Sweden in the World Cup back in 1958. It was an extensive tour, which also carried the Cosmos to the Caribbean. When it was all over, Pelé was again busy running clinics, as only he can.

A great deal has been written about Pelé, but if there is one phrase that sums up his soccer skills it has to be the words written by a Brazilian journalist after Pelé met with Prince Philip:

"In the kingdom of soccer, to whose territory all the states of the world belong, the only king is Pelé. Above his majesty only the spiritual power of Heaven can rule."

If one word is needed to describe Pelé off the field it would have to be "gentleman."

What makes Pelé that way?

A KING IS BORN

On October 23, 1940, in the poverty-striken town of Tres Coracoes, which means Three Hearts, in the Brazilian state of Minas Gerais, former soccer player Dondinho and his wife Celeste were blessed with the birth of their first child, christened Edson Arantes do Nascimento.

Except for the immediate family and perhaps a few close relatives, the event went unnoticed. For no one at the time of Pelé's birth would have dared to dream that one day this baby would become the greatest player in the long history of soccer, the world's most popular sport.

"As far as I know from what my parents told me," Pelé says, "I was an average baby, nothing exceptional, not too big and again not too small."

Two years later his brother Zoca was born, and one might well say that had not Pelé developed into a great soccer star Zoca might still be playing the sport today. In fact, when Pelé was starring for Santos, Zoca joined the team but left shortly afterward to get a college education and become a lawyer.

The dream of every aspiring soccer player in South America as well as in Europe is to own his own soccer ball—just as an American youngster playing baseball wants to have his own glove.

With barely enough money from his soccer playing to put food on the family table, Pelé's father couldn't even dream of buying the youngster a soccer ball. But ingenuity overcame this difficulty as Dondinho took an old sock and stuffed it with rags. This was to be

Pelé's training ball and day after day Pelé, now five, would run through the streets and lots of Tres Coracoes kicking the sock around. The streets, Pelé's first soccer arena, were narrow and unpaved. Sidewalks made of wood, often rotted, formed the sidelines. Although the town has now grown slightly, there were few persons walking through the streets in those days who were likely to interfere with the activities of the bouncy Pelé.

"I became pretty good at being able to dribble the sock around and even learned how to hit it with my head," Pelé would later remember.

When he was six his family moved to Bauru, in the Brazilian state of São Paulo. Bauru is slightly bigger than Tres Coracoes and offered Pelé's father the chance to supplement his soccer earnings by helping train athletes in other sports such as track and field. With many children his own age as playmates, Pelé made friends rapidly and soon was in a close-knit group of boys who played together and even cut school together.

"I would play a lot of hooky and go into the fields and practice soccer," Pelé says. "I just didn't like the rigors of education. I didn't like being forced to sit in class and listen to the teacher. Later on in my life I realized that I really wanted an education, and I got it first by getting a high school equivalency certificate and later attending junior college. But at the time I was going to what you might call grade school, I had no use for it."

The firm hand of Dondinho kept Pelé in school at least through the fourth grade. But the attendance records undoubtedly show that Pelé was out of school more often than he was in class.

His desire to own a soccer ball of his own was as strong, if not stronger, than ever and in an effort to buy his own ball and help out the family Pelé shined shoes and even sold roasted peanuts outside movie houses in town. How did he get the peanuts to sell? He would go down to the railroad depot and help himself by picking up the peanuts that fell from the cars carrying them. There were stories that he swiped them off the trains themselves but this he never admitted to me. The depot is a busy one and it's quite possible that there could be many peanuts lying around.

Obviously Pelé didn't see any harm in picking them off the ground, but ask him to explain the full circumstances of the peanut sale and he'll quickly try to change the conversation to another subject.

One subject Pelé doesn't mind talking about is the way he finally left school after the fourth grade. "One day I was playing hooky from school again," explains Pelé, "when the head schoolmaster caught me playing soccer on one of the lots my friends and I liked to use. He called my father, who came over to the lot, and in front of my friends he gave me a good spanking. It was very humiliating but it also served its purpose because it got me out of school for good."

Pelé then accepted a job as a cobbler's apprentice for a salary of just over $2 a month. The experience of being a cobbler's apprentice still shows today—he often repairs his own boots as well as those of his teammates. Since most soccer teams, with the possible exception of those National Teams who are playing in the World Cup, don't carry their own cobbler with them, most players try to fix their own boots. Pelé can match any professional cobbler at this task.

It was around this time that Pelé picked up his nickname, a name that has come to mean the greatest soccer player of all time. When asked about the name "Pelé," which has no literal translation at all in Portuguese, the native tongue in Brazil, time and again with a huge smile on his face, Pelé has given the details to thousands of inquiring reporters:

"The boys I used to play soccer with on the streets and lots gave it to me and I didn't like it. I thought they were making fun of me and I used to get into many fights with them. I asked them to stop calling me Pelé and call me by my real name, Edson, but they kept at it. The harder I tried to make them stop calling me Pelé the more they insisted on calling me by that name. I got into many big fights with even my best friends. I used to go home crying to my father, but he told me that I shouldn't be so insulted by that name since many of the top Brazilian players had nicknames that had nothing to do with their regular names. I guess after awhile I accepted the name but even today my real friends call me Edson. After all, that's my real name, the one my mother and father gave me. My mother has a nickname for me. It's Dico."

While working as a cobbler's apprentice Pelé continued his education—not in school but in soccer, as he played with a team in Bauru called Sete de Setembro.

"We didn't wear uniforms like the youngsters wear here when

they play junior soccer," Pelé explains. "And we didn't wear soccer boots. We used to play barefoot and the games were often very rough with a lot of body contact."

Barefoot soccer, called "pelada," is credited by some with helping Pelé develop many of the electrifying moves with which he breaks tackles, dribbles in crazy patterns, and comes roaring in for a shot almost unmolested.

"In barefoot soccer, especially on the streets and lots, you have to be a good mover," Pelé explains, "because if you give your opponent the opportunity to take the ball away from you he will use many dirty tricks to accomplish this. You have to remember that most of the times when we played in the lots and streets anything, and I mean anything, an opponent did to get the ball away from you was okay because we didn't usually call fouls."

Zoca also laughs when asked to describe those early soccer games. Although two years younger, he often played on the same team as Pelé and also had many occasions to be on an opposing team from his brother:

"You could say that they often got out of hand. A player would try to take the ball away from my brother and my brother would make him look silly, so he would turn around and hit my brother and my brother would come right back and take a swing at the kid who hit him. Often the games were broken off when everyone got involved in fights."

Pelé was also a constant spectator at the games his father played and says he used to enjoy watching the different players from the opposing teams coming in for a match since it gave him a chance to try to duplicate some of their moves. According to Pelé, the games were well played.

Although the players in the barefoot games didn't wear uniforms they played with regular soccer balls. The balls were of low quality, since often they had been discarded by the professional teams. Still, Pelé had the opportunity to start dribbling, shooting and heading around a regulation-size soccer ball—a far cry from his earlier days with the stocking stuffed with rags.

"Sometimes the ball was lopsided and was hard to control but we really enjoyed ourselves even with the many arguments and fights we had," Pelé remembers. "The main thing is that we were playing the game and at the same time trying to improve our skills. It was really a lot of fun and I will never forget those days. We didn't have many material things but we were almost all alike in the sense that we struggled together. The highlights of these almost daily games, many of them played after I left my job at the end of the day, were the times we would play other barefoot teams from other streets of the town. The battles were very rough, but again they were enjoyable, and I feel that because we didn't have all the luxuries of life we found a great deal of companionship with one another."

Pelé continued playing barefoot soccer in the streets and on the lots, and also engaged in pickup games in which he was often the youngest of all the players. Some of these were matches with construction and factory workers. The games took place at lunchtime or during work breaks, and although they used a regular ball there were no such things as regulation goals. Often two garbage pails or oil drums were used as replacements for the regulation-size goalposts. Some advantages of playing in these pickup games were that Pelé was no longer the brunt of many fouls as he had been as a member of the street teams. He also had the chance to impress many spectators. He dazzled everyone with his fleet style of play and his uncanny moves, which often found the older players going the wrong way as they attempted to get the ball away from him.

"Playing in these games was very enjoyable to me," Pelé explains. "I had a lot of fun and at the same time a great opportunity to learn from some of the workers. Many of them had played with top-flight amateur teams in Brazil. I guess that in many ways I embarrassed many of them with my moves, but I didn't do it intentionally. I just played the best way I knew how and I think that by now I had made up my mind that if I ever got the opportunity I would like to become a professional soccer player. But you have to remember that I was still very young at the time, and who knew what would eventually happen? After the game we would sit and talk about some of the players we had heard about. I had never seen some of the players, but I had read about them. On the other hand many of the workers had seen these stars play and I used to listen, often without talking myself, to the workers describe some of the moves they had seen the star players make in important games. It was really an education. After these talks I just couldn't wait until the day I would get the opportunity to play on a well-known team. Often when I got home from my job and from the games we played I was very tired and would skip my dinner. But to me playing soccer was even more important than eating."

And Pelé played soccer every chance he had. On his lunch break from the cobbler's job he often would skip eating for the chance to play against older workers in the area. After he finished his shift at work he'd race either onto the streets or to one of the sandlots—really nothing more than an open field—and play. He did this with the hope of one day being discovered.

THE DISCOVERY

The opportunity that Pelé talked about came almost by accident in the presence of former Santos soccer player Valdemar de Brito. De Brito, a former Brazilian soccer star, was well-known in Pelé's area and he had been very impressed with what he had heard about Edson Arantes do Nascimento—known by now as Pelé. When Pelé was twelve, he already had five years of sandlot soccer behind him, much of it against tough, older players. De Brito wandered onto the scene.

Now coach of the strong BAC team, de Brito felt that the club must start sponsoring a junior team. De Brito later revealed that many of the BAC officials were against the idea of building from the ground up, since they had not been making the type of money from the main club that they had expected. In fact, the club was suffering high losses.

Unlike scouting in American baseball, football and basketball, the scouting system in those days in Brazil was undeveloped. Many players were introduced to their teams by their parents and friends, and either they made it or they didn't. But de Brito, who might be called a pioneer in Brazilian scouting, insisted that his way was the right way and reports circulated that if the club denied his wishes then he might think of leaving them. To see just how far de Brito's idea has gone, it should be noted that today clubs like Botofoga and Santos in Brazil have over twenty teams of junior players broken down from age 8 to 15. And in Italy Juventis and Inter of Milan have 35 to 50 junior clubs. It is rare when a team playing in the first division anywhere in the world today can't, if it so desires, field a full team just by dressing players they have had in their own ranks for many years.

"I guess I made a pretty good case for the program of junior soccer," says de Brito, now a civil servant in Brazil. "I told them that we must scout the area to get players who we feel will one day be able to play for our main team."

In an effort to secure the best possible youngsters, ranging in age from twelve to fifteen, de Brito started to do a little scouting of his own, going to the sandlots and schoolyards. De Brito decided that the name of the team would be Baquinho and that the club would be composed of local youngsters. Today, many of the top clubs in the soccer world go into other teams' territory to acquire a promising youngster, but this was not the case with de Brito and the board of directors of his BAC club.

One day, de Brito, acting on what might be called a hot tip from one of his friends, went to a construction site where Pelé, two of Pelé's friends, and a group of workers were engaged in their daily routine of playing pickup soccer at lunchtime. The makeshift field was about 50 yards long by 40 yards wide and instead of regular goals they used garbage cans. The older men greeted de Brito, unaware that his main reason for being there was not to see if any of them would be able to fit into the BAC plans. De Brito saw something spectacular: a youngster dribbling, shooting, and passing rings around the older boys. Later, de Brito was to say that the minute he laid eyes on the twelve-year-old Pelé, he recognized "pure genius."

"I couldn't believe that such a young boy was able to perform some of the moves as well as the tricks with the ball that Pelé was doing," de Brito remembers. "He was making the older men look silly and in an effort to stop him they kept fouling him. But he didn't stop trying. He would get fouled and wind up on the ground but a split second later he would be back up on his feet doing the same thing again. I knew then that this boy had great talent—of course, rough around the edges—but the talent definitely was there and could be developed into something great. I knew then that this was a scene that I would never be able to forget.

"I didn't say anything at that time to Pelé, but I knew then that he was one player I definitely wanted on our junior team. It wasn't until I asked him if he desired to play for us that I really got to talk to him. I can honestly say that in all the years I have been observing promising young soccer players, no youngster ever had such an impact on me as this youngster. And I found it hard to believe that he was only twelve years old. Some of the moves he made reminded me of the greats of the game, and I myself, who was considered a pretty good junior player in my early days, had to admit that at the same number of years he was far ahead of me.

"When he agreed to play for our junior club I had a long talk with him. He appeared to me to be very sincere, but also very shy. His mind seemed to wander as if he were trying to figure out what I really wanted to know. He seemed embarrassed at some of the questions I was asking him. But after awhile I really got to know his background and I found that he had learned many of the moves from his father, whom I happened to know as a fine player. Knowing that he was the son of a player made me feel good, as it isn't uncommon that many times the son who follows in the father's footsteps becomes even a better player than the father. Of course there was no guarantee, but the gamble of giving the boy a chance wasn't too great a risk since what I had seen in practice made me sure that he would become a really fine player one day."

De Brito said that after that one talk he was already formulating a plan for the youngster's development that would take many roads, some of them very rocky. De Brito planned every step and instruction with understanding and reason. De Brito didn't just order Pelé to follow his instruction; he tried to get Pelé to understand why the moves were being used.

"He seemed to understand me when I told him that it would take a great deal of hard work for him to become a true professional soccer player, and that there were things he was doing which we would have to change in order for these moves to be successful should he eventually make the grade as a professional player.

"I understood that since his father had taught him many of the moves he was a little reluctant to change them," de Brito explained some years later. "We decided that in addition to playing with the Baquinho team and also continuing in a lesser degree with the pickup games, I would work out with him in secret. I felt that this would help speed his development and if he could make it as a big-time player, that time would come much faster than it would if he concentrated only on our junior team."

And work out they did. De Brito is the first to admit that on many occasions Pelé challenged him verbally on many of the instructions he was getting. It seemed that Pelé could not understand why de Brito insisted on the tough physical conditioning. Still, Pelé conditioned himself and carefully watched what he ate, as he does to this day. The workouts, first with the team and then privately, left Pelé exhausted, and as Zoca recalls "when he came home he just wanted to sleep. But he was also very excited about what he was learning from de Brito. Our father used to ask him questions and then go over some of what Pelé had been taught by de Brito."

The harder and longer Pelé worked out the better he seemed to enjoy the game, although there were times that he and de Brito would argue so vehemently that Pelé would wonder if it was all worth it. But he must have felt the hard work was worth it since he kept coming back for more and longer sessions.

"We worked very hard at every phase of the game," de Brito says. "We went over everything not once or twice but many, many times, and I also was exhausted but very happy as I saw Pelé start to develop. He didn't just accept what I told him to do. He questioned it and from our long discussions after we stopped playing we got to understand that together we really had a good foundation."

Pelé, still not thirteen, got a chance to play in a regulation game, on a field laid out for soccer, and against youngsters his own age. No longer would he have to be worried about feeling the wrath of the older men against him when he made them look bad. Here he got a chance to show the other players his inborn talent and the lessons he had learned from his father and de Brito. He wound up playing almost every halfback and forward position on the Baquinho team. He even practiced occasionally in goal. His speed and reflexes were unbelievable wherever he played.

To Pelé, playing for the local junior club Baquinho had a special thrill. When he joined, they handed him his own uniform, and he danced all the way home because now he could say that just like his father he too had his own uniform. "It was my very own uniform," Pelé remembers. "It may not seem such a big deal to some, but to me it was one of the thrills of my life."

Pelé wore the uniform with pride. He would play the outside wing positions, the center forward spot and the inside left as well as inside right spots. What made him so versatile was that during the sessions he had spent with de Brito the former player had explained to him that a player who could score with only one foot was not really a true overall player. He used both his feet, providing many goals for Baquinho. His head shots, dribbling and passing had the players on the opposing teams looking foolish. Pelé had already started to build his reputation but through it all remained the modest type. Even today Pelé is still the modest man—a man who cherishes a friend just like a child cherishes a new toy. Pelé is always looking to make new friends and that includes players from opposing teams.

Pelé was without a doubt the most valuable player on the Baquinho team, and many of the players from de Brito's BAC club used to make it a point to come and see the youngster play. After the games, Pelé and the other members of his junior team would talk with the members of the BAC team. There was already a friendly trade of talk going on between Pelé and the older players.

Three years after Baquinho was started Pelé was already the talk of Brazilian junior soccer. Word of his accomplishments had reached many of the bigger teams such as Santos and Botofoga. But de Brito let Pelé continue to get his feet wet in junior soccer and even though he had left as coach of BAC he continued occasionally going to Baquinho games, talking with Pelé and with others who happened to have seen a particular game that the coach himself had missed. Pelé was now being scouted by other clubs. He had scored numerous goals and added an uncounted number of assists as Baquinho swept to the local junior championship three consecutive times—a feat that in junior soccer throughout the world is almost unheard of. Pelé was enjoying himself. He now felt that he would fulfill his ambition of one day becoming a professional soccer player—something that he now admits he had strived for from the time he first started kicking around the ragged stuffed stocking years before in Tres Coracoes.

Early in 1956 de Brito returned to Bauru and asked Pelé to set up a meeting with him and Pelé's parents. The reason for the meeting was simple. De Brito felt that the time was right for Pelé to try to make it in the professional ranks. De Brito spent over an hour talking with Dondinho, and with Pelé's mother, who expressed a reluctance to see their son leave home. The team de Brito wanted Pelé to try out with was none other than the famed Santos. Finally de Brito got the answer he had been hoping for. Yes, Pelé's parents would allow the fifteen-year-old youngster to try to make it in a specially arranged tryout with Santos. So sure was de Brito that Pelé's parents would indeed consent to the tryout that he had already been in contact with club officials to arrange it. After the parents had given their approval, Pelé talked briefly with his brother and sister and told them that they shouldn't worry since he felt good. Many of Pelé's young friends gathered to say good-bye. Among those who saw him off was his boss at the cobbler's shop who wished him well. About six of his closest friends, each one of whom hugged Pelé, were also on hand to say farewell and good luck. Pelé was indeed well liked.

Before leaving, de Brito held meetings with both club officials and the coach of the BAC junior club Baquinho and got a full description of how the youngster had been doing, not only as a player but as a personality—something that is carefully evaluated by clubs looking to sign future stars.

3 HEADING FOR SANTOS

Pelé and de Brito boarded a train for the trip to Santos early in June 1956—wintertime in Brazil.

Pelé now can laugh about his experience on the train ride, but at the same time he says it wasn't so funny. He had seen many freight trains in his earlier years but this was his first true train ride and he got sick—so sick, in fact, that he begged de Brito to take him off the train and return home. Even his most dreamed-of goal—that of becoming a top notch professional soccer player—didn't seem worth it.

"It was terrible," Pelé explains. "I got sick almost as soon as the train left and I felt worse as we went on. I begged de Brito to get me off the train but like a father he quieted me down and told me that everything would be all right. I was really scared that I wouldn't be able to take it anymore. But finally the train got to Santos and I felt a little better as we got off."

On June 8, de Brito introduced Pelé to the officials of the Santos club, many of them veteran club officials who had heard more than once before that someone was bringing them a player who would one day be the best in the world. On the field that day the regular Santos team was working out and they, too, were skeptical. There had been several promising youngsters who in the previous few years had come for a tryout only to fall flat on their faces. Now the Santos regulars would have a chance for themselves to judge the youngster who was being touted by de Brito as the next great star of the sport.

Pelé trotted onto the field and started working out. All his nervousness left him as soon as he touched the ball, making the dribbles he had done with de Brito's junior team, the runs down the sidelines and across the field. It is reported that the regular Santos players stopped what they were doing and stared in amazement at Pelé's action. Club officials smiled as they watched the youngster, still not sixteen, perform brilliantly. The Santos officials were waiting for Pelé as he trotted off the field, exhausted but confident. They first explained to de Brito their happiness that the former star player saw fit to bring Pelé to them for the workout, possibly forgetting that de Brito himself had to do a great deal of talking before securing the tryout. They took Pelé aside and explained to him the facts of life regarding playing for Santos. He would not immediately be placed on the regular Santos roster. Instead he would be assigned to the juvenile team. His salary would be small, estimated at only a few dollars per month. In addition he would receive board and lodging from the club and would be expected to fulfill all the obligations that Santos demanded of all the members of their vast organization. He was told to keep his nose clean and obey all the instructions given to him by officials as well as by coaches.

As was the custom for new members of the Santos team, Pelé sat on the bench and just watched for the first few games. Pelé finally got his chance to play a regular game for the juvenile team and it was a tense event with the crowd in the stadium expecting so much from the boy. Pelé got a golden chance to become a hero but muffed the opportunity as he missed—of all things—a penalty shot and the team lost the championship. Even now, many years later, Pelé admits that he felt like crying and hiding after missing that chance, but it should be noted that in the ensuing years he hasn't missed many penalty shots. Still, Pelé so impressed the club officials with his ball control, passing, and speed that later in the year he was promoted to Santos' regular team.

On September 7, Pelé sat on the bench for the regular Santos team during the first half, anxiously awaiting the call to come in as a substitute. It was only an exhibition game against Cornintians Santos Andre but Santos took the game very seriously and used the players they expected the most of. Finally the call came and Pelé entered the game in the second half. Within a few minutes he scored the first of over 1,200 professional goals. He was jubilant and couldn't wait for another opportunity. A Swedish team called AIK was playing an exhibition match and Santos used all its starters, giving Pelé a chance to prove himself and earn an International Cap for playing in a National Team match. Pelé performed well but he still hadn't won himself a regular starting berth for the powerful Brazilian club team. When the final statistics were added up, Pelé had a grand total of only two goals for the entire eleven games he had played with Santos during the 1956 season. However, no statistics were actually kept on the total number of assists he made as his dribbling and passing set up numerous other Santos goals. The team matured steadily and was a real powerhouse at the end of the season. In his own way, Pelé played an important role for the team that year and saw action at most of the positions on the front line. Pelé's greatest contribution that first season was in setting up teammates for easy shots on goals. His passes were true to their mark and he often, because of his dribbling, would draw out two or more defenders so as to create an opening for one of his teammates.

Pelé won a permanent berth as a starter once the season got underway in 1957. A great deal of the credit was due to Pelé's tough physical conditioning. He obviously remembered the talk he had had a couple of years earlier with de Brito. When the weather was bad, Pelé would go indoors and drill for hours on every aspect of conditioning, dribbling and hard target shooting. But still Pelé had no permanent number to call his own. Sometimes he wore No. 9, when he played something resembling a center forward role. Other times he wore No. 8, because the team had him on the right side. But he would score from anywhere on the field and this enhanced his growing reputation with the press and fans alike.

He hoped that his skillful play as well as this spreading reputation would carry him to his highest dream—that of becoming a member of the Brazilian National Team. One of Portugal's most popular teams, Belenenses, were making a South American tour with a game scheduled for Brazil against the combined forces of Santos and Vasco da Gama. Pelé, because of his new-found glory and reputation, was selected to play against the Portuguese booters and emotion ran high since South American clubs, particularily those from Brazil, like nothing better than to beat a team from Portugal. The game drew a large crowd and there was a carnival-like atmosphere at the stadium. Pelé got the chance to play the fast-moving, free-style game that he says he really enjoys. He made the most of the opportunity by scoring the three-goal hat trick, and the Brazilian sports pages were already picking him for the National Team of Brazil. Pelé knew that the selections were to be announced shortly. While awaiting word he played very well in all phases of his game, leading his Santos team to victory after victory against local opposition in the tough São Paulo League.

The selection of a National Team is a complicated matter. There are sheets kept on each and every player performing in the top leagues in every major soccer power throughout the world. These sheets include playing statistics and personality reports. The personality factor is important, since a player making any country's national team is expected to uphold the dignity of his land. On more than one occasion, great players like George Best have been left off their nation's team because of their actions. Each club sends game reports in to the national soccer association, which in Pelé's case is the Brazilian Football Association. These reports are cross-checked against referee reports as well as reports handed in by the various scouts assigned by the national association. Finally, the men who are assigned to make the final selection get together and evaluate each and every man they have on their preferred list. If, for instance, one player is strong at center forward but another man might be considered even stronger, then the selection committee must evaluate the man of the lesser ratings to see how he would fit in if they tried to place him at another position. This is why, in selecting a forward line, it is quite possible that the committee could take three center forwards and no inside rights or inside lefts.

Pelé must have come through with high ratings since it was decided at the committee meeting that they would see him in person before deciding if and where he would fit in. Public opinion was running high in Pelé's favor, and the people who witnessed Santos games, as well as several of Santos' opponents, were also touting his praise. After watching him several times and talking to outsiders not associated with the Santos club, the committee came to a decision. Only when they were absolutely sure about Pelé, both as a player and as a personality who would in no way disgrace the uniform of Brazil, were they ready to reveal their decision on giving this youngster—

just turned sixteen—a chance to represent Brazil. It is reported that even hours before the decision was made there were some who still felt that the conservative committee might not be willing to take the gamble. In the event the team didn't do well, the committee might be faulted for taking this comparatively inexperienced player over some player who was more experienced in international soccer. To the credit of the committee and those who maintained their confidence in the ability of the young soccer star, the announcement was made—Pelé had been selected to play for the National Team.

"I was a little shocked at first," Pelé said much later in his life. "I knew that my name was being considered but I felt that my youth might be against me. I told everyone I knew to thank the committee for giving me this chance to play for my country."

GLORY FOR PELÉ

On July 9 Pelé, like the rest of the members of the Brazilian National Team, took his pre-game warmup and then returned to the dressing room for final words from those running the National Team. Pelé didn't expect to see any action since the game was against Argentina, one of Brazil's bitterest enemies. He was content to sit on the bench and watch the action. Just being a member of the Brazilian National Team meant that he was indeed one of the twenty or so top players in the soccer-wild nation. Brazil was losing when Pelé got a motion from the coach to enter the game in the second half as a substitute for the great Mazzola. Pelé took off his sweats and did a few wind sprints along the sideline until the referee acknowledged the substitution and signaled him to enter the game. In the game the Argentinians controlled the midfield and were able to stop constant Brazilian drives before they actually built their own scoring opportunities. Pelé scored the lone Brazilian goal while Sivori and Maschio hit the nets for the Argentinians. Despite his goal, Pelé was sad at the conclusion of the match: the Argentinians had beaten Brazil 2–1.

A few days later, the two teams were to meet again and this time Pelé was shocked as he was informed that he would start at the regular inside left position, a spot he had been playing now regularly for the Santos club. Pelé was brilliant as he roamed the field, using the wall pass, which is similar to the give-and-go in American basketball, to perfection. He was out-dribbling much more experienced Argentinian defenders, heading the ball away from much taller defenders, and the Argentinian defense was finding him a most difficult opponent to cover as he was switching all over the offensive line. In this game Pelé really started to feel that he was indeed part of the Brazilian National Team. He made the best of this opportunity to prove himself worthy of wearing the colors of Brazil. He again scored a goal and this time Brazil blanked Argentina 2–0 for a crucial victory. Pelé received acclaim by the mass of Brazilian journalists in attendance at the game, gathering praise for his fine overall performance. He was now one of the men who would be counted on to see action for the National Team in its upcoming games.

However, his age still angered many of his critics, who discredited him every time he had a bad game for the Brazil team. Many of those fans who regularly attended Santos games also seemed to single him out when the team lost an important match. Pelé admitted that the booing he received was causing him grief but he was still a regular starter both for Santos and for Brazil. On a Juventus of Italy tour of Brazil the fans were really getting to Pelé as he missed a few good scoring chances and was not up to his brilliance either in passing or dribbling. Finally he broke through the Juventus defense and sent a shot into the back of the net for a beautiful goal. The ball hooked over a defender's head and then swerved as it approached the goalie, rendering the keeper helpless to stop the shot. The famous Pelé salute was born as he rushed over to the crowd in the stands and started to punch the air in triumph. This goal salute became his trademark and he has used it ever since that day. During the 1957 campaign, Pelé had the chance to salute the crowd for each of his 66 goals in his combined performance with Santos, various All-Star teams, and the Brazilian National Team, making him the highest scorer in Brazil for the year.

Santos—and Pelé—began to gain worldwide recognition. His overall brilliance in every aspect of the game was matched by his undying stamina and equal brilliance on defense. He was not content to stay up near the opposition's goal and wait for the ball to be passed to him. He developed a deft tackling method where by a series of moves he was able to take the ball away from the opposing team's forwards as well as defenders. He could trap the ball with either foot, then quickly change direction and completely fool the opposition. His passes were there waiting for a teammate to garner in and possibly score.

Fans began to realize that they might well have the future star of the game in their midst. But to those around Pelé he was still the simple, peaceful, loving youngster who wanted nothing more than to play soccer. He still took time out to talk to youngsters, something he would be doing for years to come. He attended various team functions and was always spending extra time long after the other Santos players left to work on every phase of his game. His physical condition was among the best in the world of soccer, and he watched his diet. Those who worked with him were pleased by this attitude, and Pelé was becoming ever more popular with the press.

"Much of what I have I owe to the press," Pelé has said. "I have a job to do and I do it to the best of my ability and I realize that the press also has a job to do and they try to do it the best way they know how. Many times I feel I have been unfairly criticized, but I have made it a point never to turn my back on the press and I never criticize them—publicly, at least. Without the press I wouldn't have been able to accomplish so much on a worldwide basis."

Santos' workouts and competition in the São Paulo League kept Pelé busy for much of 1957. Much of the free time the other Santos players enjoyed was denied Pelé as he worked out steadily with the Brazilian National Team.

"A lot of the players complain," Pelé said, "but to me, wearing the uniform of my country in the World Cup is the greatest honor I can imagine and if it means giving up some of my spare time it's really a small price to pay for this honor."

The Brazilians were being talked about as a team that had only a slight chance to win the World Cup in 1958 and that is why the team worked so hard. They felt they had the talent needed to make a good run at the championship title, known as the Jules Rimet Trophy. Pelé remained a question mark as far as Brazil's future was concerned. Some still felt his inexperience and possibly the pressure of playing in the world's most popular team tournament would be too much for the youngster.

Still, by the end of the 1957 campaign it looked like a good bet that Pelé would indeed be named at least to the team that would leave for Europe a few weeks ahead of the World Cup's opening in Sweden.

Pelé later said, "I told myself that if I didn't get picked on the squad, sure, I would be disappointed—but I also felt that I still had many years ahead of me for the chance. I didn't go around asking everyone I knew if I was going to be placed on the team. I just waited to see how things would develop. I knew that scouts were always in attendance watching our games and I was sure that the committee was nearly ready to make up their minds."

What the committee did was wait until the beginning of the 1958 campaign. Pelé was playing better than ever when he received the long-awaited word that he would be on the squad traveling to Sweden.

"I cried with joy when I got the news," Pelé recalls.

5 A NATIONAL HERO

During 1958 Pelé scored a total of 87 goals, and although no official count was kept of the number of goals his passing and dribbling set up, it is estimated that at least one hundred other goals scored by both the Santos club and the Brazilian National Team came as direct results of his play. But to Pelé no goal was as important as the one he scored against Wales in the quarterfinal round of the 1958 World Cup held in Sweden. For that goal against the Welch was his first ever in World Cup competition.

His knee swollen as a result of being fouled two weeks earlier, Pelé joined Garrincha, known as the Little Bird, and Djalma Santos, another key player, on the bench for the Brazilians' first game—a dull 3–0 win over Austria. Disappointed that he still was not physically fit, he then sat on the bench while Brazil and England played to a scoreless deadlock in the Group Four competition.

Pelé went to the trainer and team doctor who gave him their permission to play the next game against the Soviet Union. This game would determine whether the Brazilians, still feeling the wrath of the European public because of their heated 1954 battle against Hungary, would advance to the quarterfinal round. Brazil had lost 4–2 in the quarterfinals of the 1954 World Cup to Hungary and after the game the Brazilians and Hungarians engaged in a fisticuff battle during which broken bottles were tossed by several players on both sides. The fight spread from the field to the dressing rooms and onto the streets when the teams left the stadium. The game is still being called the Battle of Berne.

If the Brazilians had lost to the Soviets they would have been unable to join such other teams as West Germany, the defending champion, Czechoslovakia, France, Yugoslavia, Sweden, Wales and England in the quarterfinals, a sudden-death affair where one defeat meant elimination. But with Pelé performing brilliantly in the team's new 4-2-4 system of play, which saw the Brazilians abandon their old style of having five men back (so as to give them as many as seven or eight men up front when they were on attack with a similar number of men back when the situation called for it), Brazil defeated the Soviets 2–0 to gain the quarterfinals. Now there were only eight teams left in the competition, which in reality had started some two years earlier when fifty-three nations applied to compete in the opening stages of the tournament. Playing a series of elimination contests, the clubs try to make it to the final field of sixteen. Fourteen spots in the 1958 World Cup were won by these eliminations, with only Sweden, as the host nation, and West Germany, as the defending champion, being automatic entrants.

Pelé was then selected to start in the quarterfinal game against Wales, a team that had eliminated Hungary 2–1 in the previous round. Pelé took the field along with other Brazilian stars such as goalie Gilmar, fullbacks De Sordi, Santos, N. Zito and Bellini, halfbacks Orlando and Garrincha and Pelé's front-line teammates Didi, Mazzola and Zagalo. Pelé and the rest of the front line riddled the Welch goal but to no avail as Wales' goalie Kelsey made several brilliant saves. The half ended scoreless. Then on a simple head feint and a soft shot Pelé put the ball into the Welch goal in the second half. The Brazilians held on for a 1–0 win and a spot in the semifinal round against France. In the other semifinal game, Sweden would meet West Germany.

If there is one game in which Pelé gained worldwide recognition, it was in the match against France. In that game, Pelé had room to operate. When the defenders closed in on him he would either pass the ball or dribble through two and sometimes three defenders as he put on a display that one veteran reporter described as "simply remarkable." When the final whistle sounded, the Brazilians had posted a 5–2 victory with Pelé responsible for four of the goals. He scored with the three-goal hat trick and assisted on another of his team's tallies.

Now came the final against Sweden. The Swedes were in a jubilant mood. Following their 3–1 semifinal win over defending champion West Germany, the players expressed confidence that they would be able to stop the high-geared Brazilian machine. The Swedish fans were also confident that since the game was on their home grounds Sweden would be the new champions. On the morning of the game, a light shower hit Stockholm. Still the fans kept pouring into the stadium. The Swedes were a bit disappointed on one count: the World Cup officials had ruled that they would not allow the cheerleaders who had gone onto the field against West Germany to enter the playing field this time since it had caused hard feelings. Instead, the Swedes brought to the game every conceivable type of noisemaker and came in brightly colored patriotic dress. It began to rain heavily just minutes before the start of the game. When the lineup was announced there was an air of confusion as the Brazilians had at the last minute decided to replace Mazzola with Vava. Although Vava had played well in the game against France, many had guessed that the veteran Mazzola would be given the start against Sweden. As the starting whistle sounded, there were over 60,000 fans packed into a stadium built to accommodate 50,000.

Swedish fans erupted early in the match as manager George Raynor abandoned the defensive tactics many expected him to use and started pressing the Brazilian goal. Then Liedholm beat Gilmar from ten yards out and Swedish fans were jumping wildly as their nation took a 1–0 lead. But the joy didn't last long; Brazil unleashed a powerful attack, getting two goals by Pelé, two by Vava and one by Zagalo for an impressive 5–2 victory. Some seventeen years later when Pelé returned to Sweden to play a series of exhibition matches for the Cosmos, fans were still talking about one of the goals he scored against Sweden. Pelé had his back to Swedish goalie Svensson when he received a long pass which he chest-trapped, letting the ball roll down to his left foot without allowing the sphere to hit the ground. He then flipped the ball over his shoulder and, pivoting while the ball was still in the air, was able to send a booming right-footed shot into the Swedish goal and all the goalie could do was stand there in a state of shock. As the fans leaped to their feet shouting "Pelé, Pelé!" Svensson joined in the cheers, saying later, "I have never seen anything like that before and I doubt if I will ever see a goal scored like that again. It was unbelievable."

To many that goal was the most spectacular ever scored in a World Cup title match.

Pelé and the rest of the Brazilian team celebrated their convincing victory with the traditional victory march around the Stockholm stadium. But this was only a prelude to what awaited the Brazilian team when they returned home.

Over 5,000 cheering fans greeted the team as they arrived in Rio de Janeiro. The atmosphere resembled that of carnival as the team received the equivalent of a New York ticker-tape parade. All the prominent people in the Brazilian government were on hand. Each member of the championship team was greeted individually by the government officials, including the president himself. As each player came forward to be greeted, the fans watching the reception cheered wildly and when it came time for Pelé to be honored the fans showed that he was indeed the prime object of their love as they expressed great pleasure with the way he had played. Pelé, at the age of seventeen, was certainly the youngest soccer player to claim the worldwide publicity and admiration that had been showered on him.

Showing no signs of his earlier knee injury, Pelé enjoyed every minute of the reception. When he returned to Santos the crowd was once again waiting for him and again as he trotted onto the Santos playing field he was the object of a mass greeting.

"I don't think I was ever so happy," he later said. "I had done what was expected of me and my countrymen were expressing their gratitude. I didn't think the fans would be so receptive but they were and I was a very proud man. I felt then that all the hard work we had put into making the team so strong was well worth it. We had made the rest of the soccer world come to respect us and although the championship came many miles away from Brazil I found that our people were well aware of each and every game we played in Sweden. To me this was the greatest feeling I have ever had."

During the remainder of the 1958 season Pelé had cause to feel the envy and admiration of crowds who packed stadiums throughout Brazil to see him perform. Many top players all over the world after gaining glory will disappoint fans as they play only a half or so and then leave the field, especially in an unimportant game. But Pelé wasn't one to disappoint the fans as he insisted that since he was one of the major drawing cards he be left in the game. He played every minute of every game unless injured. His dribbling, passing and shooting were a pleasure to watch. Already Santos, which had seen its early lead in the standings disappear because several of its key players, Pelé among them, had been lost to the team because of National Team commitments, was receiving invitations for a foreign tour as well as challenges from several foreign teams that were planning South American exhibition tours. Santos regained its winning ways in the São Paulo League, and at the end of the season ran off a string of eight straight wins.

Pelé finished off the year by being an almost unanimous choice for the top player in Brazil during 1958—a selection that was accepted modestly by him and by the fans with deep admiration.

POUNDING AWAY

Throughout his long playing career, Pelé has maintained an average of almost a goal a game, and one of the reasons was the glorious year of 1959. Instead of resting on the laurels he had gained in the previous year's World Cup, Pelé, the Black Pearl, came out with new enthusiasm and rapidly gained the worldwide reputation of being the greatest professional all-around soccer player and scorer of all time.

Playing with the National Team of Brazil, which was sought by many foreign clubs for exhibition matches, and with Santos, Pelé still managed to put in his time for army service. He would play for Santos on weekends and then return to his army base where he would play on the base's soccer team, in addition to doing the routine duties required of a soldier. If one man is to be credited with helping Pelé establish a record of 127 goals for the year, it would have to be Santos teammate Coutinho, who knew where Pelé would be at all times and hit him with sharp, accurate passes that enabled the Black Pearl to score many of his goals. Coutinho and Pelé worked the wall passes and the open field passes, and their dribbling skills blended well together. When Pelé scored, he was often assisted by Coutinho while a Coutinho goal would often be set up on one of Pelé's passes to the man he still rates as one of the top playmakers in the game's history. They practiced their tactics together long after the other players had left the field. They had a good relationship on the field. Off the field they were often seen together. Some say that with Coutinho in their lineup, Santos changed from one of the best teams in South America to the top soccer club in the world. Coutinho has often been lauded by Pelé, who said, "A great deal of my success that year I scored so many goals was in no small way because of Coutinho, whom I consider one of the greatest teammates I have ever had in soccer. He was a brilliant reader of the game and his ability was great."

To realize just how great a pace Pelé was setting in scoring goals, it should be mentioned that the 100th goal of his professional career was scored on July 31, 1958, and less than a year later while playing for Santos against West Germany's highly regarded Niedersachsen club he registered his 200th goal. He had played in less than 75 games between the time of the 100th and 200th goal.

With huge bonuses already in his pocket, Pelé was starting to become one of the highest paid players in soccer history. Through his scoring and overall play, he began completely to dominate Brazilian soccer. So popular a player did he become that foreign clubs inquired whether Santos was ready to sell him. Some of the offers were almost unbelievable—similar to a baseball club offering the old New York Yankees over a million dollars for the services of a Babe Ruth or a Lou Gehrig. Prior to the offer to Santos, which has been rumored at about one million dollars, the highest transfer fee in soccer history was somewhere in the range of $100,000. When examining these offers it should be kept in mind that few teams were making enough money during a season to come out in the black. The offers upset many Brazilians and some felt that Santos might just grab one to insure its financial position. However, Brazilian fans knew that even if Pelé had been sold by Santos to a club in another country, he could always play for the Brazilian National Team since the rules of the Federation Internationale de Football Association (FIFA), the worldwide ruling body of soccer, clearly state that a player, no matter in what country he is playing, must play for his native nation; even if Pelé changed nationalities, he still wouldn't be able to play for another country since he had already played for Brazil in the 1958 World Cup competition. Still, people were uncertain, and club officials were reported to be weighing the offers seriously. However, even before they had a chance to reject or accept the offer of some one million dollars for his services by a combined three-club organization in Italy, the government stepped in, declaring Pelé a "national asset, a national treasure," and thus ineligible for sale to any foreign club. If Santos so desired, they could sell Pelé, but only to another Brazilian team. Santos officials were fully aware of the reaction of their fans if they did sell him to another club. As one Santos official said later: "I honestly feel that if we had sold him to another club in Brazil our fans would have gone wild, tearing down not only our offices, but the stadium as well. They would probably have hung us for making the deal. No, as far as we were concerned, there was no way we would take the chance of letting him go to another club. Pelé knew of the many offers but he had also told us that since we had given him his chance to play in top-flight competition he wanted to stay with us, and also indicated that as long as he played soccer, he wanted to wear a Santos uniform." Even former Brazilian president Janio Quadros stepped into the story, making a personal appeal to Santos officials to inform all foreign teams that the Brazilian government would not look too kindly on their continuing offers to purchase the king of soccer. He was, as the president said, "nonexportable," which simply meant that no foreign money deal, no matter what the offer was, could be considered.

It was during the 1960 season that Santos started its run of consecutive São Paulo League titles; Pelé was again the master. Not yet twenty, he was looked on by the older players as the man they counted on—or, as one reporter said, "a traffic cop, directing the flow of cars on a busy street corner." Pelé has never bawled out a player in public, either through the press or in front of a crowd. But Pelé is a firm believer in taking a player aside and giving him an irate explanation when he feels that the player hasn't been doing what is expected of him, either on an individual basis or as part of the team pattern of play.

In 1960, Pelé's goal-scoring barrage slackened slightly, but with 78 goals he was again the highest scorer in Brazil, leading Santos to the first of its many national championships. One of the reasons why Pelé's goal production dropped almost fifty goals from the previous season was the concentrated coverage he was getting from the opposition's defenders. But despite his lack of scoring, Santos was winning and the reason was that Pelé, with his masterful control of the ball, sharp passing and speed, would take two and three defenders with him and then with several of his teammates left unmarked pass the ball to them often through the feet of a defender. He was really enjoying himself and putting in many hours of individual practice. Should he make a bad move in the game he would be the first to criticize himself. Then the following day, if not immediately after that game when the stadium was empty, Pelé would go out onto the field and work for hours correcting the mistakes he had made—although they were few and far apart.

It was during the 1960 campaign that Pelé met Rosemarie dos Reis, a Caucasian girl he would secretly court for six years, shielding her from the publicity that always followed him. Pelé recalled the meeting: "I and some of my Santos teammates decided to have some fun and drop in on a girls' basketball game one rainy afternoon. I think, had it not rained, we would have been walking somewhere, since we all enjoyed that. But we decided to have some fun and watch the girls play basketball. I myself always liked basketball and while in Brazil, I liked to work out in the gym playing the sport. Well, anyway, on that day my companions and I liked her as we watched her sit on the bench. We started to yell at the coach to put her in the game, but he wouldn't listen to us. I stopped watching the game and kept looking at her. There was no doubt that she knew who I was, and I am sure the coach also knew. But he was running the team, and she kept sitting on the bench. Later, I talked to her and found out that she was working in a record shop. Then I started to go into the shop to buy records and of course talk to her. I found that she was very sincere, and we started going out secretly. I think it was both our choices, since we knew there would be great publicity if people spotted us in public places. I feel that meeting her was one of the greatest days of my life, even if she never got into the basketball game and just sat on the bench."

Now with a social life of his own Pelé was even busier. He was still devoted one hundred per cent to improving his game, although many felt that it couldn't be improved. Pelé kept inventing new moves, and a defender who had stopped him with a successful maneuver a few games earlier soon found that Pelé had a great memory and would make sure that against this same defender in the return game he would pull another trick from his large assortment. There are some even today who feel that Pelé hasn't used every trick that he has practiced. But if he does need to use one of them one day, he'll be sure to use it to perfection.

Another milestone in his career came on May 19 of the same year, when he notched his 300th goal in an international exhibition game against Standard Football Club of Belgium, always one of Belgium's strongest teams.

Almost free from injury in 1961, Pelé had a glamorous year. Scoring a total of 110 goals—including the 400th of his career—he again teamed with his linemates to make Santos a dominant power. One of his goals led to a prolonged standing ovation from more than 100,000 fans in attendance at Maracaná Stadium, the largest soccer stadium in the world. In the 1950 World Cup finals, during which Brazil dropped a 2–1 decision to Uruguay, a crowd of over 200,000 had gathered for the exciting climax to the first Cup held after the Second World War. Pelé was playing for Santos against the always rough and dangerous Fluminese team. Pelé got the ball before he reached the midfield strip. Jumping, feinting, dribbling and jockeying the ball, he kept passing defenders as he neared the penalty area. Two defenders came in on him; with a well-executed head feint he forced them to bang into one another, leaving only the goalie to beat. Instead of shooting right out at one of the corners of the net, he waited until the goalie committed himself and then easily dribbled right around the keeper, taking himself and the ball into the net. The cheering crowd stood for over ten minutes. After giving his famous salute, Pelé walked over to the Fluminese goalie and they shook hands to the swelling roar of the crowd. Even today, Pelé still congratulates a goalie who has made a great save against him. And many goalies wave and even bow in tribute to the king when he scores against them.

Since Brazil didn't have to qualify for the following year's World Cup, Pelé spent many days and weeks traveling with the Santos team for exhibitions as the year ended and Santos again had won the São Paulo championship. More and more invitations started flowing in both to Santos and to Pelé to make personal appearances. Seemingly every shrewd businessman was looking for Pelé to finance one or another business venture. Pelé accepted some of the offers but was now spending more time with Rosemarie, even though the Brazilian public was still unaware of the love affair and only Pelé's immediate family and some of his closest friends and teammates knew what was going on.

Pelé was at the time also being approached to endorse various products which since he was the idol of the Brazilian people it was hoped they would buy, but Pelé put his foot down. He refused to endorse either cigarettes or hard liquor. When someone asked him why he was turning down this opportunity to make a great deal of Brazilian *cruzeiros,* he simply said: "I know that I have influence on youngsters, and I don't feel that I want them to think if I should endorse these products I want them to use them." To this day Pelé has refrained from endorsing tobacco or liquor, at great financial loss to himself.

In preparation for the following year's World Cup, Santos made a European tour and also played several exhibition games in Argentina and in Uruguay. Pelé's reputation had some promoters making numerous offers to bring Santos into the United States and Canada for matches against either a strong local club or a club from another nation. Meanwhile, Pelé had made a private deal with the Santos officials, calling for him to receive a fixed amount of money from each international exhibition game. Since Pelé was also working hard with the other players who would be representing Brazil in the forthcoming World Cup, however, many of these lucrative offers had to be refused. Some say that had Santos been able to play every one of the exhibition games they were invited to compete in during 1961, the club would have played as many as two hundred games.

The soccer-mad population of Brazil was optimistic as the team prepared for a South American tour that would give some of the younger players the opportunity to prove their mettle in the international soccer arena. Knowing that the competition for the 1962 World Cup would be rough both tactically and physically, Brazilian team manager Aymori Moreira decided that the series of exhibition games would include matches against foreign teams known for fouling—often brutally—some of their opponents.

In one of the games on their South American tour, three Brazilian players were fouled so violently that they were forced to leave the game, compelling Moreira to cancel a scheduled game against Peru. In another game, this one against the always-physical Uruguayans, two other players were injured. The Brazilians were being made to pay for their reputation as well as their tactics of finesse by those opponents who couldn't match them in skill.

Pelé still showed no sign of letting up. He continued to amaze his opponents with moves that left them standing as if in a daze. Often they might kick at Pelé, only to find that he had already passed them and was well on his way to another goal. Looking back at 1961, Pelé feels that in this season he began to gain the maturity and the confidence that today enable him to do anything he desires on a soccer field—with or without the ball.

A YEAR OF EXTREMES

After Pelé's 110-goal performance in 1961, Brazilian fans counted on him to score his usual share of key goals in the 1962 World Cup. Their optimism grew as Pelé scored several crucial goals, starting Santos on its romp to the 1962 São Paulo League championship. Pelé was playing at his best, and while many Brazilians were making the trek to Chile, the scene of the Cup competition, bookies established Brazil as the betting favorite. The fans also felt that with the way Pelé was playing and with the talent available on their squad, Brazil entered the tournament as the logical choice.

The Brazilians, under the direction of Moreira, were placed in Group Three against Czechoslovakia, Mexico and Spain and their matches were to be played at Viña del Mar. In the opening game the Brazilians, perhaps playing with too much confidence early in the game and seemingly uninspired, scored twice in the second half to get past a stubborn but inefficient Mexican team.

In their next game, against Czechoslovakia, Pelé pulled a leg muscle and limped off the field, not to return during the remaining games. Brazil appeared to be shattered, as they were unable to mount a sustained drive. They had to settle for a scoreless draw against the Czechs, who seemed well content with the deadlock, which virtually assured them of a spot in the upcoming quarterfinals. Suddenly, Brazilian fans were jeering their team as they took the field for a match against Spain. They were jeering even louder at the end of the first half as the Spaniards took a 1–0 lead. But Brazil, getting a verbal blast from Moreira, came out strong in the second half, put two goals on the scoreboard and came away with a 2–1 victory to win Group III. Still, Pelé would not be available for the next match—the game against England, the forerunner of several top games between the two soccer powers.

In the first half, Garrincha, the Little Bird, was brilliant, teaming with Pelé's replacement Amarildo, who hadn't expected to see any action at all. But a goal by Hitchens enabled the English to leave the field with a 1–1 half time score. Once again Moreira rallied his forces and sat smiling on the bench as his team followed their half time instructions and emerged a 3–1 victor.

Next came the semifinal round matching Brazil against host Chile. The Brazilians were nervous since it appeared that the Chileans would go unpunished no matter what kind of foul they committed. In a qualifying game, Chilean forward Sanchez had broken the nose of Italy's Maschio without receiving as much as a caution from the referee. Pelé sat in on the pregame briefing giving his encouragement and then watched as the Brazilians outplayed and outmuscled the Chileans by a score of 4–2, with Garrincha and Vava each scoring twice. Garrincha appeared ready to score the hat trick but his two goals had so incensed the Chilean defenders that they deliberately fouled him every time he either got near the ball or started one of his famous moves. Finally, with the victory all but assured, Garrincha kicked back and was promptly ejected from the game. Probably no man in soccer better knows the futile efforts of embarrassed defenders than Pelé, who later said that he couldn't fault the Little Bird for his retaliation.

In the other semifinal, Czechoslovakia outscored Yugoslavia 3–1. Now the Brazilians had the Chilean fans rooting for them in their battle against the European Czechs. Pelé wanted desperately to play in the championship game but the medics refused. In the championship game Zozimo, playing in his first World Cup that year, was brilliant at halfback, setting up many plays. The Brazilians outclassed the Czechs, beating their taller opponents to head balls and dribbling around and even through the Czech defense in a 3–1 victory. Goal scorers for Brazil were Amarildo, Zito and Vava. Asked for his reaction on Brazil's winning its second straight crown even though he had played almost a meaningless role, Pelé said, "I am disappointed that I was unable to play most of the games, but thank God that Brazil won." The victory touched off another jubilant parade in Brazil, in which even the substitutes were mobbed by overzealous fans. True to his nature, Pelé didn't try to grab any of the headlines, letting Amarildo and others enjoy the spotlight. The king was humble, feeling that he hadn't contributed.

As had been the case for most of his career, Pelé didn't stay idle for long. He was soon back in action, not only for Santos but for the São Paulo Selection team, an all-star club. Now Pelé had something else to shoot for; denied a chance to be in the final game of the World Cup, he played like a man possessed as he led Santos to the South American Club Championship (Copa Libertadores). It marked the first time that a Brazilian club had won the South American Club Championship match and the right to compete for the Copa Intercontinentale, the World Club Championship against European titlist Benfica of Portugal. Santos ran through its São Paulo League schedule and wrapped up the title early in the campaign. Pelé was again named to the All-Star League team, a position he held for nine straight years. Santos was given a better than ever chance of stopping Benfica, which appeared to be out for blood since in the previous year they had been beaten in a bitter three-game series by Uruguay's Penarol.

The opening match of the two-game Copa Intercontinentale series was scheduled for Rio de Janeiro's Maracaná Stadium. Pelé scored one goal and assisted on another as the Santos club won a hard-fought 3–2 victory. The series then returned to Portugal. If Benfica were to win, as expected, the third and decisive game would be played at a neutral site. However, Pelé, to the cheers of the Benfica fans, was brilliant as he ripped up the turf in Lisbon, scoring the three-goal hat trick as Santos won a convincing 5–2 victory. Pelé enjoyed the reception he received in Portugal, and felt the fans were very knowledgeable and fair about their soccer.

The year held still more glory for Pelé as he won the Brazilian scoring title for the fifth straight year and was voted Brazil's player of the year by the press. Though Pelé was tired and in need of rest, it had to wait until after Santos played out its committed schedule of international exhibition matches. Often the center of numerous press conferences, the fatigued Pelé could still find two hours to talk to a group of youngsters who had journeyed with their schoolmaster over two hundred miles to see the Black Pearl play a game.

When the season finally ended Pelé turned to the beach, spending a great deal of time with his future wife, Rosemarie. Together they were happy, although Edson, as she used to and still in fact calls him, knew that his privacy would soon be interrupted by the many business offers he was getting. Through it all Pelé retained his simple outlook on life.

As Pelé once said: "As long as I can give some happiness I am happy."

Since Pelé was already involved in some real-estate dealings, builders and architects, hoping to get both financial backing and endorsements, came looking for him. Often Pelé, who enjoys fishing, was pursued by businessmen as well as by the press while on a private boat. The press, on more than one occasion, chartered a boat of their own to try to find him for what they thought was an important question that had to be answered. One man, trying to get Pelé to endorse a cigarette, even chartered a private helicopter and tried to land it near Pelé's boat. However, it is reported that the water was so choppy that the copter couldn't land and the pilot abandoned the project and returned to Santos.

THE PACE ACCELERATES

Pelé was becoming a millionaire. The first millionaire soccer player (and some say that at least until the 1980s or even later he will be the only one to achieve this plateau) was still playing for Santos—and getting better, if that's possible.

Brazil was now the soccer capital of the world, Santos were the national heroes and Pelé was still the undisputed king of the game. Foreign teams were still trying to lure him into coming to their respective nations, and even the mandate set down a few years earlier by Brazil that he was a natural asset didn't stop them from at least trying. More clubs in both Italy and Portugal were threatening to try to get to him even if it meant that they would file suit in an international court.

Obviously getting tired of these rumors of his being sold, Pelé decided to clarify the issue. In a São Paulo press conference, which was attended by reporters from all over Brazil and South America, Pelé told the news media that he would never play for any team other than Santos in club competition. Still the rumors persisted and the offers continued. Pelé knew of them and seemed disturbed but grateful. He was angered by the reports, since he felt he had made it clear that Santos was his club; but he had to feel proud since it was more and more obvious that he had become the soccer world's biggest drawing power.

Pelé's fortune and business interests were growing at a rapid pace. Unlike many athletes, he didn't just jump into a possible business venture. Continually sought after to endorse various products as well as invest in various businesses, he showed much good business sense. He himself, with the advice of Zoca, went over every word in every proposed contract offer and more likely than not rejected the offer. Pelé felt that only if the investment was foolproof would he go into it; as far as endorsements were concerned, he laid down a set of ground rules for himself.

Like many an American sports hero, Pelé was also surrounded by some who are called "hangers-on," but unlike some who have been associated with American football heroes they couldn't take advantage of Pelé. They liked to be around him but he wasn't one to pick up their tabs. There are few people who have been successful in trying to use Pelé. He likes to be with people, but he also knows only too well that they could hurt him if he listened to them.

At about this time Pelé started thinking about eventually going back to school and getting a real education, although those who knew him well at the time, and those reporters who interviewed him abroad when Santos was on a foreign tour, came to realize that despite his lack of a formal education Pelé could hold a conversation on most subjects. Some say later that his desire to go back to school stemmed from his talks with Rosemarie.

Pelé doesn't, even today, just rush into a conversation but will listen carefully, and if he feels that he doesn't have anything to offer he will only listen. But if he feels he can offer something he will voice his opinion. He'll talk with anyone about music, one of his favorite pastimes. Like most other Brazilians he loves the beat of samba. And his record collection is the envy of many.

Although he was at the time still practicing every day and engaging in volleyball and basketball to keep in prime shape, he also was starting to develop his fishing interests. He would go off on a chartered boat with a few close friends and, despite the efforts of some Brazilian reporters to try for an exclusive interview by chartering their own boat and pulling alongside Pelé's boat, he really enjoyed fishing. Pelé would often be seen racing a quarter of a mile or so from the boat once it docked to a place he had to be for an important meeting.

His body condition was becoming the marvel of Brazilian doctors who examined him to see just why he was such a great athlete. What they discovered was that he had and still has about twenty-five percent better peripheral vision than other athletes; this is one of the reasons he is able to send a pass off to one of his teammates on the side while looking straight ahead. He exercised hard, continuing to build his body muscles. Santos was now winning game after game, and Pelé was enjoying himself on the field whether in practice or in a regular São Paulo League game. Brazilian newspapers asked Pelé many questions—and not only about himself or his family. Because of his ability (and probably also to help build circulation) they wanted him to analyze various games he might be attending. Pelé enjoyed this new line of work, as he got a chance to develop a theory and then put it into his own words, trying to spot the turning points of a game or the individual efforts of a player, many of whom would eventually be named to the Brazilian World Cup team of 1966.

While wrapping up another São Paulo League championship, Santos entered the South American Cup in a bid for its second straight championship. The competition was hard but the Santos team was strong and in great condition. In just one week, they played two regular league matches, an exhibition game against a touring side from Europe, and then a Copa Libertadores qualifying round game. During this amazing span they used only two substitutes, winning all four games. After this, they were considered the choice to repeat as South American champions.

Yet another milestone awaited Pelé, and it came on August 28, when Santos played their bitter rival, Botofoga. Pelé needed only two goals to reach the 600-goal mark in his professional career, and the fans were aware of it. They had come to the stadium expecting the historic event to be fulfilled. There were the usual number of vendors outside doing a good business selling pictures of Pelé and pins with his picture on them. It was a muggy night with a light drizzle falling. The field, well manicured, was a bit slippery. Still, the weather didn't dim the enthusiasm of the crowd. Pelé notched number 599 after only twenty-one minutes of play. Now the excitement was high as the Brazilian soccer fans had started the countdown long before. With six minutes gone in the second half, Pelé took a cross from the right side and with his powerful half volley he struck the ball firmly as it bounced off the soft pitch. The ball went into the goal from 30 yards out. That was number 600, and the fans responded with enthusiasm as he gave them his famous goal salute. The

Botofoga goalie was one of the first to come over and shake his hand, and Pelé responded by patting him on the head while the huge crowd jumped for joy. By this point in his career, almost every one of Pelé's goals was greeted by thousands standing and shouting in unison, "Pelé! Pelé!"

Santos won the South American Cup competition for the second straight year, while in a bitter battle with many fouls called, for the European Cup, AC Milan, featuring the finest members of the Italian National Team, beat Benfica of Portugal 2–1. The game was marred by several fistfights and many players were cautioned by the referee. The bookies rated Santos the choice to defeat the Italians in what would surely be a bitter soccer game. Games between Italian and Brazilian teams usually are bitter.

This was to be the case as the clubs squared off for the first match. Pelé, being closely guarded and often fouled, couldn't shake off his tail. The Italians put two defenders on Pelé throughout the match. One of them was Janich, who on one occasion held Pelé's shirt as the Black Pearl broke through the defense. After the referee blew the whistle Janich pushed Pelé to the turf. The rest of the Brazilian team was almost totally ineffective as they suffered a 4–2 defeat.

If Santos had hopes of winning its second straight Intercontinentale championship, they would have to defeat the Italians twice in a row—something few clubs then or today have been able to accomplish, as international play always finds AC Milan ready for action. But working hard and putting in several secret training sessions so as not to give Italian spies a chance to see the aggressive tactics they planned to use, Santos came out for the second game a changed team, willing to mix it with the Italians who seemed surprised at the aggressiveness of the Brazilians. Santos played a game in which they often humiliated the Italians by passing the ball as many as fifteen times before either taking a shot or being fouled by an irate defender. This type of passing display enabled Santos to gain a reputation as the best ball control team in the world, and in this second match they used it to perfection in beating AC Milan 4–2, setting the stage for a third and deciding contest.

With each team having one win to its credit and a couple of weeks to prepare for the rematch, Santos and AC Milan put in long hours on the practice field. A day before the match coaches of both clubs were warned by FIFA authorities that no excessive fouling would be tolerated and any player ejected for fighting would be suspended. As a result of this warning the game was surprisingly clean, unlike the first two matches.

Early in the second half Pepe (not to be confused with Pelé) set up the lone tally in Brazil's 1–0 win as he deftly dribbled around two defenders before sending a shot from 20 yards out toward the Italian goal. The ball hit the hand of one Italian defender and Brazil converted the resulting penalty shot. It may have been a lucky goal but it was still enough to give Santos its second straight World Club Championship title, and they were proud to claim the title of top soccer club in the world.

Pelé finished off the year with 76 goals and an estimated 50 or 60 assists. He even played halfback whenever the Santos team felt his ball control skill was needed there. Pelé resented the switch in position—until he found that with a swerving kick he could put the ball into the opposing team's goal from almost forty yards out. His kick would send the ball flying in an actual curve toward the goalie, who would often find the ball turning away from him at the last minute. Also taking many free kicks, Pelé developed the drop shot which dipped down suddenly although it appeared to the goalie that the ball was going over the crossbar.

As Brazilian fans turned out in record numbers whenever Santos played, Pelé was getting richer by the day by endorsing everything except tobacco products and hard liquor. There are stories that some of the leading manufacturers of these two products hired special teams to try and get the king to change his mind. Pelé would listen to their offers, then calmly refuse, saying it was not in the best interest of the children around the world. One company was so intent on getting his name on their product that it is rumored they fired at least fifteen men who, after many hours of hard work, had only Pelé's simple refusal, as well as a big smile and possibly his autograph.

Envious of his new wealth, which saw him enter a partnership with a Santos builder known only as "Fat Pepé," the opposing team saw fit to cut him down brutally to a degree even greater than in the past. Pelé started to retaliate. He was now becoming known as a fighter who didn't hesitate to argue with a referee, receiving the yellow caution card quite often. In a match against Argentina, Pelé blew his cool; two years later he recalled that incident for a jam-packed press conference.

"This one opponent," Pelé said, "seemed to have only one purpose in the game. That was to make sure I was on the ground more than I was on my feet. Every time I got the ball he would be all over me. That's okay if he does it legally, but whenever I would start to make a move he would trip and kick me. I was getting pretty angry, something I don't usually do. Finally I motioned to the referee after he had fouled me, but the referee just signaled for us to play on. It seemed he didn't really realize what fouls the Argentinian was doing to me and I got very angry. My opponent kicked me three times in about five minutes and only one foul was called against him. Then he spit in my face. That really made me mad and when he did it again, this time doing so as he kicked me, I went after him. The other players broke it up and I figured that would be the end of his fouling and as we went up the field I warned him not to do it again. He didn't —for about three minutes; then I got the ball, and again he kicked me and spat at me. This time I jumped up from the ground and kicked him back. The fans went wild. They had never seen me so angry at an opponent and they seemed to enjoy it. I didn't, because when I go onto the field I do so with the desire to play soccer. It was obvious that this Argentinian player didn't want to kick the ball, he wanted to kick me.

"Since that incident I have retaliated only two or three times but I feel that if I have to get up and defend myself because the referee appears to see nothing, I will do so. I want to play football [soccer] and I want the fans to get the action for the good money they pay to see the sport played. There are too many opposing players I have encountered who because they don't have the skill try and make a big name for themselves by being known as the man who chopped Pelé down. This really sickens me and makes me play even harder, as they soon find out."

Although he was relatively free of injuries during 1964, Pelé's goal production fell off drastically with a tally of only 60 goals, his lowest total since first joining the Santos team as a full-time starter. One of the reasons Pelé was being slowed down in putting the ball into the net was the new type of defensive alignments starting to be employed by clubs. It was almost total defense with six men back. Pelé's reaction:

"Soccer today has become far too defensive. It is no longer a show. This is bad for the public. There are many teams who do well not because they are good but because they are very negative. I don't enjoy a game in which the other team plays only defense. This doesn't allow the fans to see an exciting or even a well-played game because there are many difficulties created with the style."

On November 21, in Ribeirão Preto, Brazil, Pelé staged one of the most remarkable single-game performances of his long career. Playing against Botofoga, the magician, as some were now referring to him, hit the nets for eight goals and assisted on two of his team's other three tallies as Santos whipped Botofoga 11–0 in one of the most lopsided scores in Brazilian history. His previous high for a single game had been five goals, and some say that had he wanted to, he could have scored at least ten goals in this match. Twice he passed off when he had only the goalie to beat. Asked some eleven years later how he felt about that individual performance, Pelé smiled and shrugged his shoulders before answering:

"The first four or five goals were real fun," Pelé said, "but the game was so one-sided that I didn't really think about the other three goals. I just wanted the game to end and when it did I was happy it was over. I really felt sorry for the other team's goalie; our goalie had such an easy time of it that he could just as easily have taken a chair and sat down waiting for them to come in and take a shot on him. I don't enjoy such competition because it does little for a good player or a good team. When you can score just about every time you get the ball the fans may yell but you yourself get very careless and you don't play as well as you can. Give me a close game anytime. That I enjoy."

Late in the year Pelé scored two goals and added three assists as Brazil won a tournament in Rio called the Mini World Cup.

The following year Pelé started working out early. Under the careful eye of the team's physical health director, Pelé stressed more and more exercise in his workouts. The new trainer, Prof. Julio Mazzei had received his master's degree at Michigan State. Pelé credits Mazzei for helping maintain his conditioning for such a prolonged period of time. The professor has written many books on physical education and conditioning, and is still today the man with whom Pelé consults for a vast number of physical problems. Mazzei is dedicated to the belief that only a well-conditioned team can win important matches, especially if other conditions and factors between the two teams are similar. He feels that at the end of the match the superior conditioned team will prevail.

Pelé showed his great conditioning right from the start of the 1965 season, scoring the hat trick three times in his first fifteen games. He was once again the take-charge guy, the player the other members of the team can rely on to get them moving in the right direction. Santos ran away from the rest of the field in taking the São Paulo League title for the fourth straight time. When the season ended, Pelé had a total of 101 goals, his third 100-or-better season in seven years. He scored career goal number 700 in a match on April 15 against the Corintians. Pelé, as he had done on numerous other occasions, picked up the ball, then shook hands with the opposing goalie. With the World Cup still a year away, the Brazilians scheduled a series of top international games. Pelé, of course, was the first man selected for the National Team. Vicente Feola would manage the team, and Brazil also named Dr. Hilton Gosling as co-selector. It was the doctor's duty to whip the Brazilian team into top shape. For Pelé, this meant a double dose of training—from the doctor as well as from Mazzei. Dr. Gosling, amazed at the great physical condition and stamina that Pelé displayed, decided to try an experiment. He took Pelé to the university in Rio de Janeiro where tests were made. The testers attached wires and instruments to the king of soccer and were amazed at the results. The tests were repeated on a regular schedule, but the results were always the same. They showed that Pelé is about a half-second faster in reacting to a sudden shift in the movement of another person present in a room than is the average person. It also showed that he can make a decision in an emergency, such as reacting to a flash on the road, faster than most people. His I.Q. level, although not revealed, was among the top 10 percent in Brazil. Pelé is, according to Dr. Gosling, a man "who would be a genius no matter what field of endeavor—either physical or mental —he had decided to enter into."

That's just what Pelé's opponents have been saying for years.

It was during the later part of 1965 that someone suggested to Pelé that he enter politics; there was certainly little doubt that had he sought any elected office he would be a sure winner. Pelé remembers that he first laughed at this suggestion, and then thought about it for "maybe five or ten minutes before I said no."

"I have always stayed out of politics and race relations," he explains. "I feel that I am doing what I do best and as far as race relations are concerned I respect everybody for what they are—not for their religion or the color of their skin."

Pelé explained that Brazilian politics are rough and that he felt no desire to put his name up for political office.

"I want the people to judge me on the soccer field. I am a soccer player and that is what I am interested in. I think politics are all right for some people but not for me, and I think I will always feel the same way no matter what else I accomplish in my life."

No matter what success Pelé enjoyed on the field he still strived hard to continue to be a perfectionist. When he first broke into the Santos lineup he would put in extra hours constantly drilling over a point in his game he felt needed improvement. And even though he had gained success and high esteem, a bad play on his part during a game would see him stay after the match to try to iron out the faults. Often on the day following a match Pelé would be at practice a few hours before his teammates in an effort to work out something in his game that he felt needed straightening out.

Despite his ever-growing fame, Pelé was still a down-to-earth person, often embarrassed easily when meeting with foreign dignitaries.

During the year, Pelé met with the late Senator Robert Kennedy. Someone had forgotten to tell Pelé that Senator Kennedy wanted to meet him after a Santos game. As usual, Pelé left the field at the conclusion of the match and went straight into the locker room for his post-game shower. A messenger from the Santos club went into the dressing room with Senator Kennedy, but Pelé was nowhere to be found. Told Pelé was in the shower, the messenger walked fully dressed into the shower room where he found Pelé full of soap. He told Pelé that Senator Kennedy of the United States wanted to meet him, and since the senator had an impending meeting with Brazilian officials, the meeting should take place immediately. Undaunted, Pelé wrapped a towel around his lower torso and still soapy went to meet Senator Kennedy. He apologized to Kennedy for his soapy appearance and the Senator laughed good-naturedly.

Years later, Pelé still talked about that meeting and admitted that he was indeed embarrassed to have to meet the senator without being fully dressed.

A BIG, BUSY YEAR

The year 1966 was possibly the most dynamic in Pelé's life. He began to grow weary of the rugged arena of international soccer competition and seriously considered giving up the sport. He became a millionaire for the second time over as he expanded his vast business interests. He donated more and more money to various charities, many of which have benefited the children of Brazil. He took New York City by storm and even decided to end his bachelorhood by marrying the girl he had been dating secretly for several years. It was a big, busy year both on and off the field—one that Pelé recalls vividly.

The biggest annual event in Brazil is Carnival time, when Pelé and every other red-blooded Brazilian as well as thousands of tourists flock to the cities for the week-long festivities starting at the end of February. As a youth, Pelé used to dance and take part in the merrymaking through the night. Even soccer has to take a back seat to the Carnival, as most games are scheduled for other times.

Although still not courting Rosemarie in public, Pelé knew that the Brazilian people were more and more aware that their king of soccer just might be ready to marry—although Rosemarie would be the first to counter the claim that she was the queen of soccer. As far as she was concerned she was in love with Edson Arantes do Nascimento, the man she married during Carnival time of that year.

The ceremony could have been elaborate, but both Pelé and Rosemarie decided that they wanted a small, private ceremony and that only the closest relatives and friends would be invited. Pelé had and still has so many friends that, according to Mazzei, if he had invited them all to the wedding in Brazil "he would have to rent a large stadium and if he later on their honeymoon decided to join some of his many Italian friends for dinner there wouldn't have been a restaurant big enough to handle the number of people who would have accepted his invitation to break bread with the couple." Deciding on the priest who would perform the marriage ceremony was indeed a big chore, since many of the Brazilian clergy had been in the habit of addressing him, whenever they met him, not as Edson but as Pelé. Pelé wanted the man who would marry him to be one who on all previous meetings with him had called him Edson. According to Mazzei, Pelé's adviser and trainer, the ceremony was a simple, dignified Roman Catholic affair with about thirty people present, including several of his closest Santos teammates such as the hard-shooting Pepe. The ceremony was held in the house in Santos that had been given Pelé when he signed another professional contract with that club a year earlier. Today Pelé's parents live in the house. Inevitably, reporters learned of the impending marriage and started parking themselves on his doorstep some three or four days beforehand. Whenever a reporter asked Pelé if indeed it was true that he was ready to take a wife he would smile and refuse to answer. By the time the marriage actually did take place there were more than 50 reporters on hand, outnumbering the families of both Pelé and Rosemarie. According to Professor Mazzei, Pelé was just like any other groom on the big day—nervous and hardly able to dress himself. He was, as Mazzei said, "all tied up in knots and all thumbs whenever he tried to do something." A simple meal was served and it is rumored that Pelé sent one of the wedding helpers out to offer some refreshments to the press, who were busy flashing the news of the wedding all over Brazil and in most major nations of the world. The headlines dealing with Pelé's marriage to his secretly courted bride remained on the front pages in Brazil for at least three days. Words of congratulation flowed in from government officials and other soccer players who had come to know and respect the undisputed king of them all.

For the honeymoon, one of Pelé's most ardent followers, who owned a home (more fittingly, something like a castle) in Bavaria had been contacted and had offered the newly wedded couple its use. Honeymoon plans as well as time and date of departure were kept secret, and only when the couple arrived at the airport to depart on the honeymoon was the Brazilian public made aware of the fact that they were leaving. Even the owner of the home was sworn to secrecy, along with the hired help who would be at the service of the newly married couple. So popular had Pelé's reputation grown worldwide that whenever he and Rosemarie would go for a stroll in the immediate area of their honeymoon site people would recognize him and sooner or later word would be received by the press to rush one of their men over to talk to Pelé. While enjoying their honeymoon, Pelé and Rosemarie, perhaps using one or more of Pelé's maneuvers in avoiding opposing defenders, quickly got out of their way and as Pelé later said, "We really enjoyed ourselves, taking in everything we were able to and just relaxing."

The newlyweds then went to Italy where they were photographed walking hand in hand through the streets of Riccone, one of the cities of their choice and a city that Rosie, as he often calls her, wanted to see for its tranquil beauty. Pelé and Rosie requested and were granted a private audience with Pope Paul VI. Wherever Pelé and Rosie went, the fans followed. Italian fans are among the most knowledgeable in the world and even though Pelé helped Santos beat their team in an earlier World Club championship, they respected his ability. Many a youngster came running to him for an autograph while he was touring Rome. If Rosie was harassed, she didn't show it as she simply realized that this was her Edson—never able to turn down a youngster requesting the king's autograph. Pelé knew he would be back in Europe in four months for the eventful 1966 World Cup in England, and that he would be in the spotlight as he had been for so many years.

After the honeymoon, Pelé and Rosie set up house in Santos. Even today they laugh about some of the people they encountered on their honeymoon. As Pelé later said, "It takes all types of people to make a world, and some of the people we met while in Italy were indeed very strange, but you know me well enough to know that I love all the people I come into contact with. Some were harder to deal with than others, but they too have their rights and their desires as well as their strangeness. I loved talking to some of the little ones who came to me and sought my autograph. I never, if possible, refuse to give out an autograph." Upon hearing this, Mazzei laughed and then simply said, "I felt that if Pelé were asked by those present at the wedding for an autograph he would have held the wedding ring in one hand and with his other hand signed autographs. Maybe that's one of the reasons I love the man so. He does everything he can for people. That's his simple nature."

Now Rosie, who still misses most of Pelé's games even if she is in the same city, was ready to see him play in person. Television had been her only previous exposure to his actions on the field, because of the couple's secret courtship. After the first game she attended as Pelé's wife, Rosie revealed she was nervous and even today, after seeing him play many a game, she is still fearful that Edson will get hurt.

Meanwhile, Pelé was playing for Santos and working out in the rugged training drills and exhibition games with the Brazilian National Team, as Brazil sought the coveted Jules Rimet World Cup Trophy for an unparalleled third straight time. In addition to the time he spent with Santos and with the National Team, there were many business meetings. It was a busy time for Pelé, and he later said he felt sorry that he couldn't spend as much time with Rosie as he had hoped.

Now came even more practice time and a tough series of physical tests in which each and every National Team player was forced to undergo stress tests in which individual heart recovery rates were checked after practices and exhibition games. Brazil subjected every player, including Pelé, to the most scientific series of physical examinations ever given to any team preparing for a sports event. The preparations included "mental talks" in order to get them in the best psychological shape possible for the tournament, which was expected to be one of the best and closest of all World Cups.

Vicente Feola was back at the helm, and after a careful series of tune-up matches in South America, he arranged a tour of Europe with the team, using all its players in many of its matches. Brazil did not want to get caught shorthanded in the event of injury. While in Europe, Brazil stressed a definite pattern of play, having their four backs split in order to position one almost midway between the goalie and the penalty area markings, another center back slightly to the left of the goalie about 12 yards from him, with the two other backs some three or four yards from the right and left lines respectively joining the edges of the penalty area.

As had been the case four years earlier while playing the exhibition games, Pelé was the center of the team's drive. He was the man whom the other players were looking for. Such old-timers as Bellini and Orlando were added to the team more as an honor than for what Feola had planned for them as far as competitive action was concerned. The European soccer press besieged the Brazilians for interviews as Dr. Gosling moved the team through Sweden, getting them into peak condition for the upcoming series of matches. Pelé told an English reporter that even the boots the players would wear were carefully examined by not only the player but by the trainer, the coach and even the shoemaker, who would accompany the team on its European tour. Specially prepared food was imported from Brazil. After a lackluster 3–2 practice win over Sweden, the team was given a special practice session just a few hours after the game since Coach Feola was displeased with the team's performance. The return to Sweden, scene of his great 1958 performance, gave Pelé great pleasure as the Swedish fans well remembered the brilliant performance that shot him into prominence.

After the tour of Sweden the team went to Madrid to play an exhibition game against the strong Atletico Madrid team. A crowd of over 100,000 jammed the Bernabeu Stadium to watch the match. Pelé didn't disappoint them, netting three goals and assisting on two others. So sought-after was Pelé that reporters flew in from all over Europe, cornering him after the match in Madrid. It was there that Pelé dropped a bombshell which made front-page news in Brazil and elsewhere:

"I have thought about retiring for some time now. I have talked it over with my family. Perhaps, if I am able, I might stay another two or three years, until I am twenty-eight. For me there can be no greater experience than the World Cup in England, the home of the game. Whether we win or not, there can be nothing left to achieve. I have no reason to want to play in another World Cup anywhere else after England.

"It was a terrible disappointment to me when my Santos club prevented me from playing for the Rest of the World Team in your Centenary Match in 1963. My only ambition now is to win, if we can, in the finals at Wembley."

But Pelé during that interview also left the door open, saying: "Maybe if I were needed badly enough, I might play in the 1970

World Cup in Mexico, but I don't think so. I would like soon to play just now and then for an amateur club. I want more time with my family. Playing is not the problem, it is the traveling. I can't remember when I last spent a whole week with my family. My honeymoon in Europe was the first vacation I have ever had. The only time I get days off is if I'm injured.

"Slowly, I will drop out of the game, spending more time on my businesses. Not that money is any problem, but I must still have some occupation."

Pelé lauded the efforts of Dr. Gosling for the surprising absence of injuries incurred by team members. He spent several minutes explaining to reporters why the boots, which were carefully examined after every tune-up game as well as after each practice session, helped in his opinion to cut down the number of injuries that had hit many other teams.

"An impression of the feet of every member of the team was taken before we left Brazil," explained Pelé, perhaps calling on his younger days as a cobbler's apprentice. "It seems that the weight of the feet is distributed through three small areas, the ball, the heel and the outside, and according to the angle at which each player's foot naturally rests, the length of the studs on each part of the boot must be varied to maintain this natural position. This avoids small but constant strain being put on the ankle and knee ligaments, which can eventually lead to injury under sudden stress. To me this is very important and something that I wasn't aware of before hearing the reason why our trainer and doctor have been so careful with the selection and durability of our shoes."

The Brazilian team, which selected Lyme as their headquarters and point of relaxation, arrived in England a few days prior to their opening kickoff. Again Pelé was cornered for an interview and asked about the teams he felt would give the Brazilians the most difficulty. Pelé had seen many of them in action and was also a member of the Brazilian team that in 1964 had captured the Little World Cup held in Brazil.

"I look for a team that plays positive and not negative or defensive soccer to give us the most difficulty," Pelé answered. "I think that England will be a definite factor since they impressed me in 1964 with their aggressive style of play, and of course being on their home grounds will also benefit them. There are some other strong teams like West Germany and I feel the Italians will be difficult if they abandon some of their defensive tactics. And then there are other teams we don't know too much about. I look for a very interesting series, especially in the games when teams of different style and reason get together in an important match."

The Brazilian team worked like a well-oiled machine. Their trainers made sure that the players got just as much sleep as needed and were back at their hotel before curfew time. If any player desired to leave the area of his hotel, he had to inform a club official of his planned whereabouts and activity. Some critics felt that the National Team officials were overcautious, but they were determined to give their fans the best possible show. In order to avoid fatigue and boredom while traveling, the schedules of all buses, planes or trains were checked and rechecked by Dr. Gosling so that the players would not spend more time getting to and from games than necessary. Rush-hour trips to practice and to the upcoming matches were avoided and Dr. Gosling arranged a schedule which enabled the players to better adjust their bodies to the four-hour time difference between England and Brazil.

"Such small details," said Pelé in an interview, "don't of course, help you to win matches, but they make sure you don't lose simply because someone is travel-sick or tired. This to me at least is very important."

Pelé revealed that the players on his team were well aware of the number of fans who had traveled from Brazil to England for the hoped-for historic occasion: a third Brazilian win would give them permanent possession of the Rimet Trophy, which was to be awarded to the first nation to become a three-time winner.

"You don't realize," said Pelé, "what this World Cup means to us in Brazil. We have more supporters going to England than went across the Andes to Chile in 1962. They are even selling their cars to raise the needed money to be able to say 'I was in England for the World Cup.' "

Then showing his diplomacy which in no small way must be credited to the likes of Dr. Gosling, Pelé delighted his English interviewers:

"No other nation would we trust to take our money for tickets in

October and not receive the tickets until the next April. Mexico, Germany, nowhere else can be the same after England, with its wonderful reputation for both sportsmanship and administration. Being in England and seeing the reception my teammates and I have been getting is a great pleasure for me and makes me very happy."

An impressive opening-day ceremony marked the start of the World Cup. Pelé, along with his teammates, took his place proudly on the field amidst the members of the other fifteen competing teams. Photographers made a dash at him and the flashbulbs popped away. Pelé felt like a little boy as he stood on the field, anxious to be in action in one of the first-round games, set to begin for his Brazilian team on the home grounds of Everton on July 12 against Bulgaria. It would be a day Pelé and the rest of Brazil will always remember with deep despair.

From the opening whistle it was apparent that Brazil had too much class for its Bulgarian opponents. The Bulgarian defenders were unable to cope with the speed and finesse of Brazil's tactical, almost perfect performance. As had been the case many times before, the opponents started to foul the Brazilian players brutally, with Pelé suffering the brunt. Twice he was chopped down from behind in the opening stages of the game. The Bulgarian defender assigned to guard Pelé on a man-to-man basis resorted to calling on one of his teammates to come over and attempt to stop Pelé from making him look like a fool. The teammate did as he was asked, but instead of helping to guard Pelé he seemed to take great pleasure in ankle tapping or even kneeing and tripping the king of soccer. The referees, who had looked tough in some international exhibition matches a week or so earlier, could probably have stopped what was soon to happen. The fouling grew even more brutal. Some say that the worst thing Pelé could have done in terms of his well-being was to score Brazil's initial goal midway through the first half on a booming direct free kick from twenty yards out, which fooled the opposing goalie as it first rose and then dipped into the net. Bulgarian defender Zhechev went after Pelé again and again, forcing one press-box reporter to say that "Pelé won't finish the World Cup. It's amazing that he hasn't gone mad." There were rumors circulating in the press box at half time that the Brazilians in an effort to protect Pelé might even move him to a halfback spot. But at the start of the second half

Pelé returned to his familiar inside left spot, again receiving the brunt of punishment. Pelé frustrated the Bulgarian defenders, and even did some fouling of his own.

Still the referee appeared to see nothing. Suddenly a foul against Pelé was awarded the Bulgarians and Pelé threw up his hands in disgust. Another Brazilian direct kick, this time by the crafty Garrincha in the later stages of the game, gave Brazil its 2–0 victory, but after the gruelling match Pelé was sore. Word reached Brazil that it was indeed doubtful that he would be able to play in the team's next match against the Hungarians. Immediately the people poured into the streets and prayers were held in churches across the land. Old women lit candles hoping for their great star to have a speedy recovery. Brazil was in a state of despair as the police rushed to the Bulgarian consulate to protect it against an anticipated march by the Brazilian people. The prayers continued in Brazil for their star, now proclaimed by various hand-painted signs "Our Saviour."

Medical treatment was administered by the doctors and the trainer. Pelé himself was angry, saying he didn't feel he would be able to play against Hungary. His knees were just too sore and his entire body ached from the many fouls he had incurred. The European press criticized both the Bulgarian team and the officials for allowing such fouls to take place without ejecting one or more of the foul makers. Late into the night the lights in the hotel rooms and meeting rooms of the Brazilian National Team officials burned as they started making plans for changing the lineup should Pelé be unable to play against the fast-moving and well-disciplined Hungarian team. But they themselves knew that without Pelé there was little hope of beating Hungary and gaining a berth in the quarterfinal round.

Despite his great recuperative powers, there was no way that Pelé could dress for the match against the Hungarians, and the Brazilians were totally outplayed. They managed to leave the field at the half time with a 1–1 tie, thanks to Tostao's converting a rebound of a hard shot by Lima, Pelé's brother-in-law (who married one of Rosemarie's sisters). But in the second half, Hungary over-powered Brazil and took the lead on a brilliant goal by Parkas. Pelé was sad as, a few minutes later, the Hungarians nailed down their 3–1 win on a penalty shot by veteran Meszoli.

Pelé, his team officials and all of Brazil were now fully aware that only a miracle would enable them to reach the next round. Although Pelé was not really physically able to play against Portugal, he asked for a chance and the Brazilian coach agreed. Pelé didn't realize that he was in store for more physical punishment as the Portuguese were wild with excitement over their brilliant youngster from Mozambique, Eusebio, known as the Black Panther. The Brazilian team board of strategy made a wholesale switch in the lineup, putting Pelé back in, but placing veterans Gilmar, Bellini, Djalma, Santos and even Garrincha on the bench. With fourteen minutes gone, Antoine Simoes converted a rebound shot by Eusebio. Eleven minutes later, Coluna took a free kick which was hit by Torres and then headed in by Eusebio. Then, for a reason no one has ever been able to fully explain, Portuguese defender Morais first tripped Pelé, then brutally stepped on his knee, severely injuring him. Brazilian officials raced onto the field to help their injured star and referee George McCabe walked away from them as they argued that Morais should be ejected. He stayed in the game without incident while Pelé was forced to leave the match. It was indeed a sad sight to witness, as an English policeman covered Pelé with his raincoat while the player was being led to the sidelines. The entire Brazilian delegation was bitter, hurling insults at the referee and the Portuguese team.

But insults did not change the course of action, as the Brazilians tried futilely to bounce back into the thick of the game. At the nineteen-minute mark of the second half Brazil's hopes got a new boost through a goal by fullback Rildo. But Brazil's coffin was sealed when, with five minutes left to play, Eusebio crashed the ball into the corner of the Brazilian goal for the final tally of the match.

After the game, Pelé watched pictures of the foul, shocked that the referee didn't take any action. Brazilians were irate and the entire nation went into an unofficial day of mourning. Several fans actually committed suicide by jumping off various bridges in Brazil and most of the heavily used bridge crossings were carefully watched by the police to prevent further incidents. In Rio, black flags marked the Brazilian ouster from the World Cup while a disgusted Pelé swore that the English World Cup would be the last one he ever played in.

"It was terrible," Pelé said. "I don't want any more World Cups. The competition was too dirty in many games, and for good players it was a case of getting fouled by players who seemed to get pleasure out of their actions because they can't accomplish anything with their talent. I feel that is no longer for me."

The World Cup continued, and as it did the press began referring to Eusebio as having stepped into the boots of Pelé. Some even called him the new king of soccer. Pelé heard these remarks but made no comment as he felt that he could still help Brazil and Santos win games and titles. He could hardly wait to get back into action.

Pelé returned to Brazil and was encouraged by the fans' concern over his health and by the tremendous reception his countrymen gave him and the rest of the team, despite the fact that Brazil would now have to earn a spot through a rugged series of qualifying matches in order to get a chance to play in the 1970 World Cup, which was to be held in Mexico. Pelé again said that he did not want to play in any more World Cups and Brazilian officials, knowing how he felt at the moment of his return, decided it was best to leave him alone for the time being.

Pelé continued to build his financial empire, entering the apartment building business and endorsing various sporting goods and other products. While in Brazil he also awaited a long Santos foreign tour, for which he would receive a reported $5,000 to $10,000 a game.

A proposed meeting with Prince Philip almost touched off a bitter controversy between officials of both the Brazilian and English diplomatic corps. For days the Brazilian staff knew that the Duke of Edinburgh wanted to see Pelé play a scheduled game at the huge Maracanã Stadium in Rio de Janeiro. They also knew that the Duke wanted to meet Pelé. Their problem was how the meeting would be arranged. Many of Pelé's followers felt that the Duke should come onto the field to meet Pelé; Brazilian officials felt that Pelé should go up to the Duke's box to meet him. But on the day of the game the Duke himself settled the impending controversy when he left his box and strolled down to the field. The fans roared their approval and after the match the Brazilian press wrote a story that has been quoted again and again throughout the world:

"In the kingdom of soccer, to whose territory all the states of the world belong, the only king is Pelé. Above his majesty only the spiritual power of Heaven can rule." Though perhaps a little strong, this indicates how the Brazilian press regards the hero of millions of his countrymen. He is their king.

Fully recovered from the injuries he had incurred in the World Cup, Pelé was regaining his form and working hard for the upcoming tour which would bring him face to face with Eusebio, who was considered the biggest threat to Pelé's soccer title. Pelé and his Santos teammates put in a short tour of Mexico before coming to the United States. The Mexicans, always some of his most ardent fans, were hopeful that he would change his mind and play in the next World Cup, which was set for their nation. Brazilian National Team officials felt that Pelé would not disappoint them, once he had a chance to calm down. But Pelé maintained that as of this point, the answer was still no, and asked them to forget the subject.

After his arrival in New York, a special press conference was arranged in which Pelé and Eusebio met for a question-and-answer session. Eusebio arrived at the conference about five minutes ahead of schedule, but still there was no word from Pelé. The reporters didn't seem too disturbed, however, as the refreshments, mostly the drinking type, were well taken. When he finally arrived, Pelé saw Eusebio and immediately the two embraced. Pelé and Eusebio walked to the side of the room and chatted for about fifteen minutes. Feeling that the time was right, promoter Enzo Magnozzi introduced Pelé and Eusebio. As expected, Eusebio was asked whether he should now be regarded as the king of soccer. Eusebio asked an interpreter to repeat the question in his native Portuguese. After this, he smiled, put both his arms around Pelé and then in a clear voice gave his answer in Portuguese. The press was eager for the answer in English, and the interpreter obviously enjoyed his moment of glory, as he stepped to the microphone and said:

"Eusebio enjoyed the question but right here and now he wants to go on record as saying that he still considers Pelé to be the top soccer player in the world, or, if you prefer the only king the worldwide sport of soccer has ever had. I was pretty lucky in the World Cup and I had an exceptional series but what I did in England for my Portugal team Pelé has been doing for Santos and Brazil ever since he first started playing for them. I am very grateful that you asked me if I regard myself as being better now than Pelé, but as long as I live and play soccer to me there can never be another Pelé. He is the only man who can ever so dominate the game as he has been doing for the past ten years. I rate him Number One, and I only hope that one day I will be able to say that I am Number Two. There are many players who feel that they're the second-best player in the world, but I feel that if you asked them all they would say as I say now that Pelé is the tops and every one of them will never be able to match the skills that he has. He is a true master of every phase of the game."

Now it was Pelé's turn to comment on being regarded as the top player in the world. But before answering, he paid special tribute to Eusebio for his World Cup performance.

"I know how I felt after I helped Brazil win the championship in Sweden in 1958 and I know how proud Eusebio must be that he was able to give Portugal a brilliant third-place finish in London a couple of months ago. He played brilliantly and will get even better as he gains more experience. He is to me one of the best players I have ever had the pleasure of seeing and I look forward to the meeting between his Benfica club and my Santos club. It should be a great show and one I hope will help American soccer grow to new dimensions.

"As for me being the greatest player of all time, I can only say that I don't think I or anyone can ever be the best player in the world, because you can not excel in every position. I just feel I must play well in every match. People say beforehand that Pelé will win a match, but I don't think this any more than I think it is my fault if we lose. I just play and do the best job that I can do on any particular day. If I make mistakes I know it and I try never to make excuses for a bad performance that I may have given. I feel sorry not for myself or even for my team. I feel bad for the fans who paid their money to see me play. I might even sometimes feel that I didn't give them their money's worth."

Pelé later examined the stadium at Randalls Island where the game with Benefica would take place. There was little doubt that this was one of the worst fields he would ever play on. (Of course, there wasn't the slightest notion in his mind that one day on this very field he would play for the New York Cosmos.) As the Santos team worked out, some of the players were verbal in their blasts at the field conditions. Yet, since this was the only stadium available in New York at the time, this was where they would have to make their ball magic work. They would simply have to adjust their game to counter the bumpy conditions of the field, which literally sloped off to one side.

Meanwhile the promoters were besieged by requests for press tickets. And working in their small hotel office, they sold general tickets through such outlets as barber shops and grocery stores, finding that Americans did indeed know Pelé's reputation, and just like soccer fans around the world they too were curious to see if this man Eusebio really would become the next king of soccer.

It became obvious that the 21,500-seat stadium would be jammed for the game, and the promoters started ordering extra seats to be placed behind one of the goals, the one quite near the edge of the adjoining East River. There was also word from tour organizers in places like Fall River, Massachusetts, a strong Portuguese community, that they were hiring about thirty-five buses to come to the game. Word also came from the strong Portuguese soccer clubs located in nearby New Jersey that they too were hiring buses. It was now apparent that there would be a massive traffic jam, since the entrance to Randalls Island from the Triborough Bridge has only one lane for traffic. Appeals were made to the New York City police department, as well as to the Triboro Authority, to place extra men on the job. But even the most optimistic people working on the promotion of the game realized that it would be a messy scene and little short of a miracle would prevent a riot from fans who would arrive late at the game and find themselves unable to enter the stadium.

The day of the game arrived, and both the Santos and Benfica teams arrived well ahead of schedule, accompanied by officials of the ruling United States Soccer Federation. The knowledgeable fans knew exactly where the team buses would stop to let out the players. Inside the stadium, Magnozzi made sure that each of the gates which would not be opened were reinforced to prevent irate fans from breaking in. The fans from Fall River, most of them carrying signs written in Portuguese and many of them carrying expensive bunches of flowers for Eusebio, had been at the stadium for about two hours. When they spotted the bus carrying the team, they raced over to the runway where the players would be entering the stadium. Eusebio was mobbed and some of his clothes were torn as the fans grabbed him. Many pushed flowers in his face while some of the more optimistic begged him to sign their autograph books. Eusebio smiled, and with the aid of a flying wedge of security guards made his way into the stadium and to the Benfica locker room. When Santos and the king arrived fifteen minutes later, several of Pelé's teammates tried desperately to shield Pelé. Finally, the police arrived and pushed him through the crowd. As Pelé neared the entrance he saw a few children, patted them on their heads and smiled to the crowd, telling them that he would see them later. With both teams in the dressing rooms the fans rushed into the stadium, with or without tickets.

With the game still seventy-five minutes from kickoff, a noise from the far end of the stadium startled the officials. A gate fell down and through it rushed about one hundred fanatics who disappeared in the huge mass of fans who were now circling the stadium on the running track, since all the seats were taken. A Parks Department official estimated that over 32,000 fans filled the stadium as time neared for the two teams to make their appearance on the bumpy field.

Benfica emerged first and the large Portuguese delegations cheered wildly, as they shot firecrackers. But that was a mere prelude to Santos' entry. Pelé was mobbed by several fans who had entered the playing area and even by some who had climbed five-foot barriers to get near him. A couple of women came running over to kiss Pelé while their escorts tried to photograph the event.

After about fifteen minutes, when police and security forces had cleared the field of fans and photographers, the game started. As the game developed, the fans saw the undisputed king of soccer strongly quell the challenge of Eusebio. In a brilliant performance, Pelé directed the flow of Santos play, running from end to end; it seemed he was one second on the left side of the field and a few seconds later either on the right side or right up near the Benfica goal. Eusebio played well, but the rest of the Benfica team gave him little or no help. Santos, playing like a team gone mad, went out to help Pelé. They fed him sharp passes, both long and short, enabling Pelé to riddle the Benfica defense. The Portuguese tried to double and even triple team him, but that only left the other Santos players free to roam almost unopposed toward the Benfica goal. Also playing a strong tackling game, Pelé stole the ball away from such top Benfica players as Simoes. Pelé tallied one goal and two assists as Santos humiliated Benfica 4–0. As the crowning embarrassment, Pelé performed a brilliant piece of defensive work on Eusebio. The Black Panther from Mozambique took a pass near the midfield mark, avoided one Santos defender and came in to attempt one of his booming 40-yard shots. From his position, Pelé roared in and with a brilliant defensive tackle took the ball from Eusebio, waving to him after the play. Pelé waited for the action to get close to the runway, then suddenly pushed his way through the crowd ringing the field and seconds later he sat safe in the Santos dressing room, awaiting the siege of the press. Pelé was cordial, saying he felt that if the field had been in better condition, he would have given an even better performance. For the local press this was a shock since they had just seen him give the best soccer performance ever by any player in New York.

Pelé and his Santos teammates returned to their hotel where Pelé politely declined the offers of the promoters to join them for dinner. It was his custom to eat with his teammates, for "without them I would have nothing." Next on the Santos agenda was a match against the AEK team of Greece.

There were about 15,000 fans for the night game, and those who didn't come missed another brilliant performance. Although he didn't score a goal, Pelé was magnificent, making just about every type of play a soccer player can make. The Greek team escaped with a respectable 1–0 defeat, to the credit of their goalie, who kept them in the game. Pelé actually put the ball into the Greek net, but the referee disallowed the goal, having called a foul before Pelé shot the ball. Nevertheless, it was a great play: Pelé took the ball down the right side where he avoided the charge of one AEK defender. Another defender crashed into him, sending Pelé to the ground where he agilely flicked out his left foot and rammed the ball past the Greek goalie for an apparent score. With only two minutes left in the game, Pelé again made a remarkable play. Finding himself between the ball and the opposing goal, he scissored himself four feet off the ground and booted the ball back over himself toward the goal. The goalie somehow made a diving save and Pelé, recognizing the brilliance of the save, shook the hand of the man who had just denied him another goal in his long career.

After the game, for which Pelé was awarded still another watch as the Most Valuable Player of the match, someone asked him about the goal the referee had disallowed. Pelé smiled, as well he should since at this stage in his career he was receiving an estimated $250,000 per year from Santos, in addition to five or six times that amount through his businesses and endorsements.

"The referee made the call and there is really nothing that I could do. This is, believe me, not the first goal that has been taken away from me and I'm sure it won't be the last one. Some referees seem to get a thrill at showing me that they're the absolute power. In fact there's one referee in Brazil who has thrown me out of three games, the only three I've been ejected from. I guess he wants to get the reputation as 'the referee who throws Pelé out,' " he concluded, as he prepared to face the mass of fans who waited outside the stadium. As he approached the team bus, Pelé stopped, seeing four roses on the ground. He bent down and took one which he would later that night put in his lapel. He gave two others to his teammates and then to the delight of the fans handed the remaining rose to a beautiful Greek woman who had been waiting for her husband—a member of the AEK team.

While waiting for police to give their bus an escort Pelé leaned out a window and shook the hands of several of the Greek players. He also shook the hand of the opponent whom the game report revealed to have fouled him no fewer than six times. The night concluded when Pelé and a few of his teammates went to a nearby restaurant where the entire Greek team was eating. Pelé seemed to enjoy the music and spent three or four hours in the company of those men against whom he had just performed his steady, overall form of soccer magic.

Santos returned home the following day for a 3–2 victory against Botofoga. Pelé was brilliant, scoring twice and assisting on a tally by Edu, an eighteen-year-old he had been working steadily with—a youngster many then believed would become the next Pelé. Then it was back to New York for a game at Yankee Stadium against Italian powerhouse Inter of Milan, led by Sandro Mazzola, the son of the legendary Valentino who was perhaps the greatest of all Italian soccer players before his death along with his entire Torino team in a plane crash in 1949.

The game was scheduled for Labor Day, a bright, sunny day. Promoter Magnozzi had hoped for a crowd of around 25,000 but by game time there were officially 41,598 in attendance, and some city officials estimated that over 47,000 were on hand. The fans didn't hide their emotions as the Italian spectators came carrying huge Italian banners and signs reading Forzo Italia (Power Italy) while the Brazilian fans were there with their Brazilian flags, their bongo drums and loud noisemakers. As each team arrived near the entrance to the stadium, huge fireworks went off. Both teams went onto the field and after sprinting in full dress Pelé went out to the centerfield section where the Yankees had erected monuments to Babe Ruth and Lou Gehrig.

Once the game got underway it was not even close as the Brazilians drove the Italians crazy with their ball control to win 4–1. Pelé got one goal and assisted on both of Edu's tallies. Because the Italians were getting away with many uncalled-for fouls, the winning Brazilians decided to embarrass them as they went into a ball-control act during which they often passed the ball as many as 15 times without taking a shot. This led to more fouls by the Italians and scorn on the part of their team's action by the Italian rooters.

After the game, Pelé was voted MVP but said he felt that Edu should have won the award.

"Here is a boy who will be a great player one day," said Pelé, as if he were repeating those early words that de Brito had said about him. At the press conference, Mazzola said of Pelé:

"No matter what team he plays for—and that goes for even some of the weakest clubs in the world—he will excel. His moves are great. His talent is unmatched. He's Pelé and although we didn't play up to our capabilities today I am sure that Santos with Pelé and Edu would have beaten any club in the world."

It was Edu's turn to speak, and he thanked Pelé for all his help, saying, "He's my teacher."

Pelé, showing his goodwill for New York, added that "I like to say that now I have played in Yankee Stadium, a place my father told me about many years ago. New York is great. It's the sports center of the world and I look forward to returning here."

Pelé was invited to attend a reception that evening for the Italian team and accepted, but only after telling Magnozzi, "First I eat with my teammates."

At the party all the Italian waiters in the Greenwich Village restaurant were busy getting autographs of the Inter team, but once Pelé arrived they made a beeline for him and he signed anything available —even red napkins. He was tired but happy.

The team went to Los Angeles for a 2–2 tie against Argentina's River Plate where a record West Coast crowd of over 31,000 were in attendance. Pelé scored a goal and assisted on one by Edu, who duplicated the master's technique by feeding Pelé and then cutting sharply right to get the return pass before sending a 10-yarder into the upper right hand corner.

Pelé and his teammates returned home and the reporters wanted to know how they felt about humiliating Inter of Milan. They asked about Pelé's impressions of the United States and he gave them his feeling that it was indeed nice. Now it was time for rest, a look at how his businesses were going and free time with Rosemarie. Pelé made a trip to Tres Coracoes and was happy to find that the street where he was born on Rua Sete had been renamed in his honor.

But it was obvious that Pelé, despite all the honors and disappointments of the year, was tired. The man who slipped to only 42 goals that year and some 60 or 70 assists was allowed by his wife to rest before she gave him the news that he had been awaiting.

Yes, Pelé would be a father sometime in 1967.

"I cried when I found out that I—Edson—was going to be the father of a baby," Pelé told the Brazilian press and others who were anxious to know how he felt about his impending fatherhood. "I called my family and told my friends. I was so happy and excited. I felt great."

10 PELÉ CAPTURES NORTH AMERICA

The tremendous impact of the World Cup a year earlier on Americans and Canadians who saw the final via television brought about the formation of two professional North American leagues in 1967. One of the leagues—the United Soccer Association (USA)—was sanctioned by the Federation de Internationale Football Association, the worldwide ruling body of soccer, and by the United States Soccer Federation. But instead of staffing its teams with individual players from the United States, Canada and other nations, USA decided to import whole foreign teams for a three-month season. Santos, the first team sought out, refused because of a busy tour schedule and their São Paulo League commitments. In place of Santos, the league accepted Bangu, a fast-moving, well-coordinated team which played in the Rio League.

The other North American league was called the National Professional Soccer League (NPSL). Officials of this league sent people scurrying around the world, seeking to fill the rosters of their ten competing teams. Bob Hermann, the president of the NPSL, flew to Brazil for an avowed vacation. But when the press cornered him, he admitted that one of the reasons he came was to lure Pelé into the league. Hermann's league was considered an outlaw by both the USSF and FIFA, and any player signing a contract with them would be banned. Santos, as well as the other top professional clubs throughout the world, were further informed that they would not be allowed to accept the league's offers to play against any of the NPSL teams, or in any promotion these clubs were directly involved in.

Among those declared as outlaws were Phil Woosnam, who later became the commissioner of the North American Soccer League (NASL), Hermann and several wealthy American industrialists as well as sports personalities such as the Allyns of Chicago.

In an interview held in Rio de Janeiro on May 27, 1967, Hermann told the press who asked him about Pelé, "We can afford to buy him." But without waiting for a formal offer from Hermann, Athio Jorge Curie, president of the powerful Santos team, told the Brazilian reporters "Pelé is not for sale." Pelé himself put the final damper on any hope that Hermann may have had when he said:

"Not for all the money in the world would I leave Brazil or Santos. I play soccer for only three teams: Santos, the São Paulo State Selection and the Brazilian National Team. I am a happy man. I have a wonderful family and I have succeeded in my profession. What else would I want in life?"

It was indeed a good life, as Pelé's construction and rubber product business interests were doing very well. However, he did admit that physically, he was going through difficult times. His doctor found him at twenty-six to be as tired as a man of thirty-two. In an interview in a Canadian sports paper covering soccer throughout the world, Pelé was asked some pointed questions by Sergio Leitao. Sergio told Pelé that some people were accusing him of not trying very hard. Pelé grew angry. In a shaky voice, he countered more strongly than usual:

"Of course not. After all, I have a name for zeal. I'm just passing through a difficult period of my career, which anyone is liable to have."

Pelé was asked how many more years he expected to play, and whether his comment about never playing again for the Brazilian World Cup team was irrevocable. To these questions Pelé gave firm answers.

"Not long ago I was thinking of retiring, but not any more. I guess I'll play for at least another four years. I haven't changed my mind, however, about another World Cup. Above all, I'm not very lucky in World Cups," he added, referring to the incident the previous year and to the time in 1962 when he was injured in a key game. "No, I would say the World Cup is not in my future plans."

Santos was having hard times. With Pelé in a scoring slump, the team was losing not only on the field but at the gate and the club was experiencing some financial difficulties. Pelé was asked why Santos was slipping so rapidly.

"It's hard to say," he answered. "Some of the players are getting old and the coach is making a series of changes, but I firmly believe that in about a year, or maybe less, we shall again be presenting the fans around the world with the same top-notch performances we used to be able to present until this season. It's just a matter of time, and there are some very excellent new players on our team. Those who claim we are no longer a threat will change their mind sooner than they expect. Just wait and see. As for myself, I am not bothered one bit by those who say that I am no longer the same. After all, the same ones who now claim I'm no longer the same are the ones who once said I was the world's greatest player. It's their opinion. But I also have mine, and I think that, although I am not in my best physical shape, I'm playing just as well, only the goals do not seem to occur the way they used to. People also ask me about coaching one day, and I tell them that when I'm through as a player I will do anything but will never become a coach."

Soon Pelé began to regain his form, but the many new players on the team found it difficult to adjust their style of game to his. When he suffered a pulled knee, the team responded to his two-game absence by ripping their opposition apart. Pelé returned to the lineup and the team struggled to the São Paulo League championship once again.

The time of the rematch with Inter of Milan at Yankee Stadium was at hand and both teams had made adjustments in their roster. Inter had purchased Sandro Mazzola's brother Ferruci, and D'Amato, and were convinced that if they could stop Pelé, they would win the game. They assigned Tarsisco Burgnich, who would later become a member of Italy's National Team, to cover Pelé and they put Carlos Soldo on Edu.

Burgnich couldn't contain Pelé in the opening portion of the game, as the Black Pearl fed Edu to perfection. But Inter goalie Gulliano Sarti made two brilliant saves, and the crowd of 37,063 went wild. Pelé soon found that in place of Burgnich he had a new defender, Sergio Santarini, who did a great job without resorting to fouling techniques. Santos dominated the action, keeping the ball in Inter territory for at least eighty percent of the opening half. But goalie Sarti was brilliant, making one great save after another. Suddenly the crowd was stunned, as Pelé, with five minutes left to play before intermission, fell to the ground holding his right knee. He limped off the field but Santos, still hoping he would be able to return for the second half, didn't substitute for him; if they substituted at this point he would not have been allowed back on the field. In many international exhibition games, both coaches agree that a player who has been replaced may return later. But both teams insisted on abiding by the rules that govern regular international championship games. After all, for both Inter and Santos this was indeed a championship game.

Pelé stayed in the locker room as his teammates returned to the field. Pelé waited for the second half to get started before joining his team on the bench. The predominantly Italian crowd grew uglier by the minute, even though their favorite team now started to gain the upper hand. They seemed no longer worried about the Santos attackers. A few minutes later, this almost proved costly as with a nifty piece of footwork Edu broke through, but his shot was smothered at the last instant by an alert Sarti. As he ran back upfield, Edu was cheered by Pelé, who had leaped off the bench and was wildly cheering for Santos to win.

But it was not in the cards. Inter got a break when Burgnich picked up a loose ball in the midfield area and fed a 20-yard pass to Danish International Cap winner Harold Nielson. Nielson gave the ball to Sandro Mazzola on the wing. The son of the great Valentino came in all alone on Santos goalie Gilmar and fired a bulletlike drive that Gilmar could only deflect. The rebound came right to Sandro, who put it into the net for the eventual 1–0 victory. With ten minutes left to play, Toninho of Brazil was fouled and when he got to his feet he went after Soldo, who had fouled him. Immediately several hundred irate Italian fans raced onto the field and started punching at any Santos player they could find. As the police descended, a security guard escorted Pelé off the bench and into the safety of the locker room before the fans knew that the Pearl had escaped safely. Pelé was soon joined by his old friend Orlando, who was bleeding around the mouth, the result of several punches by a group of fans. Brazilian players had chased the fans and kicked several of them. After the game, which saw Toninho and Inter's Dotti ejected for fighting, Pelé appeared shaken by what he had witnessed, saying he felt the fans "were out of their minds to act as they did." But as he left the dressing room all hatred had been left behind as he talked with several of the Inter players as well as some of the fans who had waited for him. It was here that he gave a heartwarming example of his love for the youth, the youth of any country he plays in.

A youngster, about ten, had a small Santos banner with him as did many of the adults who wanted Pelé to sign the pennants. The older men pushed in and for a time it looked as if Pelé wouldn't even see the youngster. But he spotted him and took his hand. He signed the youngster's pennant and handed it to an adult to give back to the youth. But someone made a grab for it. Pelé yelled at the man to give it to the kid. Although he spoke in Portuguese the man got the message, the kid got the banner, and Pelé had made still another friend. After the game both teams expressed a desire to play again the following year, but the game never materialized. They went to dinner together and Sandro and Pelé were of course in the spotlight.

Pelé seemed very happy, and after a rest for recovery of his leg, he appeared to be back in peak form. He worked out almost daily, went often to his business office, and took his family on auto trips. Pelé was also happy when his sister Maria Lucia became engaged to Pelé's teammate, Davi. Pelé's brother Zoca, meanwhile, informed him that he liked school and was looking forward to becoming a lawyer and eventually handling Pelé's expanding business interests. Pelé still insisted that he would not play for Brazil in another World Cup. But he appeared to be less vehement in his statements and some Brazilian writers told the people that Pelé might reconsider. This time he made no public denial. The Brazilian National Team engaged in some exhibition games while Santos made a tour of the Caribbean. In a game in Mexico, Pelé was hailed publicly as the world's greatest athlete. In other exhibition games, he won numerous mementos of the occasions and wound up the year with a total of 57 goals and an estimated 85 assists.

Rosemarie's tally for the year included the birth of a daughter—Kelly Christina. The "Little Princess," as many now refer to her, was named in honor of Princess Grace of Monaco.

"I was so happy when the baby was born," Pelé will tell anyone who wants to listen even today.

Besides spending time with his family and devoting time to business, Pelé donated much of his spare time to visiting sick children in Brazilian hospitals. "I always have time for the children," Pelé says.

As 1968 began, Pelé again played brilliantly. But even more important, he became increasingly interested in activities other than soccer and business, the latter of which would include plans with several partners for the introduction of Café Pelé, which today is one of Brazil's biggest-selling coffees. Among these other interests was spending more time boating and fishing, helping Rosie entertain and occasionally going over to the local fields to spend time with children just learning soccer.

Santos agreed to a widespread tour including games in South America, in Europe, and in North America, against several teams of the North American Soccer League, the league which came out of a merger of the NPSL and USA. The tour was designed to give the sport in North America a sorely needed boost. The Santos tour would also include a series of games against various All-Star selections in Mexico.

And, to keep matters interesting, Pelé agreed to star in a series of films, including one in which he would play the role of a Black slave.

"I want to bring Pelé and his Santos team back to New York again," said soccer promoter Enzo Magnozzi as he began negotiations with some advance men who now handled Santos' travel plans. "Of course," Magnozzi told an agent, "there's no deal unless Pelé is with Santos. I respect the rest of the team but without Pelé I won't spend the money to bring them over here. I know that if I took Santos without Pelé I would save a great deal of money but I also know that the people in New York won't go ahead with the deal and the place will be empty." Enzo got his desire, and a game was set for Yankee Stadium against Napoli.

Pelé was playing very well in Brazil. The fans hoped that his return to top form would give him the urge to once again test himself in the World Cup. Officials of the National Team tried a new tactic: they no longer sought a firm answer from the king. Instead, they told him to let them know when he would be ready to make his decision known to all the people. They felt that, during the tour, many people would tell him of their desire to see him once again match skills against other nations. They knew Pelé could never refuse a true soccer fan.

Pelé and Santos arrived in New York for the opening of what promised to be a highly successful tour. They were desperate to stay in prime condition since they were on the verge of winning another São Paulo championship. The team, as always, was met at the hotel by well-wishers. They were promptly informed of the ground rules governing curfew, leaving the hotel, going out on their own and other such details. There was a strong feeling expressed by the board of directors that fans this year would see the true Santos team in action, and not the club that had looked so bad in the previous year's loss to Inter, after which Pelé himself was in tears, explaining, "I still have not been able to accept defeat. It hurts me but that is the way I have reacted every time we lose, whether on the road in an exhibition game or in a league game. That is one way I feel I ease myself —by crying." The team even worked out in a secret session at a small field in Manhattan for fear that if the workout was made public there would be no way that the team would be able to practice effectively. A rugged schedule of exercises was prescribed by Professor Mazzei to keep the team fit and loose. Friends from the Brazilian consulate came to see Pelé and were not allowed up to his room until Pelé himself okayed them.

The game was a Friday night affair. A few hours before the match, Napoli's Altafini, who had been a teammate of Pelé's in both the 1958 and 1962 World Cups, dropped in for a visit and was greeted by all the Brazilian players in the lobby. Pelé came almost at a run down the stairs when he was told that Altafini was there. He was also overjoyed that Napoli would field another great South American player, Sivori, from Argentina. Pelé told his teammates that the game would not be easy, and joined several of the players in singing a few Brazilian songs—another way he eases the pressures.

The team arrived at the Yankee Stadium entrance about two hours before game time. The vendors outside were having a field day by selling souvenir programs, Brazilian flags, Santos banners, huge pictures of Pelé and a wide assortment of buttons. The New York City Police Department was in force, with many of them sitting in special riot trucks. Santos went into their dressing room and then walked onto the field to inspect the conditions. Magnozzi explained that the match that night might break all existing attendance records. He was right, as the official paid attendance was listed at 43,002. This did not include some two or three thousand gate-crashers and the five hundred honored guests and press. The Triboro Bridge was backed up for six to seven miles, and police had no choice other than to cut off the approaches to try to clear up the logjam that the king's presence had caused. Police later estimated that over 15,000 fans had to miss the game because of the traffic. Some of those fans abandoned their cars on the bridge with the hope of walking across to Yankee Stadium. Promotion officials decided to delay the game for about twenty-five minutes and those in attendance didn't mind the delay too much, since the many Brazilians who had come with their drums provided some entertainment. In the aisles, already packed by those ticket holders and non- ticket holders alike who had given up their seats to get a better view of the match, the atmosphere was jovial, almost like Carnival time in Brazil. The teams were informed that there would be only a short time to work out once they reached the field, and the Santos players began doing deep-knee exercises on the floor of the locker room.

Finally Santos and Napoli received word that it was time to go to the field. The Italians came out first and were greeted by a roaring crowd as well as by the exploding of firecrackers. Then Santos made their way onto the field and Pelé was almost immediately mobbed by a group of fans who managed to enter the field. The police started shoving a few of them around and Pelé motioned to the cops to take it easy. He seemed to be enjoying the welcome.

The game started and it became immediately obvious that Napoli would be no match in technique for the high-flying Santos team, who were using every basic technique in the book as well as their wide variety of skillful, tricky maneuvers. Pelé was fouled with less than two minutes gone, and referee Jim Carr of England sternly held up a yellow caution card against the Napoli player who fouled the king. These fouls would prove very costly for Napoli later in the game. The game was scoreless to this point, with Napoli goalie Pacifico Cuman making three great saves on two shots by Pelé and a bullet drive by Toninho. Meanwhile, Altafini kept the Santos defense busy with his uncanny moves. Twice Santos keeper Gilmar had to stop breakaways by him. Cane, a Frenchman, also played well for Napoli and it looked as if all the ingredients for a truly great match were there. It is in this type of game that Pelé rises to the occasion. He was all over the field, faking Napoli defenders out of position, causing the Italian defense to double-team him, leaving other Santos players open for one of his accurate passes. Sometimes he even dribbled a few steps forward, then made either a sharp left or right turn. Despite his brilliance, the game remained scoreless. Already he had been fouled four times by different Napoli defenders who became increasingly frustrated. Late in the first half Santos broke the deadlock, but no one will ever fault the Napoli goalie. He had just made a series of brilliant saves on consecutive shots by Pelé, Pepe, the aging veteran, and Amauri when the latter's rebound came out to Toninho who booted the ball home for the first goal of the match. After the play, Pelé saluted goalie Cuman.

Santos left the field with a 1–0 half time lead and most of the fans roared their satisfaction. However, a few bitterly disappointed Napoli fans, some of whom wore shirts bearing a picture of Napoli's mascot, the donkey, waved fists at some of the Napoli players as they returned for the second half. Six minutes into the second half Napoli tied the score as Paoloa Barison sent a perfect pass to Altafini and all the former Brazilian star had to do was put a twisting header on the ball to send it swerving past Gilmar. Immediately, firecrackers exploded all over the stadium. The goal awakened the Napoli team and the Brazilian goalie Gilmar responded to the pressure, making two great saves. With fourteen minutes gone in the stanza, Lima passed to Pelé, who sidestepped one defender and sent a cannonlike shot into the back of the Napoli goal to make it 2–1 Santos. Ten minutes later Pelé was chopped down inside the penalty area and Santos was awarded a penalty shot. The crowd wanted Pelé to take it, but instead it was Toninho who took the shot, giving Santos a 3–1 lead. Napoli struck back on another goal by Altafini, who scored on a penalty shot awarded after he had been fouled inside the penalty area. But with one minute left Pelé, after faking two defenders, was again cut down inside the penalty area and Toninho converted the foul for a 4–2 victory. After the game, Pelé revealed why he himself didn't take the penalty shot:

"I used to take the penalty kicks myself. However, I hurt my knee and the team realized that Toninho was better suited to take the penalty kicks. I think tonight we proved that Santos has me and ten other very good players." At the same time a reporter asked Santos coach Antonio Fernandez how he would defend against Pelé.

"I would put one man in back of him," the coach replied, "and two men in front of him, all with guns, but I still don't think that would stop him once he got going toward that goal. Pelé is the best there ever was. They threw the mold away after they made him. And during our practice sessions before we came to New York he kept reminding the other players on the club that we had to win because we had to show the New York fans that we are better than the Italian teams. He's a great inspiration not only to the young players but to the old players themselves."

A Brazilian reporter covering the tour informed Pelé that the goal he had scored in the match was the 900th of his career and that he needed only one hundred more to gain the milestone once thought to be impossible in regulation play. Pelé smiled and gave a simple answer, one that was typical of him:

"I wasn't that aware of it because I am a player and not a bookkeeper."

Napoli begged Magnozzi for a chance to redeem themselves for their losing performance before the American public. After a ten-minute conversation, the Brazilians agreed to play another game before the two teams squared off in Toronto. Napoli should never have asked for the return match, which was held five nights later at Randalls Island. Santos had a field day before a disappointing crowd of 7,237. The Napoli defense couldn't cope with the Brazilians, who included Manoel Maria in their lineup—a man who would play an instrumental role in Pelé's future. Playing a brilliant game, Maria set up numerous Santos scoring drives. Pelé was equally brilliant, using a wide assortment of tricks. He brought the crowd to its feet when he took a long pass from Maria, trapped the ball on his right foot while running full speed ahead, and blasted the ball home for the first of two goals he would score during Santos' impressive 6–2 victory. Pepé and Toninho each scored two goals in the winning effort while Cane and Barison scored for Napoli. The fans also had a chance to witness a rarity. Late in the game Pelé was fouled inside the penalty area and asked to take the penalty kick. The king missed the net. After the game Pelé said:

"It just goes to show that penalty shots are not something that should be taken for granted. I lost my concentration just as I was about to take the kick and as a result I pulled the ball a little too much and it went wide." Altafini said he had seen Pelé miss a penalty shot about five years earlier but quickly added that "people who saw this miss should feel fortunate that they are among the few in the world who saw Pelé miss. I feel the only way you can really stop this guy is by shooting him," he added as he tried to make a pencil he was holding look like a revolver. "The guy is just too much for anyone to stop. There will never be another one like him as long as the game is played."

Napoli changed its tactics for the third and final match between the two teams, which was played on June 28, at Varsity Stadium in Toronto before a crowd of 15,514. Instead of the tight marking match that had proved so ineffective in the two previous games the team relied strictly on a quick counterattack with long passes down the wings. Santos picked them apart, using the field like a chess board. The predominantly Italian crowd booed the futile efforts of the Italians but also cheered some of the brilliant play-making efforts of the Santos team. Pelé was again brilliant. Napoli actually took the lead in the match as Altafini, seemingly the only one knowing how to counter the Brazilian's style, pushed a short pass ahead to Ferreiro on a direct free kick with only ten minutes gone in the match. Ferreiro's shot went off Gilmar's fingertips into the net. But soon Pepe scored on a swerving 24-yard direct free kick. Six minutes after Pepe's goal, Pelé showed his great anticipation when he roared in as Toninho blasted a shot at goalie Cuman, who got his hands on the ball but was unable to hold it. The ball rebounded to the ever-alert Pelé, who blasted it home. Four minutes later Toninho converted a rebound on a hard drive by Pepe to make it 3–1 at the half time break. Seven minutes into the second half, Pelé was fouled inside the penalty area and Toninho converted the penalty shot to virtually erase any hopes Napoli might have entertained. Altafini scored three minutes later but in the following fifteen minutes goalie Gilmar showed his skill as a member of the Brazilian National Team, making back-to-back saves, diving and leaping to block the shots of Altafini, Barison and Zurlini. In the last minute of play, Pelé dribbled around defender Girardo to score the final goal in Santos' 5–2 victory for a sweep of the three-game series. After the match the two teams shook hands; Napoli officials did not ask for another game.

The North American Soccer League, feeling that they could use Pelé's presence to spur interest in their young league, negotiated a tour contract for Santos. The first stop against an NASL team was June 30, a nationally televised match against the St. Louis Stars, a team comprised mostly of native-born Americans who had learned their soccer in the highly successful Catholic Youth Council program. The CYC program of soccer started after the end of World War II and has grown to over 250,000 youngsters, many of whom have gone on to play with such powerhouse colleges as St. Louis. Pelé met with the Archbishop of St. Louis and told him how impressed he was with the number of players engaged in the CYC program. He then invited many who were involved in coaching the youngsters to attend a Santos practice session scheduled for that evening.

The Stars were really up for the game, for which Santos suddenly found itself without the services of second string goalie Claudio and starters Carlos Alberto, Edu, Wilson and Joel, all of whom were called upon by Brazilian officials to play an international match in Europe. Pelé was also asked to play but declined the offer. Still, he gave the Brazilian brass great hope when he told them to ask him again in the future. Without regular goalie Gilmar, who was out with a leg injury, the stars had easy pickings against third-stringer Laercio. Casey Frankowitz dribbled the ball right around the keeper for the first St. Louis score after only four minutes. Three minutes later, to the delight of the Busch Stadium crowd of 20,116, he beat the Santos keeper from twenty yards out to make it 2–0. Then Santos awakened and Pelé cut the deficit in half on a direct free kick. Three minutes later a hand ball infraction some thirty yards out gave Santos another free kick. This time Pepe fired the ball home to tie the score. Pelé himself accounted for the final goal of the game when, with twenty minutes gone in the second half, he took a cross from Amauri and dribbled through three defenders before easing the ball into the net past goalie Vidinic, who played a strong game. Vidinic later said:

"I watched him all during the game and when I came out he just waited for the right moment before shooting the ball. Other players would have blasted the ball as hard as they could but not him. He knew exactly what to do with it and the ball was impossible to save. He may have beaten me but losing to him is certainly no disgrace. He is just perfect."

Santos celebrated America's 192nd birthday by playing against the Kansas City Spurs before a record-breaking crowd of 19,296 at Municipal Stadium. It was a routine affair, with Pelé being joined in the Santos scoring by Amauri, Elizeu and Douglas in a 4–1 win. Although tired by the rugged schedule, Pelé stood long after the game giving out his usual number of autographs.

Just two days later Pelé and Santos were in Los Angeles for a special exhibition match against the Mexican team Necaxa. A crowd of 12,418 at the Los Angeles Coliseum saw the Brazilians, although extremely tired, defeat the Mexicans 4–3. The amazing Pelé scored once and assisted on goals by Toninho and Pepe.

They returned east two nights later for a match against the Boston Beacons. It was a Brazilian holiday as they romped to a 7–1 victory in a game played before 18,431 at Fenway Park, the baseball home of the Red Sox. After Boston had taken a 1–0 lead on an early goal by Lloyd McLean, Pelé went to work assisting on the tying goal by Maria. With twelve minutes remaining in the first half he took a pass from Amauri, outraced two Beacon defenders, and sent a twisting shot past Beacon goalie Walt Tarnawsky for a 2–1 half time advantage. The second half was all Santos, as Pelé assisted on goals by Mangalvio and Toninho, followed by a solo burst down the wing by Maria who then cut for the net and scored. With eleven minutes left Pelé assisted on a goal by Elizau, and in the closing two minutes Douglas ended the runaway for Santos' biggest margin on its American tour. After the game the Boston press cornered Pelé in the dressing room and asked him for his evaluation of the Beacons:

"As far as I am concerned, Tarnawsky played a good game for Boston even if he did yield all those goals," said Pelé, "and I thought their center half [Pugh] also did a good job. But the rest of the team showed inexperience in this type of competition, for which you have to be well trained and mentally prepared."

The Santos power machine, nursing several injuries and feeling the fatigue that the rugged schedule had caused, moved into Cleveland two days later. Here Santos was beaten 2–1 by the Cleveland Stokers, a club that played the English brand of soccer and used a switching man-to-man form of the zone defense on Pelé. The Stokers played to near perfection.

"I feel that by beating them we helped boost the prestige of the league," Stoker coach Norman Low said after the contest.

"They certainly deserved the victory," Pelé said after the contest. "But I would like to play them again later and see how it comes out. We are pretty tired right now and the trip has been a rough one. But even though I, like the other players, am exhausted, please don't take anything away from the way they played in this game. I feel they are the best team from the league we have played on our tour. They didn't seem worried about our reputation and that philosophy worked well for them, as they did what they do naturally and didn't force it."

The Brazilians then returned to New York's Yankee Stadium for a match against the New York Generals, a team rated a two-goal underdog. The Generals were coached by Freddie Goodwin, a former Manchester United player who, after leaving the Generals, returned to England where he coached Birmingham City in the English First Division. The bongo drums greeted the arrival of Santos while the Generals were greeted politely. The crowd appeared to be rooting for Santos until the Generals showed that they might duplicate the efforts of the Stokers two days earlier. The Generals assigned Gordon Bradley to the Black Pearl. A night before the game Bradley had been asked by the local press how he felt about the job he was ready to do against Pelé. Bradley told the press that of course he respected Pelé, but since he had once guarded the great English player Noby Stiles he was ready for anything. At a clinic held several years later, Bradley amused the youngsters when he told them that coach Goodwin said to "guard and stay with Pelé so close that I would know the color of his underwear."

The Generals played with abandon. Warren Archibald, later to become one of the stars of Trinidad's National Team, outraced the Santos defenders down the wing; Cesar Menotti, Bradley, and goalie Geoffry Sidebottom played brilliantly, sensing their ability to beat the Brazilians. And beat them they did, by a score of 5–3 with Archibald scoring twice and Menotti, Perau and Kaszas each adding solo tallies. Santos managed only three goals, one each by Toninho and Elizeu and a gift goal when Bradley put the ball into his own net while trying to clear it. The local press flocked to Pelé after the game and the Black Pearl was gracious, explaining that the team Santos had just played could have beaten many a top foreign team.

"I liked the way they controlled the tempo of play and didn't panic when we started to press in the second half," Pelé said. "And they covered me as well as the rest of our forwards with extreme skill. They are to be congratulated."

Santos' final game of its North American tour was played at DC Stadium in Washington, to a crowd of 20,189 including a large contingent of diplomatic officials. For the third straight game Pelé was unable to score, but he did set up goals by Toninho and Pepe, the latter of whom led his team to a 3–1 win over the NASL's Washington Whips.

Finally, the tour that had started in the previous month was over. During their games Santos had drawn 188,053. The average attendance for the ten games was 18,805, which compared favorably with baseball. Pelé scored eight goals and was credited with seventeen assists as Santos won eight and lost two. It was desperately hoped that this would be just what the league needed to help insure its future.

The Santos team agreed to return the following month for several more exhibition games. They also announced that the players who had been called away in the later phase of the current tour would be back for service. They had to play a couple of games in the São Paulo League play-offs and were also scheduled for an exhibition game against the Colombian All-Stars in Bogotá. Santos' return to the more established international soccer scene was a brutal one.

Early in the game referee Guillermo Velasquez made a questionable call, allowing a goal by the Colombians. The Santos team, outraged by what they felt was surely a home-town decision, protested vehemently. Pelé was one of those players who argued that the goal should have been disallowed because of an infraction. Suddenly, the referee ejected Pelé from the field, causing his Santos teammates to assault the referee, according to reports. Immediately after the 4–2 Santos victory, the police arrived on the field and hauled the entire team off to jail, where they were detained for three hours. The team was freed only after they wrote an apology not only to the referee, who was pressing charges, but to the Colombian fans. Pelé has since made amends of his own, performing in both exhibition games and in clinics in Bogotá. Asked about that incident—the night he spent in jail—he refuses to comment.

Fresh from their brief incarceration, Pelé and his Santos teammates returned home to the friendly surroundings of Brazil. While most of the players just relaxed, Pelé was besieged by every man who had an idea about one thing or another that Pelé should invest in. Many business meetings lasted long into the night. Pelé did spend some of his time visiting his mother and father, also enjoying his baby girl whom he had not seen for over a month. He walked with Rosie, but still found little time for the beach, one of Pelé's favorite pastimes.

Santos held workouts, preparing for a brief but hectic U. S. tour which would match them against NASL teams Atlanta and Oakland, before going back to Yankee Stadium for a match against their old rival, Benfica. From there they would travel to Europe for another brief tour, before finally returning home for rest and some exhibition games against some of the good clubs from neighboring South American nations. Once back in the United States, as always, Pelé was called on to make personal appearances with the mayors and other civic representatives in every city he visited.

The opening game of the mini-tour was in Atlanta and the Chiefs, coached by present NASL commissioner Phil Woosnam, shocked the Brazilians when they took the lead at the 19-minute mark on a goal by Freddie Mwila. But that was all for the Chiefs, as Pelé took over and gave a masterful exhibition of every phase of the game, including some tremendous defensive moves when a Chief forward would dare to try and dribble around him. Pelé equalized for Santos seven minutes after Mwila's goal by putting a 15-yarder past Sven Lindberg with his left foot. Sixteen minutes after Rildo had converted a Pelé pass, the king made it 3–1 by taking a corner kick from Rildo and sending a twisting header into the Chiefs' goal. The crowd of 26,713, the largest ever to attend a game in Atlanta, saw the Santos machine roll into high gear as Pelé completed his hat trick with a bulletlike drive from twenty-five yards out. Amauri and Toninho rounded out the 6–2 romp, but not before Pelé electrified the crowd with a sudden fifty-yard bomb that Lindberg barely managed to tip over the crossbar. After the game, Pelé said he thought he would be able to shock the opposing goalie, but lauded him for the save.

"I heard about Pelé's ability to take shots like that." said the Chiefs' goalie, "but until I saw him do it I thought it was just another tale they made up about him. Believe me, that ball had plenty on it and I was fortunate to stop it."

The Santos bandwagon moved across country to Oakland. The fans were treated to a brilliant exhibition of soccer as the Brazilians played nearly perfectly, using the wall pass, the dribble and the short snappy pass to perfection. The crowd of 30,000-plus at the Oakland Coliseum saw Pelé score a goal in each half and assist on another tally by Amauri, as the Santos machine defeated the defending NASL champion Clippers 3–1. After the game, Pelé was asked about the upcoming Yankee Stadium match against Benfica and his chief rival, Eusebio.

"I am tired," Pelé said, "from playing so many games and so frequently all over the globe, but as long as I can help promote soccer in the U.S., I am ready."

And ready he was for a game that would be perhaps the greatest international match on the part of both teams ever played in North America. A crowd of 36,904 was on hand for the game, co-promoted by the New York Generals and Enzo Magnozzi. The game was part of a doubleheader. In the opening match, the Generals, paced by a pair of goals by ex-Santos player Eliseau, defeated the Detroit Cougars 4–1. Before the doubleheader Eliseau came into the Santos dressing room and talked with Pelé and his old friends. Pelé said he wished his former teammate well and Eliseau certainly was inspired as he took to the field.

The Benfica-Santos match was brilliant from the opening whistle. It was obvious that after six straight defeats at the hands of Santos, Benfica was out for revenge. The crowd was at a fever pitch, as the two clubs had been talking with equal vim about beating one another. Perhaps it was Santos' past record against Benfica, or a general feeling of tiredness on Santos' part, but from the onset the Portuguese controlled the flow of the match. The Santos defenders were double-teaming Eusebio, while the Benfica defense shadowed Pelé with one man in front and one man behind him. At the 37-minute mark, Santos halfback Rildo pulled Eusebio down inside the penalty area, and Jacinto put the penalty shot past Claudio to give Benfica a 1–0 lead. The lead lasted just five minutes before Pelé was pulled down just inside the area by two Benfica defenders. Carlos Alberto fired a bullet past Benfica keeper Nascimento to tie the score. Then, with less than twenty seconds gone in the second half, Augusto took a pass from Simoes and put Benfica ahead. The Portuguese increased their lead to 3–1 three minutes later, as Eusebio found the range, after taking a pass from Simoes. The Portuguese partisans in the crowd were frantic with delight. But Santos responded with a brilliant burst of speed which brought the fight to Benfica. With twenty-seven minutes left in the game, Santos cut the deficit to one goal when Pelé passed to his protégé Edu who sent home a booming shot while falling to the pitch, completely off balance. Pelé ran to Edu and lifted him off the ground as the Brazilian fans, who had been quieted by seeing their team behind, responded with a burst of firecrackers. Now Santos assumed command and started to tear the Benfica defense apart. With nineteen minutes left to play, Rildo crossed to Toninho, who back-headed the ball into the net to tie the match. Although many fans were yelling for overtime, it had been decided that the final whistle would end the game. The game ended in deadlock, and the fans gave both teams a standing ovation as they left the field and headed into their respective dressing rooms. Pelé was exhausted. After the completion of the team's postgame talk by their officials, Eusebio was one of the first visitors allowed into the Santos clubhouse.

The two chatted awhile in Portuguese and then it came time to tell the press their impressions of the game. Eusebio, obviously dejected, was the first to speak:

"I am disappointed," said Eusebio. "I and the rest of my team really wanted to win our first game ever against Santos but we just couldn't stop their attack when they started playing the style of play they're so great at. And the main reason for them being able to get the tie," he added as he pointed to where Pelé was standing, "was him. He didn't get a goal but he had our defense going crazy trying to guard him and also trying to figure out what he was going to do next. He's the tops in the world, but after all I said that before, and you who saw him have to agree. Without him Santos is a top club but with him they're one of the greatest teams ever to play this sport."

Pelé then took his place at the microphone and congratulated Eusebio and Benfica for their performance.

"I never saw them play that well before," Pelé said. "Eusebio is a better player than most anyone in the world and that Simoes really makes their offense go. He is tricky; ask any of our defenders and they'll tell you that if you aren't awake he'll run right over you. He passes very well and sets up his other forwards. Benfica is one of the better clubs around and with the men they have they're going to be tops for a long time to come. Maybe one day in the future we'll get to play them in another game either in our country or in their country or maybe even here. They deserve another chance to play us and I won't predict now who will win that game. I think it will be a great show for the fans no matter where the game is played."

After the game, Santos made a brief trip to the Caribbean. Pelé showed his compassion after a game against a Trinidadian team. As usual the fans came onto the field and crowded around Pelé. Club-wielding police swept onto the field and one fan was knocked to the ground, either by the police or by the other fans. Pelé, seeing the police start to swing their clubs at the man on the ground, covered the fallen fan with his own body; no further blows occurred. Friends escorted him off the field, and any policeman who would have tried to hit the man, with Pelé's body as a shield, probably would have been assaulted by the fans. Those in the crowd who weren't on the field cheered wildly as Pelé came to the sidelines to join his teammates. A few policemen were observed glaring at him.

Santos returned to Brazil, and for the first time in a long time they had no games booked and no practice sessions scheduled. Pelé and his teammates finally received a rest from physical work, although Pelé did work out on his own several times to keep his body in perfect shape. He also attended to his growing businesses, including the new plant which would produce rubber by-products. Late in the year Queen Elizabeth made an official visit to Brazil and asked that a meeting with Pelé be included on the agenda of her trip. Pelé played a game in Rio de Janeiro in honor of the queen, scored a goal, and then received a trophy she offered at the celebrities' box.

Pelé scored 59 goals in 1968, and the 1,000th of his career was not far away.

11 THE MILESTONE

Early in 1969, with the World Cup just one year away, Pelé still insisted that he would not participate. But hope flourished in Brazil that he would change his mind and honor the wishes of his fellow citizens. The Brazilian National Team selection committee was playing it cool, refraining from direct pressure, also making sure that some of Pelé's closest contacts kept a more personal type of pressure on him. It was now considered a better than even chance that the Black Pearl would once again don the uniform of Brazil and try to help his nation win its third World Cup and retire the Jules Rimet Trophy.

Late in the year Pelé let his closest friends know that he had made up his mind to play, and word leaked out. The Brazilian people were indeed ecstatic. But Pelé, himself one who sometimes seemed embarrassed by the wild rallies his presence has so often generated, still sought his 1,000th goal, which, in America, would be likened to 800 home runs in a career, or a football player soaring to about 25,000 yards gained in his career. The Brazilian people have followed Pelé's scoring enthusiastically. Meanwhile, Pelé would smile, and say, in his soft, calm tone:

"Soon it will come and then everyone will be happy, even me."

On the São Paulo League front Santos once again walked away in the pennant race. Pelé had suffered a slight pull in his thigh early in the campaign, but after only six days he bounced back to score two goals and assist on two others. The people were convinced that their hero would certainly reach the 1,000-goal pinnacle sometime during the year, even during a cold streak which saw him play four games without a goal. The Brazilian press followed every move the Black Pearl made, giving his chase of the elusive goal more and more coverage. The front pages of almost every South American newspaper were loaded with personality pieces on Pelé, and the fans poured into every match that Santos played.

It is a hot, muggy night, in November. Santos is to play at Maracaná Stadium, the largest football stadium in the world. Their opponent tonight is Vasca da Gama. One of the biggest traffic jams in the history of Rio de Janeiro occurs. Fans are coming from all over Brazil, for the Rio press as well as the rest of the Brazilian media has been saying that in this game Pelé will score his 1,000th goal. For weeks the fans have anticipated the 1,000-goal mark and although the Americans landed a man on the moon with the Apollo 12, Pelé is still the lead story.

Pelé seems nervous as he arrives and sees the jubilant atmosphere at the stadium. Banners, buttons and large pictures of him are hawked by many vendors on the scene, and scalpers are having a field day selling the better seats at the stadium for as much as ten times the official price. Pelé refuses pre-game interviews as newspapermen, radio broadcasters, and television commentators flock to the king who is making his way toward the Santos dressing room. The rest of the team goes about its usual preparations for the game. Pelé changes into his uniform, gets the same message from his coach that the other players get, and waits for the signal to get onto the field. The inside of the stadium is like a roaring festival with banners streaming from every possible location. Pelé takes the field, and the fans let out a large roar accompanied by a fantastic display of fireworks. The people, it seems, because of the many restrictions imposed on them by a stern military rule, are using the game as an outlet for their emotions. Soccer is the sport of Brazil and tonight they are ready to release their emotions in honor of their king.

The game is slow getting into gear as Santos' opponents seem to be willing to settle for a scoreless match. They must want not to be known as the team Pelé scored his 1,000th goal against. They're moving the ball around in the midfield area but as soon as Santos gets the ball they're coming back in a determined effort not to give the

Black Pearl a clean shot on goal. With 11 minutes gone, Pelé fires a 15-yarder which goes just over the bar. Then he is marked closely by two defenders and instead of worrying about getting a goal he is concentrating on passing the ball off. But his teammates want him to score and they return the ball to him quickly. But he is unable to get clear until there are six minutes left in the first half. Then he chest-traps a ball and fakes right but goes left before releasing a hard shot which speeds just wide of the right-hand corner. The crowd is up on its feet as the ball appears to be heading into the net but a scream of anguish comes from them as the ball misses target. The first half ends and Pelé, although he has looked impressive, has not scored. Still, the fans sit back, confident that the trip many of them made on the clogged roads leading to the stadium will not have been made in vain. They know their king will do it.

The stadium erupts as Santos and Pelé make their way onto the field for the second half. With the thirteen minutes to go in the game the crowd is hushed as the referee signals a foul against Vasca da Gama inside the penalty area. The fans are waiting to see who will take the penalty shot. They start chanting "Pelé! Pelé!" The Santos trainer and coach as well as many of the club officials who are on hand respond to the wishes of the crowd, and the man wearing that all-familiar No. 10 is nominated to take the shot. He waits for the referee to place the ball down on the spot twelve yards from the opposing goalie. The rest of the players, those other than Pelé and the Vasca da Gama goalie, are cleared out of the penalty area. Pelé approaches the ball and hits it with his instep, not too hard. Even before the ball finds the back of the net, Pelé starts for the goal. Later, he will say: "I knew it was a good shot. I knew that the ball was going into the goal." He races into the goal to retrieve the ball, kissing it, then patting the opposing goalie on the back. The goalie shakes his hand and the fans are nearly beyond control. Pelé has indeed scored his 1,000th goal. Firecrackers explode all over the stadium. Fans are dancing on the concrete steps. Pelé is mobbed by those fans, including police and security guards who leap for joy and race onto the field. The entire Santos bench empties and the players carry Pelé around. The Vasca da Gama players, who will lose that game 2–1, are caught up in the emotional display of the moment. They too want to shake the hand of the man who has just written soccer history.

The game was delayed eleven minutes for the demonstration. Although two other players, Brazilian Arthur Freidenreich and Austrian Franz (Bimbo) Binder, had scored 1,000 goals in their respective careers, they accomplished their feats before professional soccer was organized. This left Pelé as the only professional to reach this milestone. Fans who had never met before hugged and kissed each other. According to his trainer, Professor Julio Mazzei, Pelé was thrilled but also admitted that to score 1,000 goals "you have to be a little lucky."

"The pressure was bigger than anything I had ever experienced. Tonight I shook for the first time. Even when I played in the 1958 World Cup the strain was not so great." Pelé cried as he spoke.

After the game, fans waited outside the stadium talking to one another about their reactions. One young white secretary tells an inquiring reporter:

"I turned and hugged a black man next to me who had a grin that never quit. It seems that you forget any conception of race at Maracaná. I mean, nowhere else would I ever hug a man I'd never seen before." Another fan screamed at the top of his voice, "This is more important than anything that's going on on the moon. They have a man on the moon but we have the king of all soccer right here." Veteran reporters and photographers who had been covering games for many years were also excited. One photographer said that the people "really go to the games to swear out loud and let it all out. You know, when things get rough, and with the political situation, it helps." A political reporter who flew to the game from São Paulo proposed that Pelé enter the Brazilian government, saying, "The government ought to contract Pelé as a cabinet minister. He knows how to get people enthusiastic."

Santos went on to win the São Paulo state championship for the third straight time. Officials announced that Santos would make a tour including stops in Nigeria and Rhodesia, two nations tense with political and social unrest. Biafra and Nigeria were engaged in a bloody war, and there was concern for the safety of Pelé and the rest of Santos. But when negotiations were completed, Pelé could add yet another to his ever-growing lists of firsts: a three-day truce was declared so that both Biafrans and Nigerians would be able to see the Black Pearl perform his soccer magic.

Pelé and his teammates arrived in Nigeria for the game, which would be held before the largest African crowd ever to see a sporting event. Security measures were strict. A Nigerian army captain escorted Pelé halfway across the bridge over the river separating the two warring factions, where a Biafran captain greeted him with a warm handshake. The Nigerian captain turned to both Pelé and his Biafran counterpart and saluted them in a gesture of respect. Pelé waved farewell to the Nigerian and was escorted to the team's quarters. For the three days of truce, the two factions, who had been fighting for almost two years, reported no casualties. The day after Pelé left the country the war resumed. Maybe they should have kept him there for more games.

Pelé was now getting the equivalent of about $10,000 American money for every game he played. He encountered difficulties late in the year, when a Rhodesian customs officer asked him to open his bag at the airport. The officer almost fainted when he discovered over $100,000 cash in the suitcase, much of it packed in a little brown package. Pelé was arrested but quickly released when officials were informed that this was the way he carries his money when on tour.

Santos also played a game in Afghanistan, and Pelé and his teammates were somewhat frightened when, according to Professor Mazzei, they were greeted by over 10,000 tribesmen carrying spears. But Pelé soon forgot the fright and spent several minutes talking with the tribe's leader through an interpreter. They hugged one another and all the tribesmen raised their spears in a gesture not of war but of admiration for the man they had heard of but had never before seen. Pelé is a true goodwill ambassador wherever he goes, never, never mixing in the politics of a nation. That, some say, is the big difference between Pelé and Muhammad Ali. Once, when he was at Randalls Island, a group of Black Muslims cornered Pelé outside the stadium before he was to play a match. Pelé shook their hands but once they began to coerce him with their ideas, he quickly parted company, saying politely, "Soccer yes, but no politics."

But of all the goals he scored during the 1969 season, and there were 68 of them, one—the famed one at Maracaná Stadium—will be vividly remembered . . . and there was still more glory awaiting the king.

12 OLÉ!

Since it had not won the previous World Cup, Brazil had to qualify for the 1970 edition of the tournament in Mexico City. The Brazilians gave every indication of their readiness for international competition, as they swept through their qualifying elimination round by soundly beating Colombia, Paraguay and Venezuela.

This quieted many Brazilian soccer interests who had been at war with one another. Joao Saldanha was at the helm of the team during its qualifying victories, while Joao Havelange, who later would become president of the Federation Internationale de Football Association, used his vast power as the president of the Brazilian Sports Confederation to see that Brazil spared no expense in getting its team into top shape for the World Cup competition. However, some of the moves Saldanha was making were causing a great deal of controversy. Switching some of the promising youngsters into the role of substitutes angered some of the Brazilian soccer officials, but Saldanha's first great error was on February 28 when he sent Toninho and Scala back to their clubs in Brazil. He said that he was doing so on the advice of Dr. Toledo, the team's doctor, but it was a known fact that both of the dismissed players had had violent arguments with the coach. When both players were examined by doctors from their own team and pronounced fit, the Brazilian press started demanding the coach's ouster. Then Brazil lost a tune-up game to Argentina in Porto Alegre.

Four days later, Saldanha committed the ultimate crime. Saldanha, who had been openly critized by Pelé, decided that the king threatened the coach's control of the team. To avoid this, he said publicly that he was considering dropping Pelé from the team. Fans all over Brazil were shocked at the suggestion and it looked as if Saldanha's words might incite riots. The Brazilians had no choice but to quickly relieve Saldanha of his job. In came jovial Zagala, a man now given the task of putting together all the pieces with World Cup time only a few months away. Zagala met with all the players and Pelé swore his undying allegiance to him. Among the players he recalled were goalie Felix and forward Tostao, the latter of whom was pronounced fit to play, although later he was forced to retire because of the continuing problem of a detached retina.

In order to get acclimated to the high altitude and the intense heat, the Brazilians arrived in Mexico three weeks before the start of the event. They immediately won the favor of the host nation as they made themselves available for receptions given by various city mayors, giving autographs without hesitation. Pennants of their nation were distributed and they were always seen smiling. Young Mexicans flocked to their hotel in Guadalajara and the children, as well as the adults, were always after Pelé. They followed him wherever he went, receiving autographs and even occasional on-the-spot instructions, for the children, as Pelé said, were the future of the game.

The team then took off for their training site at Guanajuato. When they returned, their tight security precautions went into effect. Even journalists were forced to acquire from Brazilian team officials separate identity cards than those issued by the World Cup Committee. Brazil was assigned to Group 3 along with defending champion England, Czechoslovakia and Romania. From the start it was evident that England and Brazil would be the two teams to come out of this group to reach the quarterfinals.

The Mexican crowd was solidly behind the Brazilians in their opening game in Guadalajara against Czechoslovakia. The Czechs shocked the crowd by taking an early lead on a goal by Petras, but that was the day's total scoring output for the Czechoslovakians. By the end of the first half, Pelé and Rivelino were frustrating the Czech defense with their ball control, and the Czechs were falling back every time the Brazilians got the ball. Pelé thrilled the crowd when he unleashed a high, arching, 50-yard shot which was saved at the last minute by Czech goalie Viktor. But then Rivelino sent a swerving free kick home to send the teams into their locker rooms at the half, tied 1–1. Zagala knew that the Czech defense could not endure the Brazilian forwards, who were outdribbling as many as four defenders before getting a clear shot on goal. As the second half started, Gerson, one of the best passers in the history of the game, set up the second Brazilian goal with a long, left-footed pass to Pelé, who chest-trapped the ball and let it roll down to his feet where he boomed it into the goal to give Brazil the lead. While the Brazilian offense was brilliant, their defense left something to be desired as the Czechs were penetrating. Although he was making the saves, Brazilian goalie Felix looked shaky. But so concentrated and potent was the Brazilian attack that they kept the pressure on the Czechs. The final goal in the 3–1 victory came when Jairzinho outdribbled three defenders before blasting home a right-footed shot into the net.

Next on the schedule was a match against England. The English were bitter indeed on the day of the game. They had been unable to sleep the previous night, as the Mexicans vented their hostility toward the English for some derogatory statements by Sir Alf Ramsey, England's manager. Ramsey had called the Argentinians "animals" and had physically helped chase some of the Mexican press out of England's dressing room following a workout. The Mexican fans surrounded the English hotel and started a long night of disturbances. "Bra-sil, Bra-sil," they would chant, as motorcades drove round and round the hotel blowing their horns. Some fans even tried to crash the hotel but were turned away by the police. English players switched their rooms in an attempt to get some sleep, but the noise continued at the midtown hotel. Meanwhile, the Brazilians enjoyed a restful sleep and were prepared for the match, a match that many journalists were proclaiming was the true World Cup final.

Ramsey, knowing full well the terror that Pelé could cause, assigned Alan Mullery to guard the king, with Brian Labrone assigned to the stopper position in front of goalie Gordon Banks, should Pelé break through the English defense. The Brazilians demonstrated from the outset that they were not fearful of the defending champions. With 10 minutes gone in the game, Pelé took a perfect cross from Jairzinho, who had beaten the English defense. He headed the ball down hard on the bounce inside the left-hand post. Pelé was already shouting "Goal!" when Banks, somehow showing all the agility of a truly great gymnast, launched across the goal mouth from the other post where he had been stationed against the cross pass, to make what is still described as the greatest save in the long history of the World Cup.

The Brazilians and English traded missed opportunities. Bobby Moore was doing a good job cutting off Pelé whenever he would start driving toward the center of the penalty area. But with fourteen minutes gone in the second half, Tostao dribbled down the left side, drawing out the English defense. Tostao spotted Pelé in the goal mouth and without hesitation passed him the ball. The English defense immediately went to Pelé like bees to honey. Using his great peripheral vision, Pelé spotted Jairzinho on his right and hit his teammate with a perfect pass. Goalie Banks, also thinking Pelé would shoot, had committed himself. This left Jairzinho all alone to score the lone goal of the match. After the game Pelé once again exhibited the admiration he has for good plays by his opponents. Pelé sent a message to Banks at the English hotel, congratulating him for the great save he had made early in the game.

"Tell Banks," Pelé told the press, "that I hated him for three seconds when he stopped that shot . . . but I have admired him ever since. He must be the greatest goalkeeper in the world. He got up like a cat. He made one of the best saves I have ever seen, and it was not his fault that the English didn't win."

The third game of the qualifying first round was against Romania. Now assured of a spot in the quarterfinals, the Brazilians gave Rivelino and Gerson a breather and moved Piazza to the midfield area. The Brazilians wanted to rest some of their stars, but when the game got underway there was Pelé in the starting lineup. Someone later said that if Pelé hadn't played, the Mexicans would have rioted. They were now rooting for the Brazilians although their own team had already virtually clinched a spot in the quarterfinal round. Pelé didn't disappoint the fans, as he scored two clean goals and helped initiate the play for the other by Jairzinho. To the Romanians' credit, it should be mentioned that they came within a whisker of gaining a tie instead of a 3–2 defeat.

The Brazilians were matched against their South American rival Peru in the quarterfinal bracket at Guadalajara. Although managing only a 4–2 victory, Brazil was in command from the outset. Their deft ability to dismantle a weak offense was visible from the beginning. With only eleven minutes gone, a poor clearing effort by the Peru defense allowed Tostao to pick up a loose ball which he fed to Rivelino, who blasted a shot which hit the post and bounced past Peru goalie Rubinos. Tostao struck again with a hard blast to put Brazil ahead 2–0. The Peruvian team halved the deficit at the 30-minute mark, as Gallardo sent a cross past Brazilian goalie Felix, who was looking unsteady at the time. But as soon as the teams began the second half, Brazil again went to work as a long shot by Pelé was rebounded in by Tostao. Peru made a futile effort to counter by making two substitutions and for a while it looked as if they just might be able to come back as Cubillas scored to make it 3–2. But once again Brazil responded to the challenge. Jairzinho, on passes from Tostao and Pelé, scored the final tally in the 4–2 win. With it, the Brazilians gained a berth in the semifinal round against their old rival Uruguay, who had advanced to the semis with a 1–0 overtime win over the Soviet Union. West Germany and Italy had won spots in the other semifinal.

Playing the 4-2-4 system, the Brazilians started Everaldo in place of Marco Antonio. The Uruguayans had protested, to no avail, that the game be played in Mexico City instead of Guadalajara, which many now were referring to as Brazil's home field. Showing utter disrespect for Brazil's reputation, the Uruguayans shocked the Brazilians by playing offensive soccer from the opening whistle. They took a 1–0 lead when Cubilla gambled and won against the inept Felix. Cubilla dribbled down the left side and, seeing no one open for a pass, took a last second shot. It was a weak bouncer which went through the hands of Felix. Several Brazilian players gave Felix menacing looks. Pelé, however, ran back and patted his goalie on the backside. Brazil, fearing the worst, saw their players fouled regularly by the Uruguayan defense. Pelé was twice sent to the ground but no player was ejected. Pelé almost tied the game with a brilliant move of anticipation. Uruguayan goalie Mazurkiowiecz had the habit, Pelé noticed, of sending short kicks out to his defenders when he made a save. Pelé waited for his opportunity and when the Uruguayan goalie committed this fault he raced in and intercepted the ball, booming it toward the goal. But somehow Mazurkiewiecz managed to make the save.

Uruguay retained its 1–0 advantage. Because time had been lost due to injury, the whistle signaling the end of the first half did not sound after the 45-minute mark. The game continued. At this point, twenty-year-old Clodoaldo came in on the blind side and, in one swift motion, fired the ball into the net after taking a picture pass from Tostao. Pelé, knowing the feeling Clodoaldo had at the time, mobbed his Santos teammate and together they jumped for joy. Soon Brazil took command, and Tostao passed to a fast-moving Jairzinho, who sent home the shot to make it 2–1. Pelé helped set up the third and clinching tally as he drew the defense to him, then spotted Rivelino free and simply rolled the ball to him for an easy shot on goal. Pelé was still not through. With only a few minutes remaining, he came in all alone on the Uruguayan goalie. Seeing that the keeper was in a good position to make the save, he dribbled the ball away from the net, drawing the goalie with him, and then fired a shot which missed going into the now guardless net by only two feet. Although the shot was wide, the crowd cheered at the masterful ball control. After the game, the two bitter enemies shook hands as Brazil prepared for its trip to Mexico City where the final would be held against Italy, the 4–3 victors over West Germany.

Arriving in Mexico City, the Brazilians were greeted by a wild, cheering mob of Mexicans who kept chanting "Mexico! Bra-sil!" time and again. Pelé was one of the first to be interviewed.

"How will you feel after you win the championship?" a Mexican reporter asked. Pelé simply responded, "First we will have to win the game, then you will see how we react."

The game was to be held at Azteca Stadium, one of the most modern soccer stadiums in the world. A crowd of 112,000 was to be on hand for the contest. Outside the stadium the scene was one of pure madness. While his teammates were in a rush to get to the comparative safety of their locker room, Pelé told those accompanying him to stop when he observed a group of children trying to get his attention. Never one to turn down the children, Pelé waited while the excited youngsters ran over to him. There were about ten of them and Pelé shook their hands and patted their heads. He asked them if they were going to see the game and they told him that they didn't have tickets and if there were tickets to be purchased they wouldn't be able to afford them since they were living in an orphanage. Pelé was sad and told his security men to take their names and the name of the orphanage, saying he would be in contact with them. True to his word, Pelé did write to them and when, a year later, he played his final game for the Brazilian National Team, he personally extended an invitation for them to come from Mexico to Brazil. He is reported to have paid their fares. Such a man is Pelé that when the reporters saw him talking to the youngsters and began barraging him with questions of their own, he told them that he was interested at the moment in talking only with these children. Later, he told them, he would be happy to talk to them about the game and answer any questions they might have.

Inside, the stadium looked like a festival ground with green and yellow banners flying everywhere. The Mexicans had adopted Brazil as their team and they were as vocal as any soccer crowd in Maracanã. The two teams sat in their respective locker rooms until it was time to make their way onto the pitch for this, the decisive game of the 1970 World Cup. A win for Brazil would give them permanent possession of the Jules Rimet Cup. At the same time, an Italian victory would also retire the Cup, as Italy had previously won the worldwide competition in 1934 and again four years later.

The experts considered the game a soccer classic, with Brazil's dynamic offense against the Italian *cantenaccio* defensive tactics, which often see as many as nine defenders back. In this style, defenders don't challenge at midfield and are generally content with playing strictly defense, hoping for a sudden breakaway as the only way of scoring. There was no way the Italians could run against the Brazilians or match their skillful ball control technique. If the Italians had any hopes of winning they would have to rely on a sudden, long passing counterattack game similar to the style that had enabled Inter of Milan to defeat Santos in the Yankee Stadium game played three years earlier.

Brazil immediately showed its confidence in the offensive style of play. Sparked by brilliant dribbling and running on the part of Gerson and by the sharp passing of Pelé, Brazil explored the weaknesses of the Italian defense which had been regarded as almost unbeatable. With eighteen minutes gone in the match, the frenzied crowd exploded as Rivelino made one of his patented long, high passes. Pelé leaped high off the ground against his taller Italian defenders and headed the ball swiftly past Italian goalie Luciano Albertosi to put Brazil in the lead. The Italians made several thrusts of their own, using the skill and experience of Sandro Mazzola and the untiring running of Boninsegna. But they were continually stopped by the Brazilian defense, including Pelé, who often fell back to use his clever tackling ability to take the ball right off the feet of the Italian forwards. The Italians did manage to get the equalizer when, with seven minutes left before the half time break, Clodoaldo backheeled a pass toward his goalie only to have Boninsegna roar in, steal the pass, and fire a shot from the right side of the goal past Brazilian goalie Felix. The half ended with the two world soccer powers knotted at 1–1. In the second half, the Brazilians completely dominated the game, ripping apart the weakening Italian defense. With twenty-one minutes gone in the second half, Gerson left-footed a shot from outside the penalty area past Albertosi for Brazil's second goal. The Italians lost their control and were running desperately around the field, forgetting their pregame plans. Five minutes after Gerson scored, he took a free kick which Pelé skillfully trapped and flicked over to Jairzinho, who rammed the ball home for the third Brazilian goal of the match. The pro-Brazilian crowd was jubilant, as it was now evident that there was no way the Italians would be able to come back. Brazilian songs flooded the stadium as the game progressed. With three minutes left to play, Brazil rewarded their supporters with still another goal. Jairzinho passed to Pelé, who fed the ball perfectly on his right to the oncharging Carlos Alberto. Alberto put the ball into the back of the net for the final tally in the impressive 4–1 victory which gave Brazil the Cup for the third time in the last four tournaments—a feat without parallel. Many say that had Pelé been fit in the 1966 World Cup, Brazil would also have won that championship.

As the final whistle sounded, thousands of fans ran onto the field toward Pelé and Tostoa. The duo seemed to enjoy it immensely. Tostoa was mobbed by the fans who wanted his shirt, his shoes and even his shorts as they went after every Brazilian player, pulling off their bright yellow jerseys. Somehow Tostoa was able to retain his shorts—but only barely. Pelé was leaping around on the backs of his teammates when the fans got to him and divested him of his shirt. Then about fifty screaming fans put him on their shoulders and paraded him around the stadium. In places like New York's Madison

Square Garden, where the finale was broadcast on closed circuit theater television, the Brazilian fans waved banners and kissed pictures of Pelé which they had hung all over the arena. Outside the Garden traffic was blocked for over an hour as Brazilians and other soccer fans danced in the street to the music provided them by a corps of Brazilian midshipmen who had seen the game on TV, coming to the Garden from the West Side where their boat had anchored. But all these celebrations amounted to little, compared to what went on in Mexico City, Rio de Janeiro and Santos. By a minor miracle, the Brazilian players were allowed by the fans to go back to their dressing room under heavy police protection. After several minutes, their door opened to the visiting press who had come to the game from all over the world. Reporters asked Pelé how he felt and the Black Pearl, smiling ear to ear, took the microphone and said in a voice shaking with emotion:

"This is the greatest excitement I have ever had as a player, even greater than the time I scored my first goal in the 1958 World Cup and we wound up as the champions. This championship gave me tremendous satisfaction and I enjoyed the competition. It was also the first time that I have been able to play an entire World Cup without getting injured. Before this championship competition I had no luck as far as injuries were concerned when playing in the World Cup."

Another reporter asked Pelé when he knew that Brazil had the title wrapped up.

"To tell the truth," Pelé answered, "I only became certain of our victory after the fourth goal. Nevertheless, I thought we were better than the Italians throughout the game."

Then came the inevitable question. Would he play in the 1974 World Cup?

"I don't think I will be in great physical condition in another four years," he responded, "so I think I should quit as a champion. I will play only another three seasons for my Santos team and then leave the game. That I am now sure of. I can get nothing more out of playing in another World Cup. We proved to the world that we are the champions and there was no team which could beat us."

Italian coach Ferruccio Valcareggi lauded Brazil, but also complained of a call involving Pelé.

"Pelé," he said, "was clearly offside on the action of the third

Brazilian goal. Not only did the whole crowd see it but so did the linesman. He kept on flagging as the action went on, but when Brazil scored and the referee pointed to the center of the field he unbelievably put down his flag and refused to answer our player's complaint and talk to the referee.

"In any case, Brazil deserved victory and Pelé was wonderful. There is no other player like him in the world. I feel that Brazil should have had a one-goal margin, which would have been a more honest score, but after the third goal our players were brokenhearted and the Brazilians and Pelé played as if they had wings. They played today like a team more determined than anytime I have seen them in the past. They are a great team and if anyone tells you that Pelé at twenty-nine is through, then he doesn't know what he is talking about."

After the press conferences, which lasted the better part of an hour, the Brazilian team departed the stadium via a passage closed to the general public and retained their custom of eating together as a team, declining numerous invitations from high-ranking Mexican officials.

Pelé years later answered one of the most puzzling questions about his appearance during that World Cup. Asked why he had a crew cut during the Mexican World Cup, Pelé, laughing as Professor Mazzei translated the question into Portuguese, revealed the well-kept secret.

"I was a freshman in a college in Brazil at the time," Pelé said, "and all the freshmen had to have their hair cut into a crewcut."

Professor Mazzei clarified how Pelé, with only a formal fourth grade education, could attend college.

"It seems that a couple of years earlier the government issued a decree saying that anyone who felt he had the ability could take what amounted to a test of equivalency, and Pelé passed with very high honors and got a high-school degree. Pelé, when he puts his mind to it, is a very good student and his insight is brilliant. He can smell out a good deal."

Outside, Mexico City was going wild. Thousands of Mexicans paraded down the rain-soaked main arteries chanting "Me-xi-co, Brasil!" time and again. Youths in raincoats and large sombreros waved noisemakers or sat on the roofs of cars, which they parked in the

Pelé is the focal point wherever he appears.

Pelé (kneeling, second from right) and his Santos teammates, Yankee Stadium, 1966.

Inter of Milan's goalie makes a leaping save of a Pelé shot during Santos' 4-1 victory at Yankee Stadium, 1966. Note the Milan defender's illegal use of hands to prevent Pelé from attending to any rebound or fumbled ball.

In the same game, Pelé gets off a booming shot despite close marking by the defense.

Pelé's peripheral vision is one of his greatest assets. Here, his head position allows him to simultaneously scan the ball, the nearest defenders, the position of his teammates, and his own position relative to the goal.

Pelé exhibits perfect form in this simple chip-shot. His head is over the ball; his non-kicking foot points directly where he wants the chip to fly; his body leans back; and his kicking foot is locked in a right-angle position. The ball will just clear the defender as it lofts into the goal area.

As the pass approaches Pelé, the opponent on the left tries to reverse field while the one on the right rushes to intercede. Too late—the king is in the clear.

Pelé (right), in his natural role as field captain.

An opponent closes in . . .

but half a step is all the king needs . . .

and with a quick plant of his left leg he's gone.

A well-executed tackle—but note the position of Pelé's right foot, which is between the defender and the ball.

With a flick of his ankle, Pelé has beaten the first defender and gained half a step on the second.

A perfect sliding tackle is not enough to remove Pelé from the play. And neither are two defenders, both of whom have been faked badly out of position.

Only those who have never played the game describe soccer as a non-contact sport.

Pelé exhibits the flawless form (left) which brought him to the point of celebrating his 1000th professional goal (above).

A moment of relaxation at the summit of the soccer world.

The king and his court.

Pelé at Pepsi-Cola soccer-coaching in Nairobi, Kenya, where he was working in his capacity as chairman of Pepsi-Cola's International Youth Soccer Program.

Pelé.

center of streets honking their horns. At Alameda Park a band played samba music while hundreds danced on the muddy ground. Thousands more stood and cheered until they were hoarse. Others took off their raincoats and shirts and reveled in the rain. It was a Brazilian championship, but a real Mexican party.

Simultaneously, Rio de Janeiro and São Paulo had erupted into one of the wildest celebrations in history, greater even than the annual Rio Carnival. Virtually every man, woman and child in the São Paulo city of six million inhabitants joined in the post-game celebration. Firecrackers, Roman candles, horns, sirens and every other conceivable noisemaker were brought into play. Cars brightly decorated with Brazil's green and yellow colors and Brazilian flags rushed onto São Paulo's avenues, blasting their horns. Fans climbed aboard moving cars and stood on the roofs waving and shouting. Samba bands appeared from nowhere and thousands poured into the streets to dance to the music with partners they had never seen before. Sentries at the president's office jumped and were joined by ministers and other officials as everyone lost their cool, reserved look.

Guards, who were often seen pushing and clubbing Brazilian citizens in the streets, became one of the crowd hugging and kissing anyone in sight. Although times were tense in Brazil, everyone loved everyone else after the winning of the World Cup.

During the game, São Paulo had resembled a ghost town, as only a few ventured onto the street instead of watching the televised game. But now, Pelé's family came out and joined in the mad demonstration which was spreading all through Brazil. In Rio de Janeiro, paper flags and papier-mâché replicas of the Jules Rimet Cup were being proudly carried. Nightclubs announced special Carnival celebrations and the parties continued through the night and all through the following day. But the true cause for wonder would occur the following week when the team returned.

The time soon came for the victorious Brazilian team to return home for their welcoming ceremonies. From the lowest peasant in the streets to the president of Brazil himself, everyone celebrated. The president, General Emilio Garrastazu, normally careful of security because of the hatred that many Brazilians had of the military regime, threw precaution to the wind as he prepared personally to greet the returning Brazilian champions. A motorcade from the airport was arranged and the players, standing on trucks and waving to the crowd, were cheered like a liberating army in the Second World War. They arrived at the presidential palace and were personally greeted by the president, who then went onto the balcony, took off his business jacket and waved it wildly, lauding the members of the team who had come to be presented with various honors.

Now the team, or at least many of them, went to São Paulo for another wild demonstration. Pelé led the triumphal return. The fans responded to his presence with a barrage of fireworks equal to that which had greeted Brazil's winning of the World Cup in Mexico a week earlier. The team joked with the people who had taken a holiday from work, and with the schoolchildren, whose lessons that day were confined to soccer on the vacant lots and small fields around the area. Every one of the youngsters was telling his friends that he was the new Pelé.

But if there is ever to be another Pelé, although most doubt it, he may have been born on August 27 of that year. For on that day, the same birthday enjoyed by his godfather, Professor Mazzei, Edson Cholby de Nascimento came into the world, the son of Rosie and Edson, the Black Pearl.

Pelé recalls how happy he was with the birth of a son.

"I was very excited and I guess about as nervous as any other expectant father would be for the child to come into the world. I was thrilled and very excited when my daughter had been born and I was overjoyed with the birth of my son. He was a healthy baby and I was grateful. You know that before the baby was born I had a chance to be with my family, something that while I was in Mexico I had sorely missed. Now I had everything, a great wife, a wonderful daughter and a son. It is really hard to describe your feelings at the minute you learn that you are the father of a son."

After the birth of his son, Pelé spent time relaxing as well as taking care of a few exhibition game commitments he had with Santos. He began to spend more and more time with his business interests, which now included being an officer of a large Brazilian bank.

On September 15, Santos opened an American tour with a 4–3 win over NASL All-Stars in Chicago. Pelé got three assists, including one on final goal by Maria with two minutes remaining.

There was still another visit late in the year by Santos to New York for a game against West Ham United, which was being captained by Bobby Moore, the man whom some regard as one of the greatest midfielders in the game.

Pelé kept Moore waiting at a press conference on the eve of the game but Moore, showing his tremendous respect, said, "He's earned the respect and if anyone has the right to keep me waiting then he has earned it."

The game wound up 2–2 with Pelé scoring both Santos goals while Clyde Best, the Bermuda star (not to be confused with the superstar "bad boy" George Best), scored both of West Ham's goals. In the game Pelé was hardly fouled and complimented Moore afterward, telling the press: "Moore is one of the cleanest but toughest players in the world. He is what I call a real gentleman."

Together with his wife, Pelé spent time going over and over the final plans for their home, which would be ready for occupancy the following year. Pelé let Rosie handle most of the design, while he consulted the many builders involved in erecting what will one day be regarded as a national monument in Brazil.

"Rosie designed most of the house," Pelé says. "Let's get that straight right now. I helped somewhat but most of the design was hers and she is very proud of it. In fact, so am I of her."

13 THE SANCTUARY

The house that Rosie designed was opened in 1971, not as a museum or showplace, but as a true-to-life living place. Not too many outsiders have been fortunate enough to enter Pelé's sanctuary. As far as anyone knows, no business is conducted within the confines of the house.

One of those who has been allowed inside the house is Bob Beyer, the son of a Fort Worth doctor and the husband of Brazilian-born Ina. It was Beyer who housed Pelé several times when the Santos star wanted to get away from it all while in New York.

Bob was impressed by the simplicity of the house, which is estimated to have cost some $600,000 to build.

"After being in the house," Bob said, "I felt that I had visited the house of Rosie, Edson, Kelly and Adao, which is the family nickname for Edinho. I didn't feel that I had been in the home of, say, a famous movie star. It was a house of people living there and not showing off their wealth or stature.

"From the outside of the house you can't see anything, and I have often been surprised at how many tourists go there and stand around the area hoping to catch a glimpse of the house. It's impossible, since there is no way you can see anything at all. I drove up with Pelé and was impressed with the circular wall surrounding the corner lot. The wall must be at least twenty feet tall.

"Even Pelé can't get into the house unless someone lets him in. He drove into the driveway and honked the horn. I noticed the Mercedes in the driveway; when Pelé is driving around for fun or to pick someone up he'll use the Volkswagen station wagon. The Mercedes has as its license plate the number 1000 in honor of his historic goal, but Pelé told me that he doesn't like using that car too often because it calls too much attention to him and he is chased for autographs and even by those who are seeking to grab him and offer him some sort of deal. These are the people who can't get into his offices, which are nearby in Santos. On the occasion that I was with him the door was opened for us by his cousin Maria, who was brought in by Pelé and Rosie from the interior of Minas Gerais. She's working for them but she's family and that is what they want since they have a fear of robbery and an even greater fear of kidnapping, something that many wealthy South Americans have to worry about."

The house has three stories and each floor has a distinct purpose, according to Beyer, who explained the lower level.

"Maria has all the keys and I think she's the only one who knows what key fits what room. Anyway, there's Rosie's photo lab, which is very elaborate and adjoins one of the downstairs rooms. Pelé told me about it but as had been the case with him many times, he couldn't find the key to the room and only later was I shown the room by Rosie herself. There's this large projection room which is like a small movie theater and it doubles as a playroom for the youngsters with the usual assortment of toys cluttering the floor. I saw many of the toys which Pelé picked up for the youngsters on the trips and tours he made to foreign countries. The kids use the room a great deal and seem to enjoy it.

"Then there's this beautiful oval swimming pool which is about thirty feet and is sunken into a redwood deck which leads down into a small backyard play area for the youngsters. The little soccer field they have is away from the play area, and as you enter the house from here through an elaborate stone and wooden area you are impressed with the size of the garage, which can hold as many as three or four cars. There's an elevator on the first level but neither Pelé nor Rosie uses it. Mostly the kids play in there under careful supervision. Near the projection or movie studio room there are a huge sauna and two massage rooms along with the laundry. It's strictly service area and done very neatly and as quietly as you can do such an area.

"On the second floor there is an eat-in kitchen and the relatively small TV room which connects with a den by a folding door; when they're both in use as one unit, it's a nice-size area. There is also a nice game room, everything with trays and shelves for its particular purpose. In the back part there is a large living room, furnished very modernly with twelve chairs around a large modern cocktail table. The chairs, I understand, are an exact duplicate of those seen in Hong Kong in a hotel lobby by Pelé and Rosie when Santos made a tour of the Far East. They took pictures of the chairs with an Instamatic camera and when they returned to Brazil they had the largest manufacturer of furniture in Brazil duplicate the chairs from the pictures they gave him. I understand that the chairs are exactly to the specifications of those that Rosie and Edson liked so much in Hong Kong. They're beautiful. Adjoining the living room and with very little space for separation is the formal dining area which is very baroque, making you think that you're in an old manor-type house. The table is carved but not overdone, while the chairs around the dining table are dark velvet-covered and, I assume, very expensive.

"The back wall of the dining room is glass and overlooks the pool deck. The rest of the house is wood. I asked Pelé if he didn't fear fire. He told me with the humidity so high if he struck a match it would be out before it hit the floor and that he had absolutely no fear of fire at all. I told him that I was surprised but after lighting a match myself I saw that it did indeed go out within a split second."

Throughout his long career Pelé has probably collected more trophies and mementos than any other athlete in the world. But, according to Beyer, unless you ask him to show you the trophy room, he won't.

"I guess that he doesn't like to show off the room but feels that he is obligated to. From the outside of the room you would think it's a closet or some other small room. It's locked and it's between the living room and the kitchen. As soon as Pelé opened the door I was impressed with the layout of the room. The entire trophy room is about fifteen feet by fifteen feet and is in good taste. It is modern, with paths for visitors to walk along to get the full feeling of the room. There are several large presentation cases with beautiful white bases and the cases are glass-enclosed. There are so many trophies and presentations awarded to him that it is hard to recall all of them, but even now that he has added so many tokens from the United States I think the most impressive and the most meaningful to him must be the replicas of the three World Cup championships and the replicas of the Brazilian State titles won by Santos. There are also two very large sterling silver sombreros which were given to him after the 1970 World Cup by Mexican industrialists and millionaires. But what really impressed me most was the case of knives he has been presented by several sheikhs of Arabia. They're gold and encrusted with jewels. I don't think you can possibly put a financial value on these curved knives but of course to him the sentimental value is terrific. As I walked with him and heard him explain the awards, and that included the many ribbons, medals and pictures that were enclosed in glass cases on the walls, I realized that even today, although he might not like to admit it sometimes, he still gets shivers when he sees these awards and recalls what he did to earn them."

Did Bob get a chance to spend the night in the House of Edson and Rosie, as he calls it?

"No, I didn't," he explains, "but there's a good reason for it and Pelé explained it to me. It seems that when they designed the house they decided that there would be no guest rooms. He told me that if there were guest rooms relatives and friends who would come for the weekend would wind up staying a month and those who came for a month would stay there for a year. It was something, he told me, that he and Rosie had agreed on and they're happy with the decision that they made. In the event that there are those who are visiting him, he makes sure that either he or his secretary secures hotel accommodations for them. His family lives mostly in the interior while Rosie's family is from right around the Santos area, so you can see that if indeed there were visitors wanting to stay they would probably be from his side of the family.

"The white building from which he conducts his Pelé enterprise operation is also very neat. From one floor, decorated in white, green and purple, all the major operations he is involved in are run, including the many port facilities. In this office suite Professor Mazzei has his office, as do Jose Xisto, his financial adviser, Zoca, who is his lawyer and public relations or communications director, as well as former Santos goalie Edevar, who runs the port operations for the firm. Many of his friends as well as old Santos teammates have jobs with his firm, and he has a constant flow of his old friends dropping in for visits and just chatter. In the office suite's main section is Pelé's private suite of offices, which are modernly furnished. There is a private receptionist who buzzes you in through circular doors into a large waiting room where you can have either Pelé Coffee or Pepsi and keep yourself busy reading through a vast number of magazines and papers. When Pelé is ready to see you he'll buzz you in through a side door that you didn't even notice before. His private room has a covered terrace leading into a garden into which he says he often goes to meditate or make an important business decision. Rosie is not a frequent visitor to the office since she is either home or taking the children to school or to play."

Even though the people in Santos as well as São Paulo have come to know Pelé well, Bob got a chance to see how Pelé is treated on his home turf.

"We were driving near the beach into the city to go to a restaurant," Bob explained, "and Pelé was driving pretty fast. All of a sudden we came to a school crossing and the guard, seeing that the car was going pretty fast, blew his whistle asking us to stop. Pelé did and the old guard came around to the driver's side of the car and stuck his head in all the way. When he noticed who was driving the car he stuttered and could hardly speak. Pelé told him that he was sorry and the guard kept saying over and over again that it was okay. I told Pelé, 'Boy you're really the king,' and all he could say was 'I guess I was going pretty fast after all.' "

Even though he had been in the restaurant before, Pelé, according to Beyer, was immediately besieged for autographs by a group of tourists from Peru.

"These were adults and not children," explained Beyer, "but when they saw him they looked as if they were going to faint. Pelé acknowledged their greetings and then politely asked them to wait until after he had finished his meal and then he would be happy to pose with them for pictures and sign all the autographs they wanted. When we came into the restaurant they were almost finished with their meal, but they patiently waited until after we had eaten and then he fulfilled his promise, talked with them for about a half hour, posed for pictures with just about everyone of them and inquired why they were indeed in Santos. He had a grand old time and he told me that as long as they had been patient and waited for us to finish our dinner, then he wouldn't rush them in their desire to talk to him.

He's not like other athletes I have known who want absolute privacy when in a restaurant. He told me that he feels that the fans, not only in Brazil but from all over the world, have helped him become what he is.

"You have to respect him for that and it is one of the reasons why anyone who gets to meet him is immediately charmed by him. I know that when I first met him through my wife he immediately sized me up and seeing that I was not going after him for any particular gainful purpose of my own he and I became very good friends.

"After we had finished dinner we entertained those tourists and then went for a walk, something he loves to do after a meal. We talked about my wife and his family. No matter where we went that night, there was always some one running up for an autograph.

"He never hesitated to oblige, and one could see that he was indeed the king of not only soccer but of all athletes."

Unfortunately, Pelé doesn't like anyone other than his wife taking pictures inside the house, either of their possessions or of their children. Some will go to any means of deceit so as to get a chance to take some pictures. There's the story about a professional photographer who, in an effort to get into the house, disguised himself as a priest and was found walking inside the house taking pictures. Needless to say, when Pelé found out who he really was the imposter was quickly ejected—not by the man who stays outside as an unofficial bodyguard, but by Pelé himself.

Rosie also wants her children's privacy maintained and was fit to be tied when someone touring the house stole some pictures of the children and sold them for publication. Although Pelé said that he thinks he knew who did the stealing he never took action against the guilty parties but you can be sure that these "guests" were never again invited into the Nascimento home. But neither were they turned over to the Alsatian guard dog named "Black," or to the guard with the revolver who stays in the background outside the house.

Compared to his humble home in Tres Coracoes, this house best sums up Pelé's rise to the top of the soccer world.

14 FAREWELL TO THE KING

In 1971 the New York Cosmos came into being. A group of successful businessmen, who later put their various businesses under the umbrella of Warner Communications, got together and made an investment they felt would one day pay off—that of owning a soccer team. The team now is owned by Warner Communications, Inc. As their general manager, they hired former English soccer writer Clive Toye, who had in previous years been the general manager of the Baltimore Bays, and when the team ceased to exist had gone to work as the administrative assistant to Commissioner Phil Woosnam. The Cosmos would play their games at historic Yankee Stadium, which a few years earlier had housed the New York Generals with little financial success. Toye knew that New Yorkers would go only for name players. In a bold move he flew to Jamaica to see Santos and Pelé play an exhibition game. He talked with Pelé and is reported to have told the great star, "Remember the Cosmos, we'll be back when you leave Santos." The Cosmos found that they would have a chance to see Pelé on numerous occasions before the end of the year, not in negotiating sessions but as a Santos player once again making a tour of the United States and Canada.

During the year Pelé met for the first time with Cosmo officials. It was a year in which he also suffered deep emotional strain as well as joy, through the glory that was his alone.

Santos used Pelé's name to book what turned out to be another lucrative worldwide tour for the club that was now considered one of the wealthiest sports organizations in the world. Shifting players in and out to complement the talents of Pelé, the team even decided that during some of their league games they would use players of less than star quality in order to keep their stars on the exhibition tour. They knew that without Pelé and some of the other stars, people in foreign countries would not pay to see them play. Several reporters in Brazil criticized the club bitterly for their actions. The Brazilian Federation even threatened to force the team to cancel some of their foreign games unless they agreed to play their stars in several preselected games. The Santos team, fearing a denial of tour rights by the Brazilian authorities, agreed that they would play a certain number of required games with their full team.

Santos, after sweeping through a tour of Jamaica, flew into Bogotá, Colombia, for what promised to be a comparatively easy match against the DePortivo Cali Club. Santos was shocked 3–2. Onto the world soccer scene emerged Pedro Zape, who made diving and leaping saves which held Pelé scoreless. Immediately after the game Colombian fans celebrated in the streets. Zape, later to become the hero of Colombia's National Team, was lauded as the finest keeper in all of South America. Cali officials promised Santos coach Nauro Ramos a rematch, but no firm date was set.

Santos made a rare visit to France. Here, Pelé was once again treated royally. Though not the greatest soccer fans in the world, the French prepared a gala welcome for the king of soccer, including a greeting by Premier Charles de Gaulle at a reception at the presidential palace. De Gaulle gave Pelé several gifts, including a plaque and jewelry case. Then, in one of the largest parades in French history, Pelé sat atop a car and was driven right through the Arc de Triomphe to the cheers of almost 200,000 Frenchmen. He later told Professor Mazzei:

"It is most difficult to express how I felt at the moment. I know what a parade through the Arc signifies. There have been many war heroes and national heroes so honored and now they have honored me with a similar parade. It is such a great tribute and I am very, very proud. I hope to one day be worthy of such an honor."

Meanwhile, Santos continued on its way, beating almost everyone in sight. According to one Brazilian reporter, in the past seven years they had won over 85 percent of their matches against foreign clubs. Antonio Doria, a New Jersey construction executive, now owned

Santos' tour rights in North America. He arranged an exhibition series for them against Bologna of Italy. Santos agreed to the tour. Then, like the rest of the Brazilian people, Santos were saddened when on May 31, Pelé made his long-dreaded statement that he would definitely retire from the Brazilian National Team after he played his last game for them on July 18 against Yugoslavia. In his statement, which he read with tears in his eyes, Pelé said:

"Although I love to play soccer, I must think of retiring as a selection player now, so the fans can always remember me with sympathy. There is nothing that can change my mind. I must think about my family, my business and my private life. I've done enough for the selection of my country and think that it is now time for the officials to start thinking about a replacement for me. Nothing will make me change this decision." For days after that statement, while Santos was back on tour, all radio and television programs in Brazil mentioned little else than Pelé's firmness on that decision. Almost immediately, preparations were started to make his farewell game against Yugoslavia a worldwide historic contest.

Pelé and the rest of his Santos team were away during most of June. The series against Bologna included a game in Toronto and another match in Jersey City's old Roosevelt Stadium, the former home of the Jersey Giants of the International Baseball League. The game in Toronto was a wild affair, with over 21,000 people jamming the stadium and another 5,000 trying to break down the gates after the tickets ran out. Santos had a hard match against the Italians. The game hung in the balance until the closing minutes, when Pelé electrified the crowd by faking out two defenders and then heading a pass to Jader, who quickly returned the ball to Pelé who crashed it into the back of the net from fifteen yards out to give the Brazilians the 2–1 victory.

"Bologna is certainly a stronger team than we expected them to be," Pelé said. "Unlike some other Italian teams we have played against in the past, they attack more and of course their defense is very well coordinated—they work together very well."

Santos arrived in New York the day after their Toronto game. Pelé was mobbed at Kennedy Airport, not by young fans, but by workmen who were making repairs. When Pelé descended from the plane, the workmen rushed over to him and a beaming Pelé greeted them.

"It's great to be back in New York," Pelé said. "I know that I have many friends in America and I look forward to playing a good match here." He then introduced several of his teammates to the workers. "Playing with this team is just great. They're all brothers to me. I don't ask them to do anything that I myself wouldn't do, from getting the sodas in the dressing room to sometimes helping carry the bags from the locker room. Maybe that is one of the reasons we have been so successful. It's the feeling of being as one that makes us so friendly."

Pelé showed up almost two hours late for a press conference promoting the game, saying: "There were things to do for the team and then I got this call from Brazil about some business. I hope that I didn't cause you [the press] any great difficulty and I hope you understand."

It was later revealed that the business Pelé was talking about was his filming a sequence for the slave picture called *Marsha* as well as his role in an upcoming "Star Trek"-oriented series in which he would be playing the role of a private detective.

Meanwhile, Toye was busy criticizing New York City for not allowing the Bologna-Santos match to be played at Shea Stadium, which would be idle that day.

"New York City has sold its soul to the Mets," charged Toye. "Here is one of the world's great sport figures, and he's banished to a field [Roosevelt Stadium] not befitting his stature because the Mets won't let him play in a vacant stadium owned and subsidized by New York City. It's a disgrace, that's all."

The game against Bologna at Roosevelt Stadium was a true classic. The game was delayed for thirty minutes since roads leading to the field were jammed for miles outside the Lincoln Tunnel. Some fans abandoned their cars about a mile from the stadium and walked to the ancient field. Police had their hands full. "I have never seen a traffic jam around here like this one," said a veteran New Jersey police officer. "We tried to keep the people from leaving their cars in the middle of the road but they wouldn't listen. One man jumped out of his car and told me that he was getting to the field so he could see Pelé play and then he ran out and left the keys in the car and told me to move it if I wanted to. Well, he's got a surprise coming. We moved the car to the police station and he'll have to pay a fine before he gets it back. Some of the Italian fans even parked so close to the railroad tracks that train crews had to move their cars for them. This is the wildest sports scene I have ever seen, but I can only say that in the few minutes I saw of the game I was impressed with the way the man plays. He is so crafty. I'd hate to have to chase him because he could trick me right away into going the wrong way looking for him."

Pelé waged a great individual struggle with Bologna defensive ace Frederico Righi, who guarded him that night before a crowd estimated at over 25,000. After the game, which ended in a 1–1 deadlock after Pelé's late assist set up the tying goal by Jader, the two shook hands and talked about the game to the delight of the press. Meanwhile the Italian fans were busy pounding away on the back of Giuseppe Savoldo, who had scored the go-ahead goal for Bologna with 20 minutes gone in the second half. They were also busy congratulating Amos Adani, who was credited with fifteen saves, including three brilliant stops on free kicks by Pelé late in the match.

"Pelé gave me quite a busy day," said Righi, "but it was enjoyable. He's some player to go against. I just tried my best not to go for his fakes. He beat me a few times but that's nothing new. He does that to everyone. I think I did okay. He has some reputation and, believe me, once you play against him you see why. He's got moves like no other player I've ever faced. He moves one way with his feet and then twists his body in the other direction. One time I stood about five feet from him trying to figure out what to do. Finally I made my move on his third fake and luckily I was right but I just as easily could have been wrong and looked foolish. It was a real cat-and-mouse game we played."

Pelé said that he thought Righi was a fine defensive player. Speaking at a reception the two teams held later that night, Pelé said that he was pleased with the outcome, calling the game a well-earned deadlock. About Righi, Pelé said, "He didn't foul me too much and he didn't go for some of the fakes I tried against him. I think that's the mark of a good player."

A couple of days after the game Pelé and Santos returned home for the long-awaited moment of his final game for Brazil. Pelé turned up for the match by playing an international exhibition game in which he scored Brazil's only goal in a 1–1 deadlock with Austria.

Before Pelé's final appearance with the Brazilian National Team, which would be his 111th game with them, a wire story broke out of São Paulo confirming that Santos had received a three-million-dollar offer for Pelé from France's Paris Saint Germain Soccer Club. In making the disclosure, Santos president Vasco Faet revealed that the offer was a firm one calling for the French club to pay Santos two million dollars and give Pelé the other million. Faet said that Santos immediately declined the offer "because we have other plans to make more money with Pelé on our team. Everyone can be sure that Pelé will never be transferred and will end his career playing with us."

Meanwhile the pressure on Pelé not to end his career with the Brazilian National Team was growing. With the finale against Yugoslavia only a few days away, Pelé told a group of reporters who had followed him wherever he went, "When I first announced my plans to retire from the National Team everyone agreed with me. But now, all of a sudden, there has been a change in opinion. The people must understand that I am not doing this to harm anybody. I will continue playing with Santos, but if to play with Santos I must also play with the national selection, then my next step will be to quit professional soccer. I wouldn't like that to happen, but if there is a day when a player has to announce his retirement, then I have chosen mine. I know I'll suffer a lot of pressure but my answer is definite."

When a reporter asked Pelé if he still got a thrill out of playing soccer, Pelé said the thrill would never be gone. "There is nothing like soccer," he said. "Full stadium, thousands of banners. The ball shining white, ahead. A sure kick. Goal. That to me is everything an athlete can ever want."

Maracanã Stadium, July 18, 1971. The day Brazil and the rest of the soccer world bade farewell to King Pelé's membership in the colors of the Brazilian National Team. It was a day unmatched in the history of sports. So intense was the feeling not only in his native Brazil but in the rest of the world that the otherwise meaningless game against Yugoslavia was broadcast worldwide via satellite, including some fifty closed-circuit theater television outlets in the United States and Canada. The closed-circuit promoters were calling the day and the event "Farewell to the King." And in Spain, even bullfighting had to take a back seat to Pelé. The bullfights scheduled in Seville were cancelled because, as the operator of the arena said upon learning that Spain would receive a direct, live TV feed from Rio de Janeiro, "with Pelé on live television, we doubt that one tenth of the ring could be filled. I myself expect to sit home and watch the game. All the sports world owes him that much respect."

In Rio, all hotel accommodations had been booked weeks in advance. The vendors and the scalpers were having a field day. Banners with Pelé's picture on them were being grabbed up at a terrific pace. With still several hours to go before kickoff, virtually all mementos of Pelé's brilliant career had been gobbled up by those coming to pay tribute to their king by being present on this, the culminating event of his long career. Brazil had honored Pelé by issuing a stamp showing him leaping in the air, that famous grin on his face and a sweeping punch into the air. Large posters duplicating this stamp were being sold at the equivalent of about five American dollars. Fans sitting in some of the better seats at the stadium later admitted that they had paid up to one hundred dollars for seats that were usually sold for about three or four dollars. Although the game would be shown on live TV throughout Brazil, many fans felt they wanted to be part of that wild scene. Every major Brazilian political official, including General Medici, the president himself, was there to join in the historic event. Pelé arrived with the rest of the Brazilian team about an hour before kickoff and went through the regular routine of listening to the coach, getting his rubdown and then joining the other players. It was obvious, according to other players later on, that Pelé, a little slow getting into uniform that day, must have been recalling his brilliant career to himself while pulling on his famous No. 10 jersey and then securely lacing on his boots. The team was informed that in about fifteen minutes they would take the field for the pregame ceremonies. They put their arms around one another and then raced onto the runway leading to the field. The stadium was packed with over 120,000 fans; banners were everywhere. Signs proclaiming Pelé as the soccer god were prominent, and Pelé later said he shivered as he took his place on the field.

Pelé's teammates were doing everything possible to get him to score a goal. But as had been the case every time he played for Brazil, he didn't force his shots. Rather, he played his regular, controlled game and when he had the opportunity for a good shot, he took it. If he spotted another man in the open he would pass the ball off, hoping to create a goal, and making the Yugoslavian defense come to him. His faking was as brilliant as ever and his passing, whether long or short, was as accurate and sharp as it had been when he had first worn Brazil's uniform fourteen years earlier. He had lost none of the ability that had made him the undisputed king of soccer, and it looked as if he himself was trying to let one of his teammates score so that he could later recall that he scored on the day Pelé left the National Team of Brazil. The Yugoslavian defense, unlike many defensive units he had faced in international competition for so many years, did not foul him. Neither did they lie down and give him the chance to score an unchallenged goal. For this, Pelé was grateful.

He tried a hard shot midway through the first half, but the attempt was blocked in mid-air. In the closing minutes of the half and with Brazil trailing 1–0, he let fly a cannon shot that many on the far end of the stadium must have believed was a goal, as they stood and roared. But the ball had hit the outside of the net—it was not a goal. Two later shots by Pelé resulted in misses. The half ended and Pelé returned to the team's dressing room. It had been decided before the game started that he would play only the first half. What followed a few minutes later will be talked about by Brazilian soccer fans for years and generations to come.

Pelé left his team's dressing room, bidding farewell to his teammates and also encouraging them to try to win the game, which would eventually wind up in a 2–2 deadlock. He told them that although he was gone as a member of the team, he would be keeping in touch and offering any help they might need, short of donning Brazil's National Team uniform.

He then went to the referee's tunnel, stood there several minutes trying vainly to compose himself, wiping away the tears which were openly flowing from his eyes and awaiting the word that he should trot onto the field. The fans were more than ready for him; as soon as they spotted him they stood to a man, woman, and child. A chant began: *Fica! Fica!* (Stay! Stay!)

This was one of the loudest chants Pelé had ever heard in his long career. He knew then that the people of Brazil wanted him to stay, but he had made up his mind. The hundreds of photographers made a mad dash at him. Children, who somehow managed to get past the police guards, mobbed him, and Pelé, as he had always done before, stopped and signed autographs for them, occasionally stopping to shake hands with a friend or even a stranger who approached him. Now Pelé was ready to take the traditional victory lap around the outer fringe of the playing field. As he trotted around the field, joined by many children including the Mexican orphans he had flown in for the game, the crowd broke into one of the most popular songs at that time in Brazil: "Obrigado Pelé," which means "Thank You, Pelé." Pelé pulled off his jersey shirt and twirled it in the air as he jogged around the stadium. Upon completing the lap he was mobbed by fans. Many of them presented him with gifts of their own. One man handed him a small portable television set and Pelé quickly handed it over to one of his security men who was making sure that the fans didn't harm him as many strove to pull the jersey out of his hands.

Police rescued him as he was led to the comparative safety of the dressing room and with about 10 minutes gone in the second half was spotted going up to the presidential box dressed in a business suit. Along with President Medici he watched the remainder of the 2–2 game.

After the game Pelé held a short press conference and the Brazilian reporters realized that Pelé was shaken and asked him only a few brief questions.

To the all-important question of how he felt about his reception, Pelé replied, in a voice choked with emotion, "It is all too overwhelming. I had tried to imagine what this would be like, but it surpassed anything that I could imagine."

Messages of congratulations to Pelé had been received from numerous countries, many written by heads of state as well as by average soccer fans. President Richard Nixon and Queen Elizabeth were among those who had sent Pelé messages, since he had in the past met both of these world-famous people. Nixon had seen Pelé while he was Vice-President on a South American tour.

The game was reported throughout the world and in what is probably one of the most fitting tributes the London *Daily Mirror,* which many years earlier had claimed that there would be no other player who could compare with England's all-time great Sir Stanley Mathews, wrote: "Pelé is the greatest footballer the world has ever known. Pelé is unique, irreplaceable."

So ended the Brazilian National Team career of Edson Arantes do Nascimento. But he still had a lot to give in the future years.

15 THE FINALE WITH SANTOS

Following this emotional experience, Pelé had little time to sit back and brood over his decision to leave the Brazilian National Team. Santos had booked another extensive tour that would include a Yankee Stadium game against the same DePortivo Cali team that had upset them in Colombia.

The game was part of a twin bill which included a match between the New York Cosmos and Rochester Lancers. Rain caused the game to be delayed one night until August 2. On that night, Pelé's No. 10 uniform was retired by Cosmos general manager Clive Toye, who said that no Cosmos player would wear the No. 10 while the team had the same colors as the Brazilian National Team, a decision made by Toye and other Cosmo officials. Later, when the Cosmos changed their colors, the number was reinstated.

"At the time we retired the number," said Toye, "we really never did expect a player on our team to wear that number. But after about eighteen months I said to myself, 'You'll never get Pelé,' and we decided to put that number back into service for one of our players to use."

No. 10 in the rematch against DePortivo Cali was once again thwarted by the efforts of DePortivo goalie Zape, who rose to the occasion in providing his team with a 2–2 deadlock against Santos. Late in the game Zape put on a rare display for the New York area. During a twenty-second sequence, he dove to his right to tip away a bullet-like Pelé drive from fifteen feet out. The ball rebounded to Edu, who lofted a shot back toward Zape. Somehow, Zape was able to regain his feet, leap to the left-hand corner of the net, and punch the ball out—but right at the feet of Pelé, who let go with a screamer which Zape caught as he was falling to his right. After that sequence, Pelé walked over to where Zape was standing, and to the cheers of the many Colombian fans who had turned out among the crowd of 19,739, extended his hand in tribute. As Pelé turned away he was in turn patted on the back by a DePortivo Cali defender.

After the game Pelé lauded Zape while Zape in turn praised Pelé.

"I understand that he's only twenty years old," said Pelé of Zape, "and considering that many of the really great goalies don't reach their peak until much later, this boy has got a good future. I can't say that he is the best now but he's a good one and if he continues to do well against top teams not only in Colombia but throughout the world he's going to be something. He made three saves in a row in the second half that few goalies could have made. He's fast and moves well, but I still want to play against them again. I think it was a great match." (Several months later, Pelé got his wish, but once again got the collar as Zape made two spectacular saves on the king's blistering shots. Santos, however, won the game by a score of 1–0.)

Zape, when informed what Pelé had said about him, commented: "He might not have scored against me this time or last, but he's the type of player who makes it easier for the other players on his team to score. In the first half he set up both their goals by Leo and Edu with great passes. On the goal by Edu he could have just as easily come in to take the shot since I was going the wrong way, but he saw that Edu had the better angle and decided to pass the ball off. That to me is unselfishness to the highest degree, and another one of the reasons why there has never been a player like him before and I am sure will never be another player like him again. He was disappointed that Santos couldn't win the game, but that gesture of his late in the game when he came over to me after I had stopped those three shots will be something that I will never forget no matter how many times I play for Colombia or whatever honors I receive in soccer. He is not only a great player but maybe even more; he proved to me that he is a great human. That is what life is all about anyway."

Lima, Pelé's brother-in-law, also played a beautiful game. After the contest the team went to the hotel for their regular postgame meal. Having grown up with the king, and even once dating the same girl that Pelé had dated before he met Rosie, Lima talked about his relationship with the Black Pearl.

"We're real friends," said Lima, "and we spend a great deal of time off the field together. There are times when we just sit around and discuss any problem that we might have. And I'm not talking just about soccer problems.

"Many players who've had the opportunity of playing on the same team as Pelé look upon him as somewhat of an idol. I don't think of him in just this light.

"I, in my own way, try to help him with some of his problems. We had many talks about his decision to retire from the National Team and in my own way I tried to help him straighten out some of his thoughts and apprehensions over the decision. I know what he went through before he finally made that decision, and you won't find me faulting it. He knew what he thought he had to do and he did it. He did it with the same desire that he plays with. When Pelé makes up his mind he goes all-out. He's a teammate and a brother-in-law, but to me, at least, he's a friend and it's been a great pleasure being with him."

Pelé and his Santos teammates continued making exhibition stops wherever they could. Again they were criticized by some of their fans for not playing the team's best players in the São Paulo League championship contests. The team responded that they were building the reputation of Santos as well as that of Brazilian soccer throughout the world. But the fans were not satisfied with the answer, claiming that money had become the all-important thing for Santos. In response, the team returned from an exhibition tour and for four weeks played their best players, winning all of five games with ease. Pelé was not scoring as effectively as in the past, but his passing and dribbling were as good as ever. Some of the Brazilian papers, seemingly on a vendetta, again said that Pelé had become too rich and had lost the drive he once had. Pelé did not comment on these cruel blows, although after one game in which he scored two goals and assisted on three others, he told the press that he had answered their charges.

Meanwhile his vast business interests were increasing and he was spending a lot of time with Rosie and the children. He appeared happy as he told Santos officials that he would definitely retire within three years.

Pelé began negotiations for a lucrative contract with Pepsi-Cola International. From the start he made it clear that he did not intend just to pose in pictures holding the Pepsi bottle. He and Professor Mazzei wanted to build a Pepsi International soccer program and plans were started toward that goal.

The year ended with Pelé scoring only thirty-four goals, the lowest full-season total during his career. Some Brazilian papers were so bitter about his performance that they openly challenged his title as the king of soccer. Pelé was very bitter. He seriously considered ending his playing days at the close of the 1972 season when his current contract with Santos would expire. Pelé spent many determined hours on several of his new business interests. He spent his leisure time with Rosie and the children, often strumming away at the guitar and writing songs, thirty of which have been published, and two of which were pirated by people who had a hidden tape recorder going during a private party and later dubbed in the background music. Many of Pelé's songs, according to Bob Beyer, were meant to be private between Pelé and Rosie. But there always seemed to be someone around who felt he could make an easy dollar stealing one of the songs or taping it without Pelé's knowledge. Bob is certain that Pelé and Rosie were more than just a little bit disturbed when the songs were suddenly released and became best sellers in Brazil.

Early in May, 1972, Pelé signed two lucrative contracts, giving him a combined income of over a million dollars a year. While he continued to endorse various sporting-goods items, including soccer shoes and soccer uniforms, the one pact which he finally signed with Pepsi was considered to be the most lucrative ever entered into by an athlete in any sport. It called for Pelé to receive an estimated $180,000 to $250,000 a year. The contract stipulated that Pelé teach the arts of soccer to young boys in one hundred and fifteen countries. Pelé was also called on to make educational films. He supervised the Pepsi series which not only featured the master demonstrating every basic technique of the game, but also included film clips of Pelé and some of his Santos teammates during their regular drills. Pelé, under the contract, is expected to play live exhibition games under certain prearranged conditions. The other contract involved coffee endorsements, with a projected royalty payment of $50,000 to $75,000 annually.

Pelé rejoined his Santos team for an unprecedented Far East tour which took the team to Japan, Hong Kong and Australia. The large crowds were unexpected and stadiums were closed two hours before the team took to the field. In Japan, where soccer was just starting to make inroads on baseball, a crowd of over 65,000—30,000 more fans than had ever turned out for a soccer game before in that country—came to see Pelé perform his magic. The same was true in Hong Kong. During games in those two countries, Santos swept to twelve straight wins, with Pelé scoring twenty-five goals and an additional five assists. While in Hong Kong, Pelé, along with Professor Mazzei, journeyed to the edge of the colony which borders Red China. Few knew that Pelé was going to visit so close to the border. Two Red Chinese border guards, who were on duty, were informed that the man standing on the other edge of the buffer zone was Pelé. The guards put aside their machine guns, walked over the buffer zone and shook Pelé's hand in another great tribute.

Santos and Pelé made their annual visit to the New York area on June 25, playing what became a mismatch from the starting whistle. Santos and Pelé were too much for their weaker opponents, Catanzaro of Italy. In the sixty-five minutes he was on the field, Pelé scored two goals and assisted on three others as Santos ran to a 7–1 victory, causing the fans to cheer the Brazilian style of play and jeer the ineffective Italians. Both Pelé's goals were examples of the master at work. His first came on a thirty-five-yard direct free kick which hit the crossbar and bounded in past Catanzaro goalie Ponzzino. For his second goal, he outdribbled three defenders before drawing the goalie out. When the keeper committed himself, Pelé put the ball into the opposite corner of the net. After the game, Pelé talked about the team's visit to Japan and the other Far East nations.

"We had the opportunity to show our style of play to many who are really unfamiliar with top soccer," Pelé said. "Besides just playing against local and national teams, we also spent quite a bit of time giving demonstrations, and the youngsters really seemed to be enthused. Many coaches who are working with the younger players in those countries attended our demonstrations, and we noticed that they were taking pictures of every one of the moves we made as well as making a lot of notes. I think we did a service for soccer and the hospitality we were shown was tremendous."

"In the game tonight," Pelé added, "we were not as sharp as I thought we should have been even though we did win easily. But when you travel as much as we have with some sixteen games in a little over a month you are bound to lose a little."

Pelé was again asked about his future plans. He must have been tired of the same question.

"I am still under contract to Santos until the end of this year and then I will see what I will do," he answered. "But the one decision I will stick to, no matter what some might now be saying, is that I will not rejoin the National Team, no matter how much pressure they try to put on me. I feel that although I did not have as good a season back home as I had hoped for, the reason is not because of my physical condition. There were other circumstances with business that had put a lot of pressure on me."

During the season Pelé scored fifty goals but there are those who claim that he never received official credit for some of the thirty-three goals he scored on the Far Eastern tour. Pelé once said:

"What does it really matter? I never keep an accurate total of just how many goals I have scored and I really don't think anyone else should. Of course there are milestones that I am aware of."

One of the milestones came during the year against Saprissa of Costa Rica where the Santos team was playing an exhibition game. When Pelé scored, it was his 1100th official tally.

Toward the end of the year Pelé finally came to terms with Santos, signing another two-year contract with the stipulation that the entire salary for the second year of the contract would be turned over to various charities, several of them dealing with children's welfare.

"Around Christmastime everyone should remember the poor children and try to make the holiday a happy one for them. I try and do what I can so that at least around this time of the year I can see them happy. If not, I think that I would be very sad and I would cry," Pelé has said. The sincerity of these words is underscored by the fact that Pelé once owned a physical education institute in Santos specializing in physical therapy and run by Rosie as the administrator. He has since sold it, or, as is more likely, given it away, to a former Santos trainer, a Japanese-Brazilian named Tocao, who still runs the institute.

Early the following year, 1973, Pelé and Professor Mazzei made a

U.S. visit in conjunction with the Pepsi program and in New York City, Pelé's presence caused a near riot. A clinic was planned to take place in Central Park but rain forced the event to be switched downtown to a high school. Although the last-minute change in plans was kept secret, many youngsters somehow got word and they descended on the high school in droves. The Cosmos gave a brief exhibition. Then in strode Pelé. He never had a chance to say more than a few words, for as he entered the gym area, the youngsters who had come from all over the metropolitan New York area immediately raced over to him. They pounded on his back and tore his clothes, and officials, fearing for his safety, decided to cancel the planned indoor exhibition. They rushed Pelé, along with Professor Mazzei, into an office. Only after an hour was the area clear enough to get Pelé to the safety of his hotel. During the hour the ever-present press was with him. Pelé, obviously shaken from the rough reception he had received, still managed to reveal just how he felt his presence in this program could help American youngsters become familiar with soccer.

"To see many youngsters come to an outing like this is overwhelming," he explained. "I knew that there would be youngsters in the park, but to see them somehow find their way here is a great honor. I just hope that I will get another chance to give them a clinic soon and I certainly hope I can do something to help that interest continue to grow as fast as I understand it has been growing in the past couple of years."

Pelé gave a series of less violent exhibition clinics throughout the United States. During this tour he and Rosie went to the White House to see President Nixon. In preparing for their visit, Rosie spent several hours at one of New York City's better salons. Bob Beyer remembers a call Pelé got from Rosie when he returned to New York several months after the visit to the White House. According to Beyer, Rosie called from the Santos home and asked her husband to get two of each of the items that were used on her when she was being made up for the visit to Nixon.

"Pelé called me and asked me," said Beyer, "to get Rosie two of each of the things that the beautician had used on her. I called the man who made her up and asked him if he had a list of what he had used to get her ready for that visit. He told me that he did and would call me back and let me know what the cost would be. In a few minutes he called and said that two of everything he had used would come out to around $400. I told him to wait a few minutes while I contacted Pelé. I told Edson that what his wife wanted would cost him about $400 and he told me that was okay. She was worth it. I sent my secretary to pick up the stuff a couple of hours later, and she came back carrying two large bags. I gave them to Pelé and he gave me the money I had laid out. He was wondering how in the world he was going to get all the stuff back to Brazil and decided that he would use the luggage cases that the Santos trainer had with the team. He seemed surprised at the amount of stuff the beautician had used. A year later I asked Rosie if she had ever used all the stuff or had she given half of it to her sister. She didn't answer, but I later found out that she had it all in the house. I think her sister was a little annoyed that she hadn't received any of it, but they all laughed about it later."

Pelé greatly enjoyed his visit to the White House, for it was the first time he had been there. Nixon and he talked sports and toured the Rose Garden. Pelé was highly impressed with the famed Oval Room. Pictures of him giving Nixon a soccer ball were on the front pages of many American newspapers, and in Brazil it was of course Page One with big banner headlines.

Pelé played his last game in a Santos uniform in the New York area on the night of May 25, 1973, when he helped lead Santos to a convincing, riot-filled, 3–0 victory over Lazio, one of Italy's strongest teams. The Italian fans were vicious as they were tired of seeing the Brazilians rip apart their teams. The game was again about an hour late getting started as a crowd of 26,145 jammed Roosevelt Stadium. Pelé was mobbed by fans who raced onto the field when he took the bumpy pitch for his pregame warmups. Mounted police tried to make the fans leave him alone, but to no avail. Pelé was surrounded by security guards and told to go back to the dressing room while the public address announcer warned the fans to leave the field, or the game would be canceled. Finally, referee Peter McIntyre blew his whistle for the teams to come onto the field. Rather than go through the formality of announcing the players, the game immediately got underway. The Santos bench was protected by two policemen sitting atop large horses. Motorcycle cops patrolled up and down the sidelines to make sure the fans stood aside. With nine minutes gone in the game, Pelé was awarded a free kick from thirty yards out. The ball took a wicked skip and bounced right past Lazio goalie Felix Publici, for the only score of the first half.

In the second half Pelé was all over the field, setting up his teammates with those now-famous passes, challenging opponents to try to take the ball away from him, and then when they did accept the challenge, dribbling right past them. Eusebio, not to be confused with the Eusebio of Portugal, made it 2–0 in the second half. Then Pelé gave another brilliant demonstration as he dribbled the ball around, forcing three defenders to try to get it away from him. As the defense accepted his challenge, he spotted Leo Pulicio in the open and fed him perfectly for an easy goal. The Italian fans were getting angrier by the minute, and while the action was down the far side of the field, Pelé suddenly sprinted for the sideline and made his way safely to the locker room. Meanwhile, referee McIntyre had his hands full as the Lazio players continually claimed that they were being fouled. Finally with two minutes remaining, he called a foul against Santos and awarded Lazio a penalty kick. But Lazio never took it, as the Santos team saw a mob of several hundred Italian supporters descend on them. Santos raced to the sideline and into their locker room, but not before Argentinian goalie Cejas was belted on the back by a fan wielding a wooden chair. Cejas was cut, but afterward said if he hadn't raised his hand at the last moment, the chair would have hit him squarely in the face. The press was kept out of the Santos dressing room for nearly an hour while the Santos team, visibly shaken, were allowed to regain their composure.

"I wish the police had acted faster and stopped Cejas from being hurt," Pelé said. After the game, Pelé talked about his future and was firm that next year would be his last as a professional soccer player. He also said No to reporters who, once again, asked him if he wouldn't want to play in the World Cup.

"When I announced my retirement from the Brazilian National Team two years ago," Pelé said, "many people told me that I would change my mind. And although there has been increasing pressure on me to play for Brazil in next year's World Cup in Munich, and, believe me, playing in such competition is great, I have resisted the temptation. Now I feel that sometime next year I will quit soccer for good as a player. I haven't given as much time as I should to my family and to my many business interests. My children are growing up and it's time I was at home more," added the man whose income at that time was estimated at nearly three million dollars a year.

Obviously, at the time Pelé never dreamed that one day he would be wearing the Cosmo uniform, for he said, "I think that tonight you saw me play my last game ever in the New York area. To tell you the truth, I will miss coming here as a player, since I have made many friends and always look ahead to going to the many stores and doing some shopping. But the time is coming for me to go out like a man and not be carried out."

Five days later in Baltimore, Pelé and his Santos team responded to the challenge of the Baltimore Bays who played the finest game of their career. Pelé delighted the crowd by scoring three goals and adding one assist, as Santos struggled to a hard-earned 6–4 victory over the Bays and their goalie, Lincoln Philips, who had himself been a former goalie for the National Team of Trinidad.

A second game two nights later was scheduled against Baltimore, and Pelé was magnificent. He scored two goals and got one assist as Santos won 4–0. One of his goals came when he put a twist on a corner kick and the ball hooked right into the goal.

"That's the first direct goal I ever made on a corner kick," Pelé said after the game. "And what did you reporters think about my goal-keeping?"

With nine and a half minutes left to play, Santos goalie Claudio had been helped off the field with a leg injury. Cejas, who had been hurt in the previous game, was back home in Brazil. In stepped Pelé, who put on a blue jersey atop his regular No. 10 uniform. He played the remainder of the game in the nets, making two saves.

"When we practice at Santos," Pelé said, "I always try to get some practice in goal, a position I like. That practice paid off for me to-night."

During the year they also won the São Paulo League championship for the eleventh time in the past fourteen years. As a reward they took another trip to the Far East. On this trip they again visited Tokyo, where police estimate that more than 90,000 people some-how managed to get in to see the action. The team also made a visit to Indonesia, where they were greeted at a state banquet preceeding an exhibition game before a crowd of over 110,000. On to Zaire, and officials still talk about the day they beat Santos 2–1 before a crowd which included General Joseph Mobutu and other officials of the African state. The team made a brief stopover on their way home, playing a mini tour of games in the Caribbean area. Through it all, Pelé played free of injury. And without the pressure of having to start a series of practice matches with the Brazilians the next year he appeared to be enjoying himself. But could Pelé have imagined the type of pressure that he would receive both from his countrymen and from government officials alike, there is a strong possibility that he would never have played his last year with Santos.

From late in October, 1973, right up to a matter of weeks before the start of the following year's World Cup, Pelé was constantly badgered by fans and officials to change his mind. But this time there was no changing his mind even despite personal appeals from a group of political leaders including former president General Medici and newly appointed president General Ernesto Geisel, an avid soccer fan. Geisel set up a committee to coerce Pelé, and in what has to be a historic sports occasion, former president Medici led a high-ranking delegation right to Pelé's office. Pelé was cordial but also very firm. He expressed his appreciation for the honor of their visit and invited them to tour the facilities. But the answer remained a firm no.

Only one time, early in 1974, did he begin to falter. By that time, people in Brazil were very bitter that Pelé had denied them their strongest chance to win a fourth World Cup crown, which would put them two championship crowns over any other nation. Pelé was shocked when some of the fans in a personal vendetta fired two shots into his home. Some feel that but for this incident, which had occurred after he had turned down the presidential appeal, Pelé might have played.

"I was very bitter about that incident," Pelé later said. "I couldn't believe that people would be so upset, when I had only reaffirmed the decision I gave to them almost three years earlier. It left some bitterness in me, but now I have overcome it and have forgiven the people who did it. They were never caught but even if they had been I don't think that I would hold any great grudge against them."

Pelé was bowing out gracefully from the Santos lineup. Where the year before he had scored fifty-two goals, his output dropped drastically as 1974 got underway. Santos was playing several matches against some of the South American national teams who were getting ready for the World Cup. Pelé was so deeply involved in his business interests that for all practical purposes he was only a part-time player, but still one who gave his everything when he took to the field. In a São Paulo League game on January 9 against Palestra São Bernardo he recorded the 1200th goal of his career. It was greeted with a large roar of approval from the Brazilians who were still highly respectful of his talents, though disdainful of his decision.

Among Pelé's new business ventures was the Pelé Computer, which reveals at the touch of a button the exact dates and the opponents against whom he scored some of his key goals. The computer would be housed in the Pelé Museum, which would soon be built in Santos. The museum was conceived primarily because Pelé did not want to open his own home to the hordes of expected tourists. But neither did he want to keep his trophies for viewing only by his family and his closest friends.

Pelé's company, Pelé Administracaoe Propraganda, was now booming with a wide variety of businesses which included his apartment houses, rubber companies, coffee firm, the manufacturing of Pelé Clothes (often modeled by Pelé, who quickly admits that at times he is somewhat of a clothes freak), and Pelé Rubber Bands, an offshoot of the rubber plant business, and shoes, bicycles, toys, razor blades and transistor radio batteries. In many of the businesses Pelé owns a major share while in others he has only a small investment.

As Cup time approached, Pelé accepted an offer to do radio and television commentary for the event. But the arrangement collapsed at the last minute when someone in Brazil pressured the television producers into cancelling the contract. Pelé expressed bitterness over this. He felt that the Brazilians were acting very foolishly. To this day, no one admits the responsibility for the cancellation.

Upon arriving in West Germany for the 1974 Cups, Pelé was mobbed by the enthusiastic West German soccer fans. He talked with several of the teams, including the Brazilians for whom he would surely be cheering. Pelé watched the impressive early ceremonies with great enthusiasm. Then Pelé dramatically raced onto the field through a mass of West German children who leaped to their feet in an effort to touch the king. He was greeted by former

West German star Uwe Seeler and the two of them exchanged replicas of the World Cup while cameras flashed. Pelé gave Seeler a replica of the Jules Rimet Trophy. Uwe in turn gave Pelé a copy of the new Federation Internationale de Football Association Cup. While in his seat of honor at the World Cup, Pelé met with such dignitaries as U.S. Secretary of State Henry Kissinger, West German president Walter Scheel and Chancellor Helmut Schmidt, Prince Bernhardt of the Netherlands, and Princess Grace of Monaco.

After the tournament, in which Brazil was forced to settle for a fourth-place finish, Brazilian officials promptly fired National Team Coach Zagalo, and the fans echoed the censure by hanging Zagalo in effigy. Reporters asked Pelé if he felt he could have made the difference.

"I don't think any one man could have made the difference," Pelé replied. "If I had played I still don't think we could have won. We have just too many good men missing from the team we had four years ago. You don't lose men like Carlos Alberto, Tostao, Gerson and Clodoaldo, in addition to myself, and expect to have a great shot at winning another championship. But this is not the end for Brazil. We will come back in the future, of that I can assure you."

Before leaving Europe, Pelé took care of some of his business interests. He also had a chance meeting with Cosmo general manager Clive Toye in Frankfurt. Pelé gave a few clinics for Pepsi Cola and made some personal television appearances, amusing the interviewers as he had done on the Tonight Show with Johnny Carson a few years earlier. Pelé, according to Mazzei, has a great knack for entertainment. Even today the professor feels that if Pelé had put his mind to the entertainment business he could have been successful in pictures and on the stage.

Pelé then returned home to Santos. He was kept busy with his training, his enterprises, and his family. In September, Pelé was asked if he truly intended to wind up his career in two more months. Rumors had circulated that Pelé might sign an additional one-year pact with Santos. Without hesitation Pelé answered that he had received all an athlete could expect from a career.

"I am about to become Mr. Edson Arantes do Nascimento," Pelé said, "an industrialist, an average father, and a husband. This is my ambition and nothing will change my mind right now." Pelé continued, "Lately I have been going more frequently to places that I could never go to before in Santos. My idea is to eventually become just another person, to be able to go places without being bothered by autograph hounds." He was quick to add that giving autographs made him happy. "I am just happy that I can sign the name Pelé instead of my full name because I don't think my fingers would be able to take the strain of signing all the autographs I sign using my whole name. There are some to whom I sign more than just Pelé or another short name."

Pelé also revealed that he was not interested in coaching a professional team but felt he could become a good soccer teacher for children. "I have an ambition to teach kids how to play soccer. I want to help Santos find new stars and once again establish their team as the best not only in Brazil but throughout the soccer world. That would give me a great deal of pleasure, and I'm looking ahead to the day I will be able to discover what might turn out to be another Pelé." His final game for Santos was against Ponte Preta. Word came that the few tickets which had not already been grabbed up would be placed on special sale a few hours before the game. It was evident that the Santos Stadium would be completely sold out. Some felt that Santos should have switched the game to Maracaná Stadium, but feeling that their fans had been loyal throughout the years, Santos officials decided to sacrifice a great potential profit. Pelé spent the night before the game playing with the children, who would not go to the stadium, talking to Rosie, who was still undecided about going, and simply walking around the garage with its four cars: a Mercedes, two Volkswagens, and an Opel. He puttered around the house, trying to relax, his mind recalling all the events leading from his first game with Santos, to this, the game he believed would end his playing career.

Finally, the time came for him to go to the game. He kissed the children and some of the friends who had come over to wish him well. He told Rosie that he would meet her at their ranch as soon as possible after the game. He left, waving to the neighborhood children who always made sure they were on the scene when Pelé left the house for a game. He avoided the large crowds around and outside the stadium, and joked with the players as he entered the dressing room and took his usual pregame rubdown. Some of the players had tears in their eyes as they greeted him. Even Pelé was not without emotion as he bowed his head toward his lap. This was undoubtedly one of the most emotional days in his long, brilliant soccer career.

Bob Beyer remembers, "It was pure madness. The vendors and the scalpers were having a great day. Scalpers were selling tickets for over one hundred dollars apiece and the people were fighting with one another to buy the available tickets. Even the police who usually try to chase the scalpers away weren't doing anything to stop the sale, since they must have figured that, had they prevented someone from buying a ticket, they might have been smacked. Zoca and I went to the main door of the stadium and being with Zoca showed me what respect he commands. Before I went to Zoca to pick up my tickets at Pelé's office I had misunderstood and believed that Zoca was going to leave the tickets for me at the stadium. The police and guards wouldn't let me get near the dressing room or even into the Santos office. The vendors were again out in force selling every type of souvenir possible and getting a pretty good price for them. Zoca and I walked up to the main entrance gate. We looked at one another and Zoca said to me, 'You really don't want to see this game. It's too sad a sight to witness. Let's go.' I replied, 'That's a great idea.' Together, we decided to go to the beach and have a couple of beers."

After the game, Pelé didn't hold his usual postgame interview, which would have seen the reporters asking him if he was planning a comeback one day and how he felt about the fact that in this his last game he hadn't been able to score at least one goal although the other Santos forwards were setting him up. (Some say that the opponents were playing as many as three defenders back on him, and that whenever Pelé would spot an open teammate he would pass the ball over to him only to have the teammate quickly pass the ball, like a hot potato, back to Pelé, who was then converged on once again by the Ponte Preta defensive alignment.)

Pelé left the stadium through a series of secret corridors. But according to Professor Mazzei, the king was so emotionally drained that he had requested club officials to make sure that he was not bothered by reporters. "Tell them," Mazzei later said, "that Pelé will see them soon but this was just too much of a strain for him. He is drained not only physically but mentally and wants to get away to the seclusion of the ranch."

Rosie had insisted that when she and Pelé were on the ranch, a couple of miles away from their Santos home, there would be no visitors allowed—friends or teammates. "She knew," said Beyer, "that Pelé was in need of privacy. In fact the only person who got there before anyone else was a television man who was going to install a color antenna."

Still, business pressure could not wait. Pelé would have to close down the Fiolax rubber firm, which was losing about $35,000 a month and later was declared bankrupt. Pelé had been advised earlier by Zoca and Xisto to close up the firm he had co-signed for. Pelé himself accepted responsibility for putting additional cash into the firm. He did not want to put so many people out of work, so he absorbed the loss himself. But now Zoca and Xisto were going to the ranch to persuade him to sign the necessary papers, putting an end to this financial drain. Rosie grudgingly let them in.

When they arrived at the ranch, Rosie almost stormed out of the house. If a phone had been available to them and if they had then been able to call it is a certainty that Rosie would have told them to wait another week or so to let Pelé compose himself.

When he returned to Santos from the ranch, he described his plans for filling his spare time. "Whatever spare time there is away from business interests I will spend with my family and take them to the beach. That is something that I have been promising them for a long time and now I have the chance to do just that."

But even as Pelé took his family to the beach, the wheels which would eventually see him play with the Cosmos were turning. Much of this took place in extreme secrecy with meetings held in strange surroundings, such as in a waiting room at Kennedy Airport in New York where Toye met with both Pelé and Mazzei. At the time Pelé was on his way to Canada. But no matter where the meetings were held and whom they were intended to include, Pelé remained firm. He might occasionally play a charity game or make a guest appearance for a certain cause or play in a benefit match where all the money, minus expenses, would go to a retiring player's family. But he would not be back in uniform on a regular basis.

Pelé did not score in that final game against Ponte Preta. He had scored his 1220th goal a couple of weeks earlier, on September 22, against Guatani. It was ironic that the final goal of his great career in Brazil would come in a match with the same team against whom he had missed a penalty shot in his first championship game for the Santos juvenille team 18 years earlier.

Pelé often talks about that missed penalty shot.

"I still shiver sometimes when I think about it," he says. "The feeling that I might miss sometimes haunts me."

Of Pelé's 1220 goals, 1096 were scored for Santos, another 95 for the Brazilian National Team in 111 games, 14 for the Brazilian Army team, and an additional 15 in various all-star games.

16 THE NEGOTIATIONS

It was a little past four in the afternoon. Clive Toye, the Cosmo general manager, was talking with some of the press who had gathered in the eating room adjoining the main auditorium at the Rockefeller Center headquarters of Warner Communications. Warner had been pouring money into the North American Soccer League's New York Cosmos in what best could be described as a futile effort.

Finally John O'Reilly, the Cosmo public relations director, informed Toye that it was time for the press conference to get started. The press and the hangers-on who had somehow got wind of the announcement politely went into the main room, although some hesitated, making sure they had a drink to take with them. It took a while for the crowd to quiet down on this third day of June, 1975. But when Toye took the podium and slowly, almost deliberately, pulled out a shirt with the name Pelé printed above the number 10, you could sense history being made. Toye, slowing his pace in order to enjoy every minute of his performance, calmly unfolded the shirt and held it up for everyone to see as he spoke.

"Today we have the shirt, tomorrow we will have the man."

So ended the Cosmos' worldwide chase after Pelé. The Cosmos had first put Pelé on notice that there was in fact such a team as the Cosmos when Toye went down to see Santos play a series of exhibition matches in Jamaica. At the time, as Toye informed Pelé back in 1971, the Cosmos had not played one single game in the NASL. Toye revealed much of the struggle for Pelé, who had entered retirement only eight months earlier. The chase involved many people, including Pelé's brother Zoca (his attorney), Professor Mazzei (his confidant, trainer and personal adviser), and Jose Xisto (his financial adviser and the man with whom Pelé rarely disagrees), Warner Communications President Steven Ross, Jay Emmett (head of the Licensing Corporation of America, a subsidiary of Warner Communications), Rafel de la Sierra (a Warner Communications vice-president), Jim Carradine (the organization's financial adviser) and Toye.

Toye disappeared from the New York scene in July 1974. In Frankfurt, he met hastily with Pelé, who had just witnessed Brazil's fourth-place finish in the World Cup. Professor Mazzei was also present. It was there that Toye made his first firm offer to Pelé to come to the Cosmos after he finished his playing days with Santos in a few short months.

"There were many journalists there in Frankfurt," Toye recalled, "and they told me that I really didn't have a snowball's chance in hell of getting Pelé to play with the Cosmos. Many of them felt that I was wasting my time, but I figured that I really had nothing to lose—so why not try? When I met Pelé, I was asked if I had an offer and I came up with one right on the spot. They didn't say anything firm but told me that they would be in touch with me sooner or later."

Although no figures of that initial offer were ever made public, it was estimated to be about $300,000 a year for regular league games with a bonus of about $10,000 for every additional exhibition game.

Two months later, at Kennedy Airport's Air Canada Terminal, Toye again met briefly with Pelé, Professor Mazzei and Xisto. Tentative arrangements were made for Toye to go to São Paulo the following month for a series of four meetings with the trio, also including talks in Santos. The Brazilians started to get wind of the negotiations, although no public statements were made at the time.

As of January the Cosmos had one reason to hope for Pelé, and another to fight for his services. They had signed an old Pelé teammate, Manoel Maria of Santos. The Cosmos made the offer for Maria after learning that Pelé himself wanted to see his friend play. Since an auto accident two years earlier, Maria had been nothing resembling his old self. That he survived the auto crash was considered a miracle, but to play again in top-flight Brazilian competition seemed impossible. Pelé and Maria had always been close friends and it was felt that Pelé's asking that he play with the Cosmos might one day help the New Yorkers get the Black Pearl into their own uniform. Cosmo officials declined comment on this possibility.

At the same time, the Cosmos held an elaborate press reception for George Best, the superstar bad boy who has grabbed almost as many headlines for his antics off the field as for his brilliance on the field. Best had more talent than anyone in the game—with the exception of Pelé and possibly Johann Cruyff of Holland—but high living had caused him to be jailed on charges ranging from drunken driving to causing fights. Finally, when he skipped training and went absent without leave, Manchester United suspended their Irish international star. Toye went after Best and all the papers were worked out to have him transferred to the Cosmos with the option to buy. Best came into New York and was more than polite with the press. He announced that it was ninety-nine percent certain that he would come back and play for the Cosmos. The deal made the front pages in England, and the New York papers also gave it a big blast. But when Best got back to Manchester he met with his business partners in discotheques and other interests. They decided that although Best wanted to play, he could not leave his businesses.

Toye and the rest of the Cosmos were disappointed. More importantly, the creditability of the Cosmos was now on the line, and unless Toye could land a player of superstar caliber, then the team, playing at the old Randalls Island, would suffer the wrath of the New York fans. Toye was in touch again with Pelé and his advisers, but it wasn't until February that he got the indication he had been waiting for from Professor Mazzei. There was now a possibility that Pelé might come out of retirement and play with the Cosmos.

Pelé was invited to play a special exhibition game along with a group of soccer all-stars in Brussels in March. Toye, not wanting to pass up the contact with Mazzei, arrived for four days of meetings with Pelé, Mazzei and Xisto. A lot was accomplished, and Pelé was closer to ending his self-imposed retirement than ever before. The press was alert to the dealings and stories began to appear not only in the American and South American press, but throughout Europe as well.

In April the chase returned to Europe, where Pelé played a game in Rome, as well as giving soccer clinics. Toye flew to Rome in the presence of de la Sierra and Carradine and met there with the familiar trio: Pelé, Mazzei and Xisto. Pelé told Toye that he would let them know within a week. Toye flew home feeling confident that he had made the needed breakthrough. It seems that the breakthrough was accomplished via a proposed tax package that was never made public.

On April 22, Pelé said he would play for the Cosmos only if the New Yorkers upped the ante from $4.5 million to his terms: $5,000,000 or $2.2 million tax-free for the three-year pact. The following week in Santos at a press conference Pelé turned down the offer, saying, "I have to take care of my family and my business obligations."

Informed of Pelé's rejection, Toye refused to give up hope. "As far as I am concerned," Toye said, "the deal is not dead yet. I will go to Brazil and try and get the deal completed."

Toye added company on his May 11 visit to São Paulo, Santos and Guaruja. With him on the trip were Jay Emmett, Nesuhi Ertegun, who was the president of the Cosmos at the time as well as the head of WEA International, and de la Sierra.

Saying that he was aware that Cosmo officials were in Brazil, Pelé added, "That won't change my mind. Nothing will make me change it now. I will not resume my career and will only take part in benefit games."

This did little, if anything, to throw the Cosmos off his trail, as they met with some of Pelé's closest advisers. The deal was so attractive that apparently Pelé's signature on the contract became almost a mere formality.

Meanwhile, Pelé's friend Bob Beyer decided to call Santos on Monday night, May 19, and talk with Professor Mazzei.

"He told me," Bob said as he put down the phone after talking with the professor for about fifteen minutes, "that Pelé is coming to play. As far as he is concerned, it's all decided. The financial terms have been settled and he told me there was only one problem still to be resolved.

"I didn't press him on it but I figure it's what type of tranquilizer Pelé is going to give the Brazilian people. The professor told me that Pelé and he will be fishing over the weekend and I assume that they will work out a statement to the people."

Bob says that the professor asked him what he thought of the deal, and Bob replied, "Tell him if he doesn't take it he would be dumb not only for the money but for what he had previously said about being able to help American soccer." He reminded the professor that a couple of years earlier when Pelé had been in Los Angeles he had got one of the biggest thrills of his life when he watched a group of youngsters playing soccer.

The professor expected Cosmo officials to fly to Brazil later in the week in order to finalize everything.

One important cause of Pelé's hesitation was his concern about the education of his two children. The professor had explained to him that the Cosmos were in the process of looking into the school situation. For the time being it appeared that the children would be placed in the United Nations School to get an English education during the summer.

Cosmo officials did go to Brazil later that week. For all practical purposes, the deal was finalized. All that awaited was Pelé's signing of the proposed agreement, which now ranged from $4.5 to $11 million for the three years. One of the main reasons for the wide range of figures was that Argentinian sources for example were convinced that Pelé would receive about $5 million for a two-part movie series on his life that they felt was part of the deal.

A press conference was called for May 28, but because Pelé missed his plane out of Vancouver, where he had gone to be inducted into the British Columbia Hall of Fame following honors bestowed on him in Mexico, he would not be available until that night at Randalls Island, where the Cosmos were scheduled against the Vancouver Whitecaps. The television crews and still photographers were present hours before the game.

While a preliminary game was going on between two groups of young players, everyone made a mad rush for the open end of the stadium. A helicopter was set to land and from it would emerge Pelé, Emmett, Ross and several other dignitaries. Pelé touched down and as he emerged he waved not to the crowd but to the youngsters who had been busily engaged in their game. A group of the youngsters posed for pictures with the king of soccer. Pelé smiled ear-to-ear as he shook hands with some of those he had previously known, such as Beyer and a few Brazilian reporters. With Cosmo security forces leading the way into the tunnel to the prearranged press interview,

Pelé chatted with Toye. He looked unhappy with both the field and the dressing room, but Toye told him, "Next year it will be better, much better."

During the press conference, in which Pelé answered every question, the king made it "sixty to seventy percent certain" that he would play for the Cosmos. But listening to his reasons, one could hardly be criticized if he said that Pelé was all but signed and delivered.

"I would like everyone to understand my principles," Pelé said through interpreter Mazzei. "If this offer had come from West Germany, Spain, Italy or even Brazil I would have to say No. But to return to playing in the United States would be a different principle. I love soccer. I've been playing it almost twenty years around the world. Why should I not come to the United States to play and help the game? New York is great for sports. I really feel if I came here I could give something to U.S. soccer."

Pelé was asked about the expected bitterness on the part of the Brazilian public.

"If I come back," Pelé said, "the Brazilian people would prefer that I come back to playing in Brazil. But I think the people would be proud of me if Brazil in some way can gain through me playing here. I believe there are no real problems if I come over here to work with Warner Communications as I do with Pepsi in their youth soccer program. If I sign it would be a great deal for Brazil."

Before going out to watch the game, Pelé was asked to compare the standard of play between U.S. and international soccer.

"The U.S. standard is not as high as international," he replied, "but as soccer grows in this country I believe the standard will be improved."

A few Brazilian reporters took Pelé aside and asked him if he was coming back to soccer because his businesses were losing a great deal of money.

"I don't need the money, although the offer is a very good one," Pelé answered. "If I didn't want to play again then I still could live well on what I have. Money is not the main thing for me. I have enough to keep my family and myself very comfortable, so please don't say money will be the determining factor if I do sign."

Pelé then watched the Cosmos lose a 1–0 decision to Vancouver. After the game, Pelé was asked by a pool reporter what he thought of the match in which Vancouver clearly looked like a better-organized team.

"It is difficult to make a judgment on one game," said Pelé. "The Cosmos do have some good players but seem to lack organization on the field."

Pelé and Mazzei stayed in New York for more meetings with Warner Communications but left late Thursday night, leaving Xisto behind to talk with Toye on Friday and with Pepsi Cola on Saturday. Meanwhile, the translators were busy drawing the contract up in both English and Portuguese. They transcribed everything they had agreed to verbally, so that when Pelé and Zoca got the pact from Xisto, everything would be clearly defined, including the provisions which would ensure that Pelé's contract with Pepsi did not interfere with Pelé's proposed Cosmo contract.

Pelé had promised the Cosmos an answer on Monday, June 2. But because of the complexity of the pact, no decision was announced until late the following afternoon, at the time Toye displayed Pelé's new Cosmo shirt.

After the initial announcement, Toye said that the following announcement was being made jointly in Brazil:

"Pelé has told us he will be happy to play with the New York Cosmos for the remainder of the 1975 season and for the 1976 and 1977 seasons," Toye said. "The contract has not yet been signed. Pelé's legal staff is presently going over the voluminous contract in Santos. True to his word, Pelé has already told the Brazilian public that he intends to play soccer in America. Pelé had promised the Brazilian people that he would let them know first. We are proud and pleased that Pelé will sign with us. We felt that he had retired far too early from professional soccer. There are only two things in doubt at this point. They are the exact arrival date of Pelé in the United States and the date of his first game. One thing he talked about regarding the contract was that he wanted one clause not to be included. That clause was that he would be subject to draft by another team. We were only too pleased to have that clause stricken from the proposed agreement."

An English journalist asked Toye if the Cosmos were still interested in obtaining George Best. Toye replied, "We have The Best. We don't need George Best."

Back home, Brazilians were racing into the streets with the news.

Pelé knew that his announcement would be something of a time bomb, but as he said, "I feel I am still in good form or else I wouldn't come back. I returned because of my love for soccer and besides I want to contribute to the growth of the sport in the United States. And I want to keep making publicity for Brazil abroad."

Because Warner Communications is one of the larger and more diversified corporations in the United States, many financial writers cornered their executives to ask why the company decided to plunge ahead with the money to Pelé.

"We've been offered five basketball, two baseball and several hockey teams in the past," said Emmett. "We feel that soccer is the fastest-growing sport. It's unquestionably the sport of the future."

Among Warner's hopes for their Pelé investment were the following:

•If average attendance were to rise from the five thousand to the twenty thousand level for the forty games they are scheduled to play at home over the next three years (the years of Pelé), the team's gate would increase by up to three million dollars.

•The team could realize about $750,000 from the gate sharing on the road.

•International tours would give the Cosmos another $300,000 a year.

•Under the contract, Pelé would be a worldwide representative of the Warner-owned Licensing Corporation of America. At the time of his signing, LCA was already negotiating for Pelé endorsements of soccer shoes, track suits, toiletries, sneakers and games.

•Pelé's presence, it was hoped, would garner the NASL a nationwide TV package and might help Warner's Cable TV division. "Three, four, five years down the road," said Emmett, "soccer could be very important to us when pay cable comes into being on a wide scale."

In light of these considerations, one might say that Warner executives were, after all, shrewd negotiators.

Even Secretary of State Kissinger, himself a fan of the negotiating table, sent a telegram through diplomatic channels to Brazil and to Pelé: "Should you decide to sign the contract, I am sure your stay here will substantially contribute to closer ties between Brazil and the United States in the field of sports."

The influential Brazilian newspaper *Folha de São Paulo* ran a banner headline, commenting on the influence of Kissinger: "Kissinger roots for Pelé."

The reaction throughout South America was widespread and varied. Rio de Janeiro's *O Globe* newspaper printed a poll it had taken. A twenty-one-year-old student was quoted as saying: "I think he should play for Brazil and not the United States. If he doesn't play for Brazil, he doesn't play for anyone." But in the same poll, a fifty-one-year-old public servant countered: "I think it's great. The idea is to roll in the money to stabilize his life. Money is the bread of the world."

Editorials appearing in South American newspapers were equally varied. The popular *O Estade de São* Paulo said in its main editorial: "For the first time in eighteen years, the ambitious dream of the man overpowered the frigidity of his myth, causing him to fall into contradictions. The myth always said that Pelé was famous for being a man who kept his word. Nevertheless, some North American businessmen, always smiling behind their enormous cigars and millions of dollars, changed his mind."

But Pelé gained support in an editorial from *Ultima Hora,* a paper in Rio: "Finally the King will drill into the United States some love of the soccer ball. Pelé will possess all of heaven and earth in New York."

On June 9, Pelé was in Bermuda. There he signed a contract with Warner Communications, which, according to wire reports, would tie up his playing time with the Cosmos and channel his promotional activities through Licensing Corporation of America. Still, as far as the average fan was concerned, the formal signing was set for the following day at the 21 Club. What happened at the 21 Club in the Hunt Room far surpassed any press conference ever staged for an athlete of any sport.

As usual, Pelé was late, giving the reporters, photographers, and the invited guests time to partake freely of the liquor and small sandwiches. Some of the photographers were already jockeying for space where they could get their pictures and get out in a hurry. Others forgot about their jobs and were busy drinking and eating. The members of the media were getting uglier as they waited for the king of soccer to arrive, which he did three quarters of an hour after the originally slated time. Warner Communications security men had their hands full trying to keep order in the room.

Pelé, wearing a black silk brocaded lounge suit with white shirt and red and black tie, came into the room to be introduced to the press. With him was his wife Rosemarie, looking trim in a tight-fitting purple blouse and skirt.

Almost immediately some of the photographers jumped up, blocking the view of their comrades. A Brazilian photographer and an American photographer suddenly traded blows, with glasses flying all over the room. It looked like an official signing would never take place as others started to join in, making sure that justice was done. Pelé looked disturbed but not as much as the Club 21 proprietor Peter Kriendler, who had never expected the crowd to be as large as the three hundred who packed the room.

Pelé tried to calm the battlers, but it was five minutes or more before cooler heads prevailed and the press conference was allowed to begin. Still the photographers and the reporters were battling for the right either to take pictures of Pelé being kissed by Rosemarie, or to ask their own questions.

The Cosmos were trying desperately to settle the crowd down and John O'Reilly, the team's public relations man, kept saying over and over again, "We *must* have order. Let us have order! We can not go on unless we have order." At one time he even threatened to pull Pelé out of the press conference. Finally, with the exception of one or two stubborn reporters who kept demanding that Pelé reveal how much money he would receive, the proceedings started to flow in a somewhat normal manner.

To the all-important question of why he was going to play again, not in Brazil but in the United States, Pelé answered, "Everybody has a mission. Everybody has a goal. It was my dream that the United States would some day know soccer as does the rest of the world. I feel I can do something to help soccer grow in the United States. That is my goal."

The few reporters and columnists who started the afternoon by barraging Pelé about the financial aspects of his contract finally had their chance when one of them yelled: "Why can't you tell us how much you're getting? Other athletes do."

Pelé had an answer which silenced them for a time. "The confusion is with the press," Pelé said. "The press says I get one million, four million, nine million. I cannot say. The contract is very involved with many clauses."

Pelé was then asked how he could perform brilliantly at the age of thirty-four.

"If you take care of your body as I have," answered Pelé, "it is possible to play until you are forty-five or fifty. My talent is the gift of God—I am only what He made me."

The flow of the interview went to Pelé's willingness to play with the Cosmos, a team that couldn't be considered a world class team.

"On every team," answered Pelé, "there are great players, good players and just players. I have seen the Cosmos. We have all classes of players. If as I said before the Cosmos hope that my coming to them will automatically result in a championship then they are mistaken. Every player on the team must work and be willing to work together to build a strong team."

When the press conference ended, it took forty-five minutes to get Pelé to his car; some of the press who were hanging around waiting for the bus to take them to Philadelphia that night for the game between the Cosmos and Atoms stood around and talked to Zoca as well as to Bob Beyer. Beyer later recalled part of the conversation. Pelé, although he doesn't endorse liquor, will occasionally take a short slug. He also hates cigarettes, and on one occasion while in New York with Santos he went to an extreme to prove why he feels they're bad for people. While in a restaurant with several of his Santos teammates and Bob Beyer, he asked for a cigarette, saying, as Beyer reported, "I bet you think I don't know how to smoke. Give me one and I'll show you." Then after taking one puff he started choking—not in jest but in earnest. "Some of us at the table," said Beyer, "were really worried that he would choke himself. Since then I've never seen him smoke again—a cigarette or anything else. Pelé certainly respects his body all the way."

While Pelé was back in the hotel getting some rest, the foreign reporters flashed the news home of his formal signing. The inevitable criticism emerged the following day. A leading Brazilian columnist claimed the multimillion-dollar player returned to professional soccer because he was in deep financial trouble. Another reinforced this, saying that not only was Fiolax filing bankruptcy, but that two previous Pelé-backed companies, Sanitaria Santusta and Planasa, had cost Pelé a great deal of his own money. Another Brazilian newspaper criticized Pelé for not appearing in an exhibition game on the night he was on his way to Philadelphia with the Cosmos, saying that Pelé was fearful of being booed by the fans who had loved him so much for so long a time. *Opiniao,* a weekly Brazilian magazine, said Pelé was lured back on the field by "nine million dollars . . . from the sky for a man who literally is on the verge of bankruptcy." Ibrahim Sued, a daily columnist for *O Globe,* said that he had information revealing that "Pelé lost plenty of capital on an unsuccessful business deal. The Cosmos came at the right time." Helio Fernandes, a respected publisher of the newspaper *Tribuna da Imprensa,* wrote in his column: "Pelé himself preferred not to play any games in Brazil before going to New York to sign with the Cosmos. He did not want to play because he was afraid of receiving a colossal booing from the fans."

But probably the most devastating headline that hit the papers that day appeared in *O Estado de São Paulo* and simply said: "June 9, Brazil's First Day Without Pelé."

17 IN A COSMO UNIFORM

Brazil no longer had Pelé, but the United States did. Pelé was now ready to see his new teammates in action in a game at Veteran's Stadium in Philadelphia the very night of June 9. The owners of the Atoms had been informed a few days earlier that Pelé would be at the game only as a spectator. In an effort to try to get their fans to understand this they offered refunds to all those who had purchased tickets with the intent of seeing Pelé perform. Still, a crowd of 20,124 showed up, twice the usual Atom home crowd. Pelé was given a standing ovation as he walked onto the field. A young girl presented him with a beautiful bouquet of flowers and after kicking out the first ball Pelé trotted to where his new teammates were sitting to have a few words with them. Then, in the company of security men, he went to the owners' box high atop the stadium to watch the New Yorkers play what may have been the worst game of their five-year history. Pelé shared the dignitary box with Professor Mazzei, who had been placed in charge of whipping the Cosmos into peak physical condition. Also in the box were Pelé's wife, Mazzei's wife and Xisto. The party, including many of Pelé's closest friends, had arrived in five chauffeur-driven limousines. As soon as the game was over, Pelé headed for the dressing room downstairs and then into the special press room where he would be interviewed by the Philadelphia scribes. Then it was on home, long before the team would be coming back to New York.

Upon entering his suite in the Essex House, Pelé and Professor Mazzei got together over the notes they had been making all through the Cosmos 1–0 defeat. Pelé was polite enough to stop for a few minutes when the New York press got to the hotel. In evaluating the game he had just seen, Pelé maintained his policy of never criticizing a teammate in the open:

"As was the case with the Vancouver game, which I saw two weeks ago, I found the Cosmos have a number of good players but their style is too individual. I thought the Cosmo defenders played well but their forwards were too slow. They were disorganized on the field and they didn't play well together as a team.

"I feel from what I have seen here the game is more of a running game, where in Brazil it is more technical. But that doesn't mean that you can't use the technique that you have."

The following day Pelé and Mazzei met with coach Bradley and went over some of the ideas they had. It was agreed that Pelé would work out with the team Thursday at Hofstra University on Long Island. He would then play his first game as a member of the Cosmos on Sunday in a special exhibition game against the Dallas Tornado. The Tornado featured Kyle Rote, Jr., the son of an American football hero. The younger Rote had turned away from the grid sport after his first year in college and is now one of the leading players in the North American Soccer League.

On Thursday morning Pelé arrived at Hofstra University. Since it was raining very hard, the team had switched their practice indoors. Pelé seemed confused, since in Brazil a practice session is held where it is scheduled, rain or no rain.

By the time Pelé donned his green sweat suit the Cosmos were well into their workout. Having gone through their warm-up drills, they were in the process of kicking the ball around on the basketball court which had been converted into an indoor soccer pitch. Pelé was accompanied into the gymnasium by Pedro Garay, Pelé's assigned body guard, and by Professor Mazzei, who made sure that Pelé did not interfere with ongoing practice. Pelé ran around the outer fringe of the basketball court and then went through a series of amazing limbering-up exercises. He ran, sprinted, jogged, did his push-ups and knee bends, and then amazed the crowd when he lay on his back and—with Professor Mazzei holding his legs straight—proceeded to touch his toes with his head.

"That is one of the reasons why Pelé is Pelé," Mazzei explains. "He has the strongest abdominal muscles I have ever seen. It's these muscles which are the key to every good soccer player. Without strong abdominal muscles a soccer player can't be a complete player."

Pelé joined his teammates for practice and seemed embarrassed as every player on the club stopped what he was doing and applauded. "He wants to be treated just like every other player," Mazzei said. "He doesn't like it when his own teammates clap and shout for him."

Pelé played a small four-on-a-side pickup game and then took part in a full-court, six-on-a-side indoor game in which he played very well and had a chance to score an easy goal against Sam Nusum, a member of the Bermuda National Team, who was then the starting Cosmo goalie. However, seeing that his shot could have decapitated Nusum, Pelé just smiled and pulled his shot back. "Thank God he didn't shoot," said Nusum later.

After he had been given time to shower and dress after the workout, Pelé spotted a group of youngsters who had been held back while Pelé was interviewed by the working media. One of the youngsters gave Pelé a ball and the greatest soccer player of all time immediately broke into a loud laugh.

"You know what I would have given to get a ball like this for myself when I was very young? This is one of the nicest gestures anyone has ever done for me. It reminds me of all those American youngsters who wrote to me when I was busy making up my mind if I would or wouldn't come over here to play with the Cosmos. Don't fool yourself. The letters they wrote to me asking me to come over here had a lot to do with my finally saying yes. Imagine, American children writing to me in Brazil telling me that they wanted to see me come over here and play soccer for the Cosmos. I bet there were many of them who had never seen a professional game before, but they were interested and they took the time to write to me and for that I will always be most thankful."

Pelé was asked by one of the youngsters how many goals he would score while playing his first season for the Cosmos.

"I told those at that big press conference," Pelé said, this time without the aid of Mazzei as his interpreter, "that I would score maybe fourteen or fifteen goals in the fifteen games we still have to play. Mr. Toye told me that maybe I should put that down on a piece of paper in my own writing but I refused," he added with a smile that could calm a lion, or at least an angry opponent.

Pelé was told by a reporter that his English was getting better and he revealed that he was taking lessons and soon would soon answer all questions in English.

The following day Pelé was one of the first of the Cosmo players to arrive at Randalls Island for a brief workout. Pelé was brilliant as he took to the Randalls Island pitch with enthusiasm and skill. He dribbled the ball in the way that fans across the world have come to expect of him. He sent his forwards up the wings and then hit them with pinpoint passes. To top off the practice session he put one of his patented somersault kicks into the upper corner of the goal.

"I don't think anyone who comes to the game will be disappointed in the way he performs," said Professor Mazzei as the pair left the stadium locker room for a luncheon appointment.

Indeed, the Cosmos, and the rest of the world waited . . . for the Sunday, June 15 game against Dallas and the start of a new chapter in the long history of Pelé.

Soccer had never received such widespread coverage in the New York area, or for that matter anywhere in the United States, as it did in the six days leading up to Pelé's first game as a member of the Cosmos. Pelé was being photographed everywhere he went. His pictures were plastered in the local newspapers. He was interviewed time and again and tapes, sometimes heavily edited and translated, were on almost every radio station. Film clips of some of his great world-class moments were televised nightly, while the Cosmo office scrambled day and night trying desperately to fulfill ticket requests for working press credentials not only from the American press but from the foreign press. At game time, the press alone would number in excess of three hundred. Special seating and standing arrangements had to be made to accommodate the regular television crew which would broadcast the game live throughout the United States and Canada. TV Globo would also send the game to South America and on feed to some fourteen foreign countries. Special telecopiers were rushed in so that the world press would be able to flash the result not only of the game, itself an important exhibition match, but of Pelé's moves before, during and after the game. If one entering Randalls Island a few hours before game time thought he was in the wrong place he might well have been excused, since on the field were a couple of men busily painting the bare spots on the bumpy field with green paint so it would look better on television. More than one player that afternoon was to come into the dressing room after the match and find a nice green stain on the back of his jersey. To say the least, Pelé made things happen on the day he donned his Cosmo uniform, for not one of the reporters who had come to Randalls Island that morning could remember seeing anyone working to improve the field—until Pelé became a Cosmo.

Pelé ate with the rest of the Cosmos and then arrived at Randalls Island about two and a half hours before kickoff. He had eaten his usual pregame meal of steak, with a little bone and fat to make it more appetizing. He appeared to be nervous as he entered the Cosmo dressing room accompanied by Mazzei and a few others, including Pedro Garay, his bodyguard, and Louis Luca, who is head of security for Warner Communications. Pelé stopped just outside the door to once more sign an autograph for a youngster who reached out to touch the sheepskin red jacket Pelé was wearing, a jacket he had purchased for $210 along with a white one and a blue one a month earlier in Istanbul. Police reported that traffic was already starting to build up in the area and many cars were seen turning back to avoid getting shut out of the parking lots. Their occupants were now racing home in order to catch the game on television.

Inside the stadium, Brazilian and Santos banners and flags were waving. There were signs saying "Thank You Brazil" and others saying "Happy Father's Day Pelé." As Pelé emerged from the dressing room tunnel he received a tremendous ovation. New York City Mayor Abraham Beame stood and applauded loudly. Pelé was a happy man, waving to the crowd, throwing kisses in all directions. Rosie was nervous before the game got under way, holding her mustard-colored "worry beads," which perfectly matched her outfit. The pregame ceremony called for Pelé to present Kyle Rote, Jr., with a Brazilian flag while Kyle in return would give Pelé an American flag. Now after the formal introductions the game was set to start and a new chapter in Pelé's life would start to unfold.

The Cosmos appeared lost in the opening phases of the game. Pelé would go one way, expecting a pass or a teammate to cut in a certain direction. But the teammates he now had were not the Santos teammates who had become familiar with his every move. This rendered most of his moves virtually useless. He adopted the role of a traffic cop, directing the flow of play, pointing to where he wanted one of his teammates to go, where he wanted the ball to be passed and urging his men to utilize the wings. With nine minutes gone Dallas took a 1–0 lead as Alty McKenzie broke away for an easy tally. Six minutes later Pelé showed that, although only five feet seven, he can out-jump most taller defenders. He leaped high and belted a bullet-like header which hit the crossbar and bounded away. Dallas goalie Ken Cooper played the role of spoiler brilliantly as he made two diving saves on shots by Pelé late in the first half. Next, the Cosmo defense gave the Tornado a goal. David Chadwick had come in alone and when his shot was partially deflected the Cosmos' Mike Dillon, from England's Tottenham Hootspur, accidently pushed it in past goalie Sam Nusum.

The Cosmos went into the locker room at half time trailing 2–0. It was obvious that Pelé would have to abandon his traffic-cop role and help his teammates bring the attack to the Dallas goal. In the locker room Pelé was an inspiring force. He kept telling the players that being down 2–0 wasn't the end of the game.

With twelve minutes gone in the second half Pelé fed a thirty-yard pass to Julio Correa, the diminutive five-feet-four Uruguayan. Then, in contrast to the first half of the game, he got the ball back in the perfect execution of soccer's give-and-go play known as the wall pass. Pelé dribbled the ball about five yards and then spotted Mordechai Shpigler, a member of the Israeli World Cup team of 1970 and more recently a player whom the Cosmos had obtained after he played in France. Shpigler knew exactly what was in Pelé's mind as he raced downfield and perfectly trapped Pelé's lofted pass to send an easy shot past Cooper. Because soccer did not stop even for television commercials (something that the North American Soccer League was able to change later in the year as they allowed a thirty-second break when a goal kick was declared), a good portion of the play was lost to the viewing audience. With a goal on the scoreboard, the Cosmos pressed the attack. With 20:54 gone in the second half, Shpigler sent a perfect cross to Pelé, who outleaped three Dallas defenders before sending a twisting head shot past Cooper to tie the score.

Despite elaborate security precautions, many fans and photographers raced onto the pitch to mob Pelé as he jumped for joy with the 1221st goal of his professional career.

The game ended in a 2–2 deadlock. A statistical breakdown revealed that Pelé handled the ball seventy-five times, completed fifty passes, took nine shots on goal and had the ball taken away from him only five times. He was fouled five times by the Tornado defenders while committing only one foul himself. A press conference was held in the runway leading to the field after Pelé had a chance to cool off.

Kyle Rote, Jr., was the first to address the press conference, even as some fans who had gotten wind of the conference chanted "Pee-lah." Kyle received a good hand from the onlookers as he approached the microphone. In his calm voice he said, "Pelé has great skills. He handles himself very well out there. What amazes me is the way he uses his peripheral vision. He knows where everyone of his teammates is at all times. He didn't use that great speed of his too often but I'm sure that within a few weeks he'll be almost as fast as he always was. And of course he's tricky out there. He has some moves that I have never seen before. The heel pass is not an easy pass to master but he performed it brilliantly. An opponent of his can certainly learn something playing against him. I look ahead to once again playing against him although I'm not sure that our goalie [Ken Cooper] is so eager. Ken played a great game—if he hadn't, then we would have been beaten."

Pelé took time out to acknowledge Rote's ability as he said, "To see an American-born boy with such good soccer skill is very pleasing. He really surprised me with some of the moves he made out there."

Zoca said that he knew "my brother was very happy to be here today." Meanwhile Rosie broke her usual silence, coming out with the statement that "yes, the game and the occasion were very exciting. I'm sorry but that is all I can comment on now." Pelé has been known not to like his wife to make statements in public too often.

After the game, Mazzei was asked to give an evaluation of Pelé's performance. The man who had been closer to him in the past decade than any other on or off the playing field said, "All the other ingredients are still there. He played better in the match than I had expected him to, since you have to remember he has had only two workouts with the team. He's ahead of the schedule I had worked out for him and I would say that right now he is about seventy-five to eighty percent of top efficiency. He also completed almost every type of play that he should be required to in a match, such as the quick heel pass, the lofted pass right on the head of a teammate, the swift behind-the-back shot, the trap and quick release and the instep and outside-of-the-foot kicks. To me he did everything and maybe even more than the fans could have expected of him. To me he was Pelé. That's all."

The Cosmos' next home game was scheduled for the following Wednesday night at Randalls Island against the Toronto Metro-Croatians, a team which has been known to knock down an opponent when they cannot get the ball in a fair tackling situation.

The Cosmos' front office and their staff at the stadium were completely unaware of what to expect, for the Toronto game was coming just three days after the Dallas game. Before the contest Cosmo officials were predicting a crowd of some 15,000. But an hour before the game, with Pelé already in the dressing room, it was obvious that there was going to be a complete sellout of 22,500. Traffic was backed up for at least five miles and police had tried to direct the flow of traffic from the Triborough Bridge to other avenues away from the one feed road into the stadium. But many of the drivers, waving tickets in the faces of the police, refused to leave the long lines and decided to wait. Many of those who had chosen to wait didn't get into the stadium until the second half got underway. The crowd was once again in a holiday mood as they waved their banners and flags. When the Cosmos took to the field, Maria, Pelé's old Santos teammate, started his custom of spotting the Brazilian and Santos flags and then running over to Pelé to point them out to him. Pelé would acknowledge the flags and wave to those fans holding them.

The game itself was not one of Pelé's better efforts. Numerous times he came in for what appeared to be sure goals only to shoot the ball either wide or over the crossbar. But his passing was flawless and his teammates often found themselves free. The first half ended scoreless. But in the dressing room, Pelé told his teammates that since he was being covered by two and sometimes three defenders, they should be able to get in for some clear shots once he passed the ball to them. With twelve minutes gone in the second half, English-born Barry Mahy passed to Julio Correa, who banged the ball home. With sixteen minutes left to play in the match, the Cosmos iced the victory as Pelé passed to Maria, who fed the ball to Correa, who in turn gave the ball back to Maria. By now the Toronto defense was caught completely asleep and all they could do to prevent Maria from scoring was to foul him. The crowd roared for Pelé to take the penalty shot which had been awarded. To their frustration, the shot was taken by Shpigler, who boomed it past Toronto goalie Zelko Bilecki for the final tally of the match. That the Cosmos only won the game 2–0 was a surprise as they completely dominated the action from the starting whistle.

After the game, Pelé was asked how he missed some apparently easy goal-scoring chances.

"The ball here is softer and lighter than it is in Brazil and if you hit it as hard as you do in Brazil it's going to go off on an angle and take off over the bar. It will take me some time to get my kicks adjusted to the ball, but I'm not really worried," Pelé explained, before commenting on the crowd as well as some of his teammates.

"It was nice to see all the women and children with their families here. I knew that we had a good crowd here on Sunday and I didn't know how many we would see for this game. When I came to America I said I had a dream, a mission and a goal to see the sport become popular here. I think these crowds in my first two games here prove that the game will be a success here.

Correa, who had been the brunt of many of the skeptical fans because of some earlier, erratic performances, came toward Pelé and said, "Playing with that man is certainly a lesson in soccer. Once I passed him the ball and I thought he was going to send it to someone else. Instead he gave me a signal with his hand and I moved where he told me to go. All of a sudden the ball was there waiting for me. It was almost as if the play was some sort of magic."

Pelé shrugged off questions about the Toronto defenders who had fouled him six times, twice knocking him to the ground.

"They were tough," Pelé said, "and that is just what I expected them to be. After all, they were playing in a league game and they wanted to win just as much as we did. I don't think anyone really wants to go out there and hurt me."

Gene Strenicer, who along with Emir Jusic guarded Pelé throughout most of the game, was asked to give his opinion about taking the Black Pearl.

"The way he trapped the ball and the way he was able to release the pass to his teammates was something that you read about. But until you get the honor of playing against him you can't believe the way he handles himself out there. I think he can do anything with the ball he wants to. He knows exactly where everyone on the field is at all times and that doesn't only include his teammates. Once he saw that one of our defenders was going to intercept a pass near our goal and he looked at this player's feet and headed to where the ball eventually was going. It's almost unbelievable but I guess that is why they call him the best ever."

Pelé's other names include the French La Tulip Noire (The Black Tulip), the South American Perola Negra (The Black Pearl) and the Chilean El Peligro (The Dangerous One), and the Italian Il Re (The King). After the game against Toronto he became known in American soccer circles as "The Missionary." The Cosmos were now ready to reap some of the dividends that Pelé's signing had given them. Through a unique arrangement with the North American Soccer League, the Cosmos would get a bonus of fifty percent of the gross ticket sales, above the team's pre-Pelé average for every game they were on the road. But two nights later, in Boston, Pelé came within inches of paying the ultimate price for his worldwide popularity.

Before Pelé joined the Cosmos, the Boston Minutemen had signed the great Black Panther from Mozambique, Eusebio. In Beantown, on the night of Friday, June 20, at Nickerson Field, the home stadium of Boston University, the two old rivals would get together for a game. Boston and the Cosmos had been bitter enemies for the past couple of years. Manning the goal for the Minutemen would be Shep Messing, an ex-Cosmo goalie with no love lost on his old New York organization. The Cosmos knew that a tremendous crowd would be on hand and that Nickerson Stadium did not have adequate security forces. The Cosmos sent their own security men up to survey the scene. Although ticket sales were going briskly, when the Cosmos asked for extra police protection they were told in no uncertain terms that hardly anyone comes to a soccer game in Boston and that the police department was shorthanded anyway. Nevertheless, the Cosmos were assured by the Minutemen that there would be ample protection on and off the field. However, just in case they would be needed, the Cosmos decided to fly in some of their own men. This would prove a smart gesture.

When the Cosmo bus arrived at the stadium the crowd was already starting to flock to get on line. The stadium holds 15,000 at best, but an hour before game time it became evident that there would be many more fans in attendance. Those with tickets who were stuck in the back of the lines could do nothing other than push their way into the gates leading into the stadium. Then some Boston operator decided to try to accommodate everyone in line. He motioned to the people in the stands to come over the walls and gather around the outer fringes of the field. The eager fans responded and by the time the Cosmos and Minutemen took to the field, fans stood five and six deep around the field with hundreds of others standing on the balcony overlooking the field from walks that were only used for students going to and from their dormitories. That the Cosmos let the game start at all is a mystery, for it was obvious that if the crowd were to get unruly, there would be no way for the limited security men on the scene to control them. One of the reasons later given was that if the Cosmos tried to leave the field before the game, or if Pelé didn't play, a full-scale riot would have broken out with many injuries. Pelé and the rest of the Cosmos were not as effective as they had been against Toronto since they were having trouble adjusting to the artificial surface of the field. The more highly skilled a player is, the more he likes to play on real grass. Some say that an artificial surface makes the average player closer to the better player.

With two minutes gone in the game Pelé was pulled down from behind and awarded a direct free kick from twenty yards out. Boston goalie Messing made a brilliant punch save of the shot and the crowd roared its approval. Messing later admitted that he was out to prove Pelé right when the star had been quoted as saying that the "first true great American soccer player would be a goalie."

Eusebio broke a scoreless deadlock in the second half as he was fouled by Pelé, and then converted his own direct kick from twenty-seven yards out, sending a cannonlike shot zooming over Cosmo goalie Sam Nusum's head into the upper left-hand corner. The Cosmos fought back and with eleven minutes left to play, Pelé scored the tying goal as he booted home a rebound from a shot by Maria. The crowd couldn't contain itself any longer. When Eusebio had scored his goal, a few of them came out and shook his hand and pounded away on his back. But when Pelé put the ball into the net they turned out by the hundreds and pounded away at him, knocking him to the ground. Some tried to rip off his shirt and shoes.

"I never saw a soccer crowd go crazy like that before," said Messing. "I saw Pelé was hurt and I came out to help him. This guy jumped me and I just pushed him off. Then the security men got there and helped him. He was hurt."

The public relations man of the Minutemen informed the press that Pelé, who was now taken off the field on a portable stretcher, was not hurt and that the stretcher was being used as a play to fool the fans, thus forcing them to disperse. The press, which had already flashed the news on the wire services that Pelé was hurt, quickly got to the one phone available to them and told their news desks to kill the story. Following the incident, the Cosmos walked off the field. When they returned ten minutes later they were informed by referee Paul Avis that Pelé had not scored a goal. The goal was disallowed, since Maria's shot had hit a fan standing near the goal post before bouncing back onto the field. Without Pelé and Eusebio, neither of whom returned after the incident, the fans settled back to see the remainder of the match. Mirko Liveric crashed into Messing at one point, and Shep started to go after him but thought better of it since it might have resulted in another riot. With ninety seconds left to play in regulation time Liveric took a pass from Maria and scored the equalizing goal, forcing the game into sudden-death overtime. Nine minutes into overtime, the Minutemen's Wolfgang Suhnholz took a pass from Don Welbourne and beat Nusum for a 2–1 Minutemen victory.

Dramatically, the press was informed by a fellow reporter that Pelé was indeed hurt and was limping with ankle and knee injuries. The extent was not known, although Pelé still planned to catch a plane the following day for Santos and a reunion with his wife and children. After a brief rest, they would all return to New York.

"I don't think the injuries are too bad," Pelé said, "but right now I'm in some pain. I don't think what happened should have been allowed to happen."

Pedro Garay, Pelé's bodyguard, recalled the incident in the hotel later that night.

"When I got to him the fans were all over him. I yelled to him, 'It's Pedro, it's Pedro,' and he looked up at me. I covered his body with mine and I took a few good kicks from some of those fans. Finally we were able to get someone to bring the stretcher over and get him off the field. He was really afraid that he would get hit again."

Mirko Liveric said that if the linesmen had made any calls against the Minutemen they would have been in trouble.

"With all those fans on the sidelines," said Liveric, "I think any linesman who called something against them would have been pulled back into the crowd and never heard from again. It was almost unbelievable the way the fans acted."

Toye was furious, informing the press that he would protest the game and ask for a replay on the grounds that the Cosmos' best player was not available for the remainder of the match. He also sent out a firm warning to the other clubs in the North American Soccer League.

"Only if," Toye said, "the men we send in advance to cities where we will be playing report to us that security regulations are expected to be enforced will we put Pelé on the field. But if our advance men report to us that they are not satisfied with the security arrangements, we will play the game—but without Pelé. These men will get there two or three days ahead of the scheduled game and they will thoroughly check out every phase of the security regulations. In the past we requested that certain security be set up. Now we are demanding it. What happened to Pelé was a disgrace. One of the biggest problems in Boston was that they oversold the stadium. We will not allow this to happen again in any league city where we are to play. It's simple. This is now our mandate to the other teams and to the league."

Dennis O'Donnell, the sports publicity director at the United States Merchant Marine Academy at Kings Point, New York, reported that one of his members of the Kings Point soccer team was in Brazil the night Pelé was mobbed. He informed Dennis that the people in the streets were angry and even at one time threatened to attack the United States Embassy. Pelé might not be playing in Brazil but he was a Brazilian, he was hurt, and the fans were angry.

Pelé spent a few days in Brazil. Instead of anger he now found that the Brazilians were indeed interested in American soccer. After his first game, local stories read to the effect that it was too bad Pelé had to play with such amateurs. He was far and away too good for his teammates. Two of the leading Brazilian magazines had given Pelé their front cover; one dressed him in a Statue of Liberty outfit and the other dressed him as Uncle Sam. Some of his closest friends told him that because the Dallas game would be shown on tape later in the day they had decided to get a local radio station to place a call to Bob Beyer's home and have someone at the house put the phone alongside the television station so that they could capture the excitement and action of the crowd. This was achieved at the cost of about $3 a minute, with the bill totaling almost $300.

Pelé took care of some of his business needs before returning to New York with his wife, daughter and son. He acknowledged that he was completely healed of the injuries incurred in Boston and that he felt the caliber of soccer, although still a far cry from top international competition, had improved tremendously since he had seen league games a couple of years earlier.

He arrived in New York in almost complete secrecy and was soon on his way to Rochester for a game against the Lancers who had been a bitter opponent of the Cosmos for the past five years. There was the usual press conference where the routine questions were asked. The obligatory signing of autographs, visits to City Hall and meetings with local dignitaries followed. An all-time Lancer home crowd record of 14,562 showed up for the game, and for a time it looked as if Pelé had a new teammate to perform with. Giorgio Chanaglia, a member of Italy's World Cup team, was trying to get his release from his Lazio team, and Toye and several other Cosmo officials had been in constant touch with Italy all through the day. There was even a uniform for Giorgio, who had expressed his desire to remain in the United States with his American wife in New Jersey. But about an hour before the Cosmos were to leave for the stadium and the Friday night contest of June 27, word was received that Lazio was not ready to sell the six-foot-two player who has one of the deadliest head shots in the sport today.

"That is too bad," said Pelé, "because I have seen him play and he could score goals for us. He is a fine player."

The Cosmos gave a brilliant performance, winning 3–0 in a game that would have been much more lopsided had it not been for the effort of Lancer goalie Ardo Perri, who made several spectacular saves. Pelé fell victim to Perri on three separate occasions as the

Lancer goalie came out to cut down angles and dove to either side with the grace of a ballet dancer. He showed great mobility as he would bounce right off the ground from one diving save and leap to either corner to deny another ball earmarked for the goal.

Pelé was directing the team, pointing to a spot and then hitting Liveric and Correa and others with pinpoint passes. Finally, with thirty-one minutes gone, Correa took a hard shot which hit the crossbar. In raced Pelé for the rebound, converting the shot with a header that Perri could only look at futilely as the ball went into the net.

"I don't know where he came from," Perri said after the game. "I was watching their entire forward line coming in for the rebound and I never saw him. He must have been about twenty-five yards back when the first shot was taken and then all of a sudden he's heading the ball into the net. He must have flown out of nowhere to score that goal. You can't take your eyes off him for a second. I guess that I was lucky making those early saves on him. I just decided to come out and throw caution to the winds. I've been playing against top forwards all my life, but, believe me, there is only one Pelé."

In the second half, Pelé put on a textbook demonstration of soccer skills with ball traps on his chest, his thighs and even one in which he stopped a flying ball with the back of his foot. So exacting was his performance that late in the second half one of the Lancers who had been guarding him stopped and applauded when the king chest-trapped a ball and let it fall to his feet where he connected on a long pass to Liveric without ever breaking stride. Pelé played the last fifteen minutes of the game as a midfielder, directing the flow of traffic. When Jorge Siega, a native of Brazil who had been living in the United States for fifteen years, converted passes from Correa and Shpigler to score the final goal, Pelé raced over and lifted Siega to the cheers of the rest of the Cosmos.

"I felt a lot better in this game than I have in the other three games I played for the Cosmos," Pelé told a press conference after the match. "And scoring that first goal certainly felt great. I think the team played very well. We were moving the ball better and slowing it down so as to let it work for us. In the first couple of games we were outrunning the ball. Now we're playing it the right way and making the ball do things for us. I was also very pleased with the defense, and their fine play enabled me to move up closer on the attack than I did in the beginning when I first joined the team. It was a difficult game with both teams fighting for every ball. I was fouled seven times and some of the fouls I feel were uncalled for, but I have come to expect these fouls in my career."

Cosmo goalie Sam Nusum lauded Pelé for falling back on occasion to stop Lancer breakaways.

"I saw him come back and with either a feint or a legal tackle just take the ball away from their great forward Frank Oddi," said Nusum, who remarked that while sitting in the team's hotel he had twice been approached by people asking him for his autograph thinking that he was indeed Pelé. "Pelé has been a great help to the entire defense with the way he is able to set up the wall we use against direct free kicks."

The Cosmos were in a good mood as they returned to their hotel after the game, especially when they were informed that NASL Commissioner Phil Woosnam had ordered their protest of the Boston game upheld and ordered a replay of the match.

While most of the Cosmos were just getting down to the breakfast table the following morning, Pelé, Mazzei and a couple of other Cosmo officials were on their way to Washington where Pelé was to meet with President Gerald Ford. The team would meet Pelé later that afternoon and get a brief workout for the next day's game against the Washington Diplomats.

The meeting between Pelé and President Ford at the White House was well covered by the American as well as foreign press corps. Both Pelé and the President seemed to have a good time.

President Ford officially welcomed Pelé to the United States in a brief ceremony on the steps in the Rose Garden. Then the two moved to the White House lawn where Pelé demonstrated his skill after the President said, "Show me how to do it."

Pelé bounced the ball several times off his foot and then gave it to President Ford, who failed to duplicate the move. Pelé asked the President to show him how to throw an American football and the pair lobbed the ball back and forth while the cameramen had a field day.

"I would center one to you but all these people, photographers and newsmen are just waiting for that," said Ford who was the center on the Michigan football team in the 1930s. Pelé then put on another show of ball control, moving it upward and outward off his forehead and then off his left shoulder, all the time never touching the ball with his hands. Ford made another attempt to bounce the ball lightly off his foot, à la Pelé, but the ball went forward instead of upward. "Maybe I can do it better with my head than my foot," laughed Ford. "I'm awfully clumsy. But I won't try it because they're waiting for that, those photographers and newsmen."

In his formal remarks, Ford said, "I've never played soccer so I'm not familiar with the game. I appreciate excellence. You are the best. I am sure that your presence will increase America's interest in soccer."

Pelé gave Ford a small green and gold Cosmo pennant and the president said it would hang in his private White House office.

Pelé showed some of his diplomacy when near the end of their meeting he told the President: "In your game you were one of the best. It was a great pleasure to be with you." Pelé then invited Ford to Brazil to see what he described as the best in soccer and Ford said that he would think about it.

The Cosmos and Pelé played their finest game of the season the following afternoon at Robert F. Kennedy Stadium. Playing on a new field which had never been used before, the Cosmos and Washington Diplomats drew a record NASL season crowd of 35,620. Pelé was brilliant, scoring two goals and assisting on two others as the Cosmos tied the NASL single game scoring mark by beating Washington 9–2.

After the game, Pelé lauded the new Prescription turf, which got its first use. "The minute I stepped onto the field," said Pelé, "I knew that we would play a good game. It's the best field I've ever played on in this country. You can really make the ball work the way you want to on this type of surface.

"Today we played the type of game that I felt we were capable of. We fell behind 1–0 but instead of just sending long passes upfield in the hope of getting the equalizer we worked the ball around. We passed more than we have done this season and at one span we completed fourteen straight passes before taking a shot. That's the type of play championship teams all over the world use. We were able to spot their weakness and take advantage of it. I'm proud of the way the men played and I promise we're going to get even better as the season progresses."

Pelé didn't get an assist on the Cosmos' first goal but he was a big factor in it. He fired a thirty-yard direct kick which Washington goalie George Taratsides deflected off the crossbar. The Diplomat goalie was so shaken that when he attempted to throw the ball out after catching it off the crossbar he threw it right at Correa who fed Shpigler for the tying goal. In the next twenty minutes the Cosmos added three more goals with Pelé feeding Fink for a goal from fifteen yards out. Then Shpigler scored and minutes later Pelé boomed a twenty-five yarder which twisted past the Diplomat goalie. Barry Mahy, off a pass from Pelé, and Maria on a breakaway made it 6–1. After Washington's Gerry Ingram scored the Cosmos went back to work with Pelé scoring on a rebound of a shot by Maria, Johnny Kerr firing in a thirty yarder and Americo Paredes, from Uruguay, scoring the last goal with twenty-five seconds remaining.

After the game Pelé held court for the press and some of the younger fans who were allowed into the dressing room. While speaking with the press he noticed Roy Willner, a former Junior College All-American at Cantonsville Junior College, who had spent a frustrating afternoon trying to stop his tactics.

"I have never asked an athlete for an autograph in my life," said Willner, "but after what he put me through this afternoon I've just got to get his name on my game program. Since our coach Dennis Viollet told me last week that he was putting me on Pelé, I've had a lot of suggestions on how to stop him. I got hold of some game films and studied his weaknesses. Believe me, it's useless. There's no way to stop that guy without knocking him down and out, but I'm not that type of player. Twice I thought I had him stopped before he was able to start downfield. Both times he made me look like a fool. Once he went right around me and the other time he feinted in one direction, went the other way, and I found myself bumping into one of my teammates. I've never seen a guy jump so high without running. I'm five feet seven, and that's about what he is and I've been proud of the way I can jump against even taller players but he was outjumping me. He's got tremendous spring in his legs. In fact he's got more spring in his legs than I ever saw before."

Pelé signed not one but three autographs, for Willner and some of the other Washington players who had come into the Cosmo dressing room to pay tribute to the king. One of the players was Randy Horton, who had been captain of the Cosmos before being traded to the Diplomats at the beginning of the season.

"That's the first time I ever played against him," said Horton. "He's everything and even more than they say about him."

Willner said after pocketing the autograph, "He's not only the greatest soccer player in the world. He's one of the nicest men I've ever met."

With hundreds of youths waiting outside the dressing room, security men linked arms around Pelé and escorted him to the safety of the team bus. Pelé still found a way to give a few of the youngsters autographs. He begged his security men to "be careful. Don't hurt the children." Outside the team bus the youths kept screaming, "Pelé, Pelé!"

"That's the future of soccer in this country," Pelé said. "That is why I am here. I believe the game will make it here."

It should be noted that the next time the Diplomats played at home they drew less than 4,000 fans.

The Cosmos then took their Pelé road show on a western swing, where they ran into trouble. Pelé was on national television the night before their July 3 game in Los Angeles against the Aztecs. Those watching the Tonight Show, this one without Johnny Carson, had to be amazed at the progress Pelé had made in mastering the English language. Along with Joe Fink, a Cosmo teammate, Pelé gave a demonstration that included his famous penalty and scissor kicks. He said afterward, "It was a lot of fun making those shots for the American people to see. It won't be so easy scoring goals on this trip as everyone now wants to beat the Cosmos and me."

The Aztecs drew 12,174 fans, a park record for them. Promptly, Pelé fed Shpigler to put the New Yorkers ahead 1–0. That was all the fans rooting for Pelé had to cheer about all night as the New York defense came apart at the seams and up the middle as the Aztecs put five straight goals in against Nusum, who had a terrible night. After the game Pelé said, "The way they played against us they could have beaten most any team in the world. They played smart and when they fell behind they didn't rush the action. It was not one of our better games and I am disappointed. We allowed their speedy men to break right through and our defenders were often caught going the wrong way. This was a game that you best like to forget."

Then Pelé was asked about the NASL rule which differs from the rest of the soccer world in that a player can't be called offside (that is, when he hasn't got two defenders plus the goalie between him and the goal when he's inside the opponent's end of the field) until he's thirty-five yards from the opposition goal. The NASL had adopted their version of the offside rule to prevent opposing defenders from coming up to their own midfield line to prevent the other team's forwards from entering into their attacking territory until after the ball had been passed to them. It had been hoped by league officials when they instituted the rule three years earlier that it would beef up the scoring, but it didn't.

"I played in over 1200 games under the worldwide offside rule, and when I signed with the Cosmos and found that their league offside rule is different from that in the rest of the world I was worried that I wouldn't be able to adjust. But now after playing six games I feel very confident. I think the rule creates more offensive action while in the rest of the world the trend has been toward more defensive soccer. I think the fans come to see goals and more attempts at possible goals and this rule gives them that opportunity."

Now the Cosmos were off to Seattle for a nationally televised game against the Sounders, and Pelé was not overjoyed when he found that the game would be played on artificial turf. He relaxed in the hotel the day before the game and wrote another chapter in his amazing life history.

Pelé, who likes to fish whenever he gets the chance, was in his second floor suite with Professor Mazzei. Having heard that there were fish in the harbor surrounding the motel, the two decided to throw their hand-fashioned rods and reels out the window. Within a few minutes Pelé was screaming. He had latched onto something and he reeled it in. It was a two-and-a-half-foot baby sand shark. Minutes later he started to reel in a four-footer, but as the shark was almost in the window the line broke and the catch plopped into the harbor.

"I didn't know what was going on," said Louis Luca, the Warner security head. "All of a sudden Pedro [Pelé's body guard] comes running into my room yelling in Spanish. I thought that someone had come in and attacked Pelé. I got to the room and there were Pelé and the professor banging the shark on the head. I never laughed so hard in my life."

Since it was July 4 when the Seattle press conference was held, Pelé started the talk by announcing, "I am glad to be here on America's birthday. Who is playing baseball? I used to practice hitting a baseball. There was this group of Japanese men in Brazil and they liked to hit a baseball around. My father helped keep them in shape by training them and I took to hitting the baseball, sometimes. Most of the time in the beginning I would miss the ball when they threw it to me but it was always a lot of fun."

It was during this press conference that Professor Mazzei was asked just why Pelé was so good an athlete, and the professor answered: "Pelé would be a great decathlon man in the Olympics because he has the knack of catching on quickly to every sport he tries. Also while he's in training his heartbeat is 56–58 as compared to 90–95 for the average athlete. He likes to train and work hard and he has to be admired for that, since at thirty-four he is in better shape than a lot of athletes ten years younger than he is. He can still run the one hundred meters in about eleven seconds and that's really good."

Pelé would rather forget his performance on the field the following day, as the Cosmos looked terrible in losing 2–0 on the artificial field surface. The Cosmos, to the delight of the fans—a record crowd of 17,925—could do nothing right against the home Sounders. There were signs openly declaring that the Sounders were number one and Pelé was only number two. During the game Pelé became so incensed with a call that he received a yellow caution card, the first he had picked up in the NASL. After the game he complimented the Seattle players for playing a good game, but rapped the playing conditions.

"I was never so tired in my life after a game," said Pelé. "The heat was bad and my feet are still burning. The bottom of the soles of many of our players are blistered and part of my shoe burned off. You stand down there for a few minutes and the heat gets right to your feet and you can't play the type of game that you're used to on this type of field. Soccer was made to be played on real grass fields. There is a great difference between how the ball rolls and runs on a real grass field and how it travels on a field composed of an artificial surface. There are certain passing plays in soccer when you feed the ball to a teammate running downfield. The play calls for the ball to slow down so the man can catch up to it. But on an artificial surface the ball just keeps on rolling and goes out of bounds.

"A good example of this is the pass I tried early in the first half. The play was supposed to be a short pass, the lead type of pass to Jorge Siega who would then cross it over to me in front of the Seattle goal. But Siega couldn't catch up to the ball and the play was dead. On a real grass field I would have been able to put backspin on the ball but you can't backspin a ball and have it stop where you want it to on an artificial surface. I also find that it is very hard to make long solo runs on these types of surfaces, and it takes you longer to switch direction when you trap a ball."

When Pelé was informed that eight of the twenty league fields had an artificial surface he shrugged and said, "I guess that I'll have to adjust my game when we go on these types of fields but give me grass anytime. That is where soccer was meant to be played."

"I'll also be trying out a re-enforced tennis sneaker in our next game in Vancouver and this I hope will be able to give me some feeling that I'm playing on a real grass field."

Former English National Team player Mike England said that although he stopped Pelé, he felt that there was no guarantee that the next time the teams met he would be able to do the same.

"I kept watching his feet throughout the game," said Mike, "and I tried to outguess him. I imagine that I was pretty lucky and the field surface certainly didn't allow him to play his usual type of game."

The team went back to its hotel after the game just in time to catch the replay of the match. Pelé and the professor watched the action. Pelé seemed a bit annoyed as he followed the movement of some of his teammates on the screen.

"We didn't deserve to win the game, the way we played," he said after the telecast was over. "If we are to get into the playoffs we'll have to play much better as a team working together."

Before returning home for the resumption of the regular season, the Cosmos had to play an exhibition game two nights later in Vancouver, a game which didn't exactly suit Pelé or some of the other members of the team.

"Some of the boys, including myself, are pretty tired right now," Pelé said. "I'd rather get back to New York and rest up for our league game coming up, but since we have this contract for the game we'll have to make the best of it."

Pelé, as is his habit, took a quick cat-nap on the short flight from Seattle to Vancouver. Professor Mazzei remarks, "As long as I remember, Pelé has had the ability to fall asleep as soon as we were on the plane. That is why he often misses his meals in flight but we make up for it when we get where we're going and he has a good steak dinner."

Pelé and the professor received a great steak and lobster meal the following day at the home of Vancouver chairman of the board Herb Capozzi. The Whitecaps were going all out to promote the game. Cars and buses moved through the downtown area throwing out miniature soccer balls announcing the game. The hard work paid off as an all-time high Vancouver soccer crowd of 26,495 turned out for the game, which was won by the Cosmos 2–1 on artificial turf. Wearing his new sneakers, Pelé was brilliant not only on attack but late in the game when he broke up a desperate bid by the Whitecaps to tie the game in the final seconds.

Many who came to the game expected that since it was only an exhibition match Pelé would play the first half and only a brief part of the second. But although he was tired and the Cosmos were playing under a prearranged agreement for unlimited substitution, Pelé told coach Bradley that he felt fine and wanted to stay in the game. He set up the first Cosmo goal when with twenty minutes of the second half gone he passed to Correa who fed the ball off to Shpigler who sent a short shot past Vancouver goalie Peter Greco. The goal ended a Cosmo scoreless streak of two hundred and sixty-five minutes. Two minutes later, another Pelé executed goal-scoring play followed. Here he broke through defender Lee Wilson and passed to Shpigler, who booted the ball home. Pelé then went back on defense and aided substitute goalie Kirt Kuykendall who had started the second half in place of Sam Nusum.

"Even though it was an exhibition game," Pelé said, "it feels great to get back on the winning side after our defeats in Los Angeles and Seattle. It was a very good game. It was open and clean. Although the field isn't grass, it's a lot better than the one we had in Seattle. At least we were able to work on some good passing plays and that is what we will be doing hopefully on other nongrass fields. But don't get me wrong. I still don't like these types of surfaces."

Lee Wilson, who was assigned the task of guarding Pelé, lauded the king as he became another member of Pelé's fan club.

"Some of our players were telling me before the game," Wilson said, "that since this was only an exhibition game Pelé wouldn't go out there killing himself. After the game I told them anytime they wanted the assignment of guarding him, they're welcome to it.

"I was faked out many, many times. When I backed off him expecting him to try to dribble, he would put a loft pass right over my head onto the feet of one of his teammates. Then when I'd try and get real close to him he'd back off the ball to get a running start and then take off. I've never seen a man read the game so well in my life. After the game he came over to me and told me that he thought I'd played a pretty good game. I'm glad he told me so because I think he made me look like a fool in so many different ways. Many times I braced myself expecting him to come up with some fancy move and he'd anticipate this and beat me with a very basic pass play or a simple cut. There is no way in the world that you can go into a game against him expecting what every one of his moves will be. He's just got too many different tricks he can kill you with. That is why he's the best ever. He proved it to me here tonight and I think I came out of the game a better player for it."

The following morning the Cosmos departed for home. While waiting to board their plane Pelé was mobbed by a group of Japanese businessmen who were in Vancouver on a convention. They told him, through an interpreter, that they had seen him play with Santos while the Brazilians toured Japan. They claimed that soccer was really booming in Japan, and Pelé appeared pleased to hear about its growth. Finally the team departed with a one-hour stopover in Winnipeg, which led one Cosmo player to remark to the amusement of all, "I wonder if they've got time to get us another exhibition game."

Pelé never seems to tire of Maria's actions. Although he will not join in the horseplay, he always comes up with a smile or a laugh when his former teammate goes through his routine, which includes singing and dancing in the airport, helping elders carry their luggage to where they're going or even putting on an apron to help the stewardesses serve the meal.

"He has always been like this, ever since I first knew him," says Pelé, who recalled an incident when the Santos team was playing a game in Bogotá. "Maria was having a good time, dancing and everything, when someone asked him who he was. He got insulted because they didn't recognize him and he finally told them that he was the man who played with Pelé. Then they asked him where Pelé was and he told them that I was in the hotel because he said I didn't like to dance. That is not true. I love to dance as much as anyone else."

The Cosmos finally arrived home less than twenty-four hours before their scheduled Randalls Island game against the Boston Minutemen. They were a tired group as they collected their luggage at the airport. Pelé said, looking forward to meeting Boston and Messing, "I thought Messing did a wonderful thing when he came out to rescue me from those fans. "You have to respect a man who does that. I'll make it a point to tell him so before the game. But in no way will that affect my play against him. I'm going out there to win just as I am sure he'll be doing."

The scene outside Randalls Island the following night resembled a card-carrying convention. Many Portuguese fans from Fall River had journeyed into New York to see Pelé and Eusebio once again come head to head. There were signs saying "Lisbon Connection." Eusebio waved to the crowd and then waited inside the entranceway to his Boston dressing room for Pelé to arrive. Pelé stopped outside and signed his usual quota of autographs before coming into the stadium. Seeing Eusebio, he hastened his pace and the two hugged each other.

The game was a rough affair. The Boston defense caused the crowd of 18,126 to boo loudly as Pelé was continually knocked to the ground. Referee Gordon Hill was severely jeered when Pelé was tripped by two men inside the penalty area; play was allowed to continue without a penalty shot being awarded. Pelé kept throwing up his arms in disbelief that the referee was not calling fouls. Once Hill blew his whistle on a foul against a Boston defender on Pelé inside the penalty area, but instead of awarding a penalty kick he gave Pelé an indirect free kick. The Minutemen took the lead when with 5:54 gone Brazilian Fernando Nelson took a cross from Ade Coker and headed a shot past Nusum. Eusebio was devastating, as his cannonlike shots came booming toward Nusum. But with twenty-five minutes gone, Eusebio fell on the wet turf and was forced to leave the game. Boston was able to hold its lead and went into the dressing room at the half with a 1–0 advantage. The Cosmos, playing more aggressively, tied the score with fifteen minutes gone in the second half on a goal by Liveric. Ten minutes later Luis de la Fuente, a former Real Madrid player, put the New Yorkers in the lead on a twelve-yarder which sailed over Messing's head into the upper left-hand corner of the goal. Three minutes later Pelé electrified the crowd as he took a short pass from Kerr, faked two defenders and then fed the ball back to Kerr who blasted home the final tally in the 3–1 New York victory.

"Once Pelé got the ball on that play," Messing said after the game, "I thought he was going to let loose. Once he switched the play and fed the ball back to Kerr I had no chance to stop the shot since I had already committed myself."

"It's on plays like this," explained Professor Mazzei while tending to Pelé, who had just come out of the whirlpool, "where Pelé really excels. Everyone thinks he's going to shoot and he fools them with a swift return pass and the goalie is out of position. To me, Pelé played one of the best games he has played in the past year and a half. He gave a total effort on offense as well as defense and we won and now are back in first place."

Coach Bradley echoed Mazzei as he said, "Pelé played his best game for us tonight. He kept bouncing up from hard tackles and fouls and he was sprinting forty yards to take the ball away from a Boston attacker. It was his type of game. The man has this more than anyone I've known," he added, pointing to his heart. "He was incredible. He was being pushed away from loose balls and was fouled several times when he seemed to be on the verge of scoring but he didn't stop hustling. Many of his passes were right on target and would have resulted in goals but the wet turf was causing many of our boys to slip."

"I knew," Pelé said, "that even though we were down 1–0 at the half we could win. Their defense was slower than our forwards and it was only a matter of time before we would score. I'm sorry Eusebio had to leave the game so early because whenever we play against one another it's a tough battle. Sometimes it winds up with me taking him when he has the ball and other times he takes me. But after the game he came in to congratulate me.

"At the half I told our players that we were concentrating too much on defense and were giving the Boston attackers time to build up their game. Once we started challenging them more for the loose balls and pressing them when they had the ball we were able to take over control of the match."

Pelé was asked about the roughness of the game.

"At times it bothered me," he smiled as he replied. "But at times I enjoyed it. I think every player really likes to mix it up once in a while."

With no further games scheduled for a full week, Pelé and Professor Mazzei spent a great deal of time together discussing the Pelé business empire and plans they had for the postseason Pepsi tour, as well as formulating clinics in the metropolitan area. The team practiced three times at Hofstra, and whenever Pelé arrived with the professor in their chauffeur-driven car there were youngsters waiting for him to sign autograph books.

The week off seemed to work against the Cosmos. They took the field on Wednesday night, July 16, for a Randalls Island matchup against the Portland Timbers, who would eventually finish as the runners-up to Tampa Bay in the league championship. Before the game Pelé was just like any proud father as he carried his son into the stadium before joining his teammates in the locker room. Pelé was asked if his son might one day play soccer. The youngster has practiced with the old man on a piece of property adjoining their house, property designated strictly for soccer practice. He has shown such skill that there were several offers by major clubs to invest in the boy's future development.

"I want him to get an education, a good one," Pelé said after hesitating slightly before answering. "About soccer, I will give to him what my father gave to me, the knowledge of the game. If he wants to become a professional player one day I certainly won't stand in his way. But first he must get an education."

Pelé didn't mention that the boy's family background, where his father is the king of soccer and his grandfather was according to Pelé, "the best player in the world," is certainly in the youngster's favor in one day becoming a top star.

The boy has maybe unwillingly taunted his father on occasion, thanks to the pressure of some of Pelé's former teammates at Santos. Pelé went home one day, the story goes, and asked his son how he liked the soccer practice at the Santos stadium.

"You have the name but I have the talent," the youngster was reported to have told his father. Pelé's answer was never revealed.

The Timbers was the only team in the league that was not required to maintain a minimum of five American or Canadian citizens on their team, and coach Vic Crowe, himself the former pilot of England's Aston Villa, had raced over to his native land and grabbed up First, Second and Third Division players who didn't seem to have any better way of spending the summer. The three token Americans Crowe signed sat on the bench and watched. The Cosmos also spent their time watching that night, as Portland played a very conservative, dull type of English soccer and forced the Cosmos to duplicate their style. When the final whistle sounded it was 2–1 Portland, and Pelé was a bitter man even though he did score the lone New York goal.

"This was the poorest game we've played since I joined the team," Pelé remarked as he held interviews while sitting in the whirlpool bath easing an ache in his left thigh. "We did everything wrong. Portland might have won 2–1 but they didn't play much better than we did. Considering the way we had been improving lately I am very disappointed. But I'm not giving up. Even when I was at Santos there would be games like this, although not too often I'm happy to say. One of our more successful plays since I joined the team has been the pass I give to one of the other forwards and then run in for the return pass. Tonight there weren't too many passes being returned to me. A lot of our guys were losing the ball or kicking it poorly. It was very frustrating."

This was one of the few times in his career that Pelé was critical of his teammates' performances in public. Usually he saves the words for the players themselves in the privacy of the locker room.

Pelé lauded Nusum for keeping the New Yorkers in the game. Sam made five great saves in the opening fifteen minutes before yielding a goal to Peter Withe midway through the opening half.

"Sam can't be blamed for that goal," said Pelé. "The defense, which has been strong lately, messed up the play as they didn't see Withe free in front of our goal. By the time they spotted him and decided to try and cut off the man coming up the wing [Willie Anderson], it was too late and we looked bad. During the game we made mistakes that a professional team should never be guilty of. You just can't kick the ball downfield and hope you score. You have to work the ball downfield, make your passes to the open men accurately and try to exploit the opponent's weakness. We didn't do any of that tonight. And after we did tie the game we handed it right back to Portland. We made a foolish foul which gave them a free kick from thirty-five yards out, and we took too long to establish our wall against the direct kick. Their man [Brian Godfrey] found the hole in the wall and put the ball right past Nusum. I don't think Sam can be faulted for that goal either, as the wall should have been set up quicker—and of course better."

The one bright spot for Pelé was his goal which came fifteen minutes into the second half. De la Fuente slammed a thirty-five yarder, which appeared to hit inside the goal past keeper Graham Brown. But referee Peter Johnson waved play to continue, indicating that the ball hadn't hit inside the net. Pelé, following the ball, headed it in for the score.

"I thought the ball was in," de la Fuente said after the game, "but the referee missed it. I'm just happy that Pelé followed his instinct and headed it into the goal. It's only too bad that was the only goal we got all night. We all made mistakes tonight and Pelé let us know after the game how disappointed he was in our performance. When it comes from a guy like him, you listen."

The Cosmos next journeyed to Toronto for a Saturday night, July 19, game against the Metro-Croatians. Varsity Stadium was jammed to the rafters. Toronto went all out to attract a record-breaking crowd of 21,753, even while Pelé spent the day before doing film interviews and radio recordings. The Metro-Croatians acquired extra security, since a week earlier Toronto had been rocked by a soccer riot involving one of its amateur clubs. Cosmos security forces surveyed the scene and requested that mounted police patrol the area immediately behind their bench in order to prevent fans from bothering their players. Elaborate ways of bringing Pelé on and later off the field were worked out by Louis Luca and several Toronto officials. The team bus was surrounded by police as it arrived at the stadium for the game whose attendance probably saved the Toronto franchise from going out of business, as one Metro owner admitted.

At a pregame interview, Professor Mazzei mused, "Pelé feels at home wherever and with whomever he meets, otherwise he wouldn't be so outgoing. When Pelé is in Spain, the people there believe he is Spanish. When he is in England, they feel he is English and that goes for any place in the world he might be. Pelé, to me, is not an athlete. He is an international phenomenon, and that is why there has never been a Pelé before and I am sure there will never be another one like him again."

The Metro defenders who guarded Pelé that night showed no respect for the king, as he was butchered for the first time in a league game. Every time he got the ball there were two defenders on him, one pushing him from the back and the other tripping him. The field was soaked from two hours of rain. Pelé was received warmly by the fans but that was about the only kindness shown to him all night as Toronto's defense made him pay dearly for his flashy style of play. The Cosmos suffered a vital loss in the opening minute of play when captain Barry Mahy fell while trying to kick a ball. He had broken his ankle in the effort. Off the bench came De, a former teammate of Pelé, who had arrived from Brazil only a few hours before kickoff. De showed little on the field and it was felt that his weariness or perhaps the emotion of being once again with Pelé and Maria was the cause.

With 9:46 gone in the match, Harijan Hradvic fired a twenty-five-yarder at Nusum which the Cosmo goalie stopped, only to have the ball roll out of his hands onto the foot of Ivan Lukacevic, who booted home the rebound. As Pelé and the Cosmos pressed for the equalizer, Toronto goalie Zeluko Bilecki made two brilliant saves on shots by Pelé and Liveric, while his defense cleared two other shots off the goal line as they appeared heading into the net. Then Correa blew a wide open net as the Toronto keeper left his position and was caught flat-footed. The Cosmos came storming out for the second half. With six minutes gone in the period, Luis de la Fuente's high shot was headed off the far corner of the goal by Toronto defender Ian MacPhee. Four minutes later, Toronto scored the second goal with the help of a lucky deflection. Marino Perani fired a soft shot toward Nusum, who appeared to have it well under control when Peter Roe turned his back and had the ball hit off his backside into the goal past Nusum.

"I don't care what they say about that goal," said Nusum. "I swear he used his hands to help push that ball into the goal. The referee saw it but he was afraid to call the goal back."

As the ball went into the net, Pelé threw up his hands in disgust, drawing jeers for his actions from the Toronto fans who, of all fans who had come to see Pelé on the road, certainly showed him the least respect, even taunting him at times with bitter and nasty remarks such as, "Go back to Brazil. That is where you belong." After Roe's goal, Pelé put on one of his patented moves, dribbling right through one defender and then around another. When he started to pass a third defender he got a kick in his upper left thigh for his efforts by two separate Toronto players, sending him to the ground hard. Many felt that Pelé should come out of the game, but according to Bradley, "We were losing and since Pelé likes to lose less than anyone else he made his own decision to stay in the game. If he wanted to come out he would have signaled to me to take him out."

For the remainder of the game Pelé was ineffective as he started to run with a limp. His passes were as sharp as ever but he wasn't getting off his runs and he was steadily outjumped for loose balls. The Metro-Croatians wrapped up their 3–0 victory as Roberto Vieri converted a penalty shot called when Werner Roth, the captain of the United States National Team, fouled Brazilian Ivair Ferreira inside the penalty area with nine minutes remaining. In the dressing room after the match Pelé was in obvious pain, holding cold packs to his thigh. The kids waited outside for the king to emerge and even though he was in pain he still accommodated the youngsters who flocked to his side as he emerged from the dressing room. So security-conscious were the men hired by the Metros that Pelé's bodyguard Pedro Garay was knocked to the ground by two burly law enforcers and had to be restrained from engaging in a battle himself. Two of the special security guards employed by the Metros tried to stop Pedro from going into the locker room after the game. One hit him and another kicked him as he went down. Pedro was furious and only quick action on the part of Lou Luca, head of Warner security, stopped him from retaliating.

While the team waited in their hotel to depart for their next game in St. Louis, an exhibition affair, the Cosmo officials contacted St. Louis officials and advised them that Pelé would be unavailable to play. St. Louis, fearing a riot if Pelé didn't play by the 10,000 ticket-holders, asked the Cosmos to postpone the game. The New Yorkers agreed, and about two in the morning the players were informed that they would be going home instead of to St. Louis. They spent almost the entire Sunday in Toronto waiting for available airline passage to New York.

Later, Pelé was examined by Dr. Jeffrey Minkoff, who ruled that if he stayed off his feet until Wednesday, he could play that night at Randalls Island against San Jose's Earthquakes. Because the fans doubted Pelé would be in top shape, the game that night drew only 11,137. But those who turned out saw Pelé give a brilliant exhibition despite the fact that he was in pain for most of the game.

"There's still pain here," he said later, pointing to his thigh. "I need to put these ice bags on to keep the muscles from swelling."

The Cosmos were a happy and confident bunch after their 2–1 victory, achieved when they outshot the Quakes 4–3 in penalty shooting after the two clubs had tied 1–1 in regulation time and a fifteen-minute sudden-death overtime session had failed to resolve the deadlock. Kurt Kuykendall, the American goalie, survived a shaky start as he was given the starting nod over Nusum, while Uruguayan World Cup captain Juan Masnik saw his first action as a fullback since the team's opening game when he had suffered a knee injury which required surgery.

"Both Kurt and Juan played well," said Pelé, who himself had been an aggressive force all through the match. Jimmy Johnstone, the spark plug of Scotland's Glasgow Celtics, stands only five feet four, but he drove Kurt and the rest of the Cosmos crazy in the opening stages of the game with his daredevil dribbling, his nonstop running, and his sharp passing. With 18:20 gone in the match he faked Kurt out as the Cosmo goalie prepared for his anticipated shot. But Johnstone stood firm, opened his legs and let the pass from Boris Bandov go right through his legs onto the foot of Art Welch who booted the ball into the Cosmo goal. Pelé was passing well, but Liveric and Correa were losing balls they should have trapped with ease. Pelé showed his disappointment by yelling at them for making bad plays. Pelé came out for the second half with new-found determination, outjumping opponents much taller than himself, and fighting for every loose ball. With 4:48 left to play in regulation time, Pelé tied the game with a deft fifteen-yarder, forcing the overtime in which he was one of the four Cosmos who were successful in putting their penalty shots past San Jose's towering six-foot, four-inch goalie Mike Ivanow.

"I liked the way Masnik played on defense and the new player we got from Toronto, Brian Rowan, also impressed me," Pelé said. He was then asked to comment on Kuykendall's statement that the victory was owed to the Lord and that "whatever happens now goes to Him. God has raised me to play soccer. He's my best friend. I would have thanked Him for the opportunity he gave me even if I had lost the game."

Pelé refused comment, saying that "I don't comment on religious issues. If that is his belief, then he's entitled to it."

Two days after the San Jose game, Pelé was off to Dallas for an exhibition game against the Tornado. There was a hectic schedule of press conferences, a visit to the site where the late President John F. Kennedy had been assassinated, and the honor of being inducted as a citizen of Texas. He also appeared at the tryout session for the selection of a U.S. Junior Team. The Tornado had been going all-out for the match at Texas Stadium under the lights and a record-smashing crowd of 26,127 turned out to see and pay tribute to Pelé. Over five hundred youngsters were on the field. When Pelé asked what they were doing there before he trotted onto the pitch he was informed that they would bow to him. He almost refused to go through with the ceremonies, in which he would receive a ten-gallon Texas hat, as he said, "The children don't have to bow to me. They don't have to bow to anyone." Finally he was persuaded to trot onto the field and as Louis Luca ran alongside him, Pelé constantly asked his security boss "not to hurt the children. Please don't step on them."

Pelé said after the ceremony that he cried with joy.

"Seeing all those youngsters on the field bowing to me made me shiver. Many youngsters were yelling my name and the feeling was tremendous. It was one of the most emotional experiences of my life."

For seventy-two minutes Pelé thrilled the crowd with his running and passing. He outdribbled the entire Tornado defense which had come to him every time he got the ball. His accurate passes were of every type. Then suddenly he was upended as he broke through the Tornado defense, going down hard to the artificial surface, grabbing his left thigh. As he limped off the field he was given a standing ovation, and Tornado defender Albert Jackson grabbed him and hugged him, telling him that he "did what no man had ever done for soccer before."

The game was tied 1–1 when Pelé departed. He had played a part in the goal, feeding Shpigler who then blasted the ball past Tornado goalie Ken Cooper. After Dallas had tied the score, Pelé had again set to work and only some brilliant saves by Cooper kept the match tied. With six minutes left, Maria scored to give the Cosmos a 2–1 lead but then questionable calls by referee Toris Kibritzian enabled the Tornado to tie the score. He twice violated international rules in the final minute by stopping the clock with the ball out of bounds and then with five seconds remaining he called a hand ball infraction against De, giving Mike Rensaw a chance to tie the game on a penalty shot which forced the match into overtime. De and Masnik went after the referee and Masnik was ejected, forcing the Cosmos to play shorthanded during the scoreless fifteen-minute sudden death. The extra period came as a surprise to the Cosmos, since they had been informed before the match that should the game end in a tie after regulation time, no overtime would be played.

"I never touched the ball with my hands and that referee knew it," claimed De after the game, while Masnik had a few choice words for the decision. Pelé and Professor Mazzei were also disturbed.

"I was very upset about the final result, even though it was only an exhibition game," said Pelé. "I am happy that Maria scored what should have been the winning goal. But to have the victory and then lose it the way we did does not make me happy.

"It was very hot out there and even though it was evening the field retained much of the heat it had absorbed during the afternoon. I think that not only the players were uncomfortable but the fans also seemed to be bothered by the heat."

"I wonder if there really was a referee on the field during this game," said Mazzei. "There was someone running around out there making signals but I don't really think he was a referee."

Even the Dallas press took the opportunity to blast the referee's action.

Cooper lauded Pelé after the game, saying, "The pass Pelé gave on New York's first goal was impossible to believe. There was hardly any space at all, but he managed to find what little room there was. I feel that the Cosmos have improved tremendously since that first game we had against them in New York because now they're starting to anticipate Pelé's movements. I made a couple of lucky saves against him tonight, but three of his shots could easily have wound up as goals. It's amazing. Even though he was obviously not feeling one hundred percent fit, he never stopped driving and hustling all the time he was out there. That is a tribute to him."

When he left Dallas, Pelé felt that he would be able to play in the team's next game against Rochester. But Professor Mazzei warned that the injury might be more serious than Pelé believed it to be. Mazzei's fears were realized when, upon examination, Pelé was informed by Dr. Minkoff that unless he rested the injury he might suffer permanent damage to his thigh. Pelé was heartbroken. The Cosmos had just obtained English-born forward Tommy Ord from Rochester and still had a chance at the playoffs, but Pelé missed the remaining four regular season games, in which the Cosmos defeated Rochester 2–0 on two Ord goals, looked terrible in losing 3–1 to the Hartford Bicentennials, and then on national television in Boston, with the Minutemen's Eusebio also sidelined with an injury, the Cosmos were disgraced 5–0, which eliminated them from the title race.

"It was one of the worse exhibitions of soccer I have seen over here," Pelé said about the New York performance. He worked out the following day and was declared fit to play the season finale against Boston. But the morning of the game he felt a pull in the muscle and sat out the Cosmos' 1–0 victory.

The season was over but there was still plenty of action for Pelé, both on and off the field.

The Cosmos announced that they would make up an exhibition game against St. Louis and then journey to San Jose for another exhibition game before taking off for Europe and the Caribbean for a series of international matches.

Pelé also had some Pepsi-Cola clinic commitments ahead of him, as well as other pleasant chores—like signing two lucrative commercial endorsement contracts and acting as a goodwill ambassador for soccer in general in several other areas.

"We must immediately start building for next year and the championship," Pelé said after the final game of the regular season. "We can't wait for next year before we get new players and see who we will keep from this year's team. If we wait too long we will just be losing time. Every team must after a season evaluate its players and see what has to be done to strengthen a team for the year ahead."

18 AFTER THE SEASON

On August 10, Pelé returned to the Cosmo lineup as the club journeyed to St. Louis for an exhibition game against the Stars, a team consisting mostly of American-born players who had learned their soccer in St. Louis, the heart of amateur and youth soccer throughout the United States. Joining the Cosmos were two former Santos teammates Ray Mifflin of Peru, and Nelsi Morais.

The game was sold out as the Stars' field at Washington University bulged with ten thousand fans. Pelé passed to Ord who fed the ball to Liveric to put the Cosmos ahead 1–0 with eleven minutes left in the first half. But making a wholesale list of substitutions hurt the Cosmos in the second half as St. Louis stormed back on goals by John Carenza and John Pisani to win 2–1. After the game Pelé was disturbed over a decision by game officials which he felt had cost the Cosmos a victory.

"In the second half a referee took away a goal by Tony Donlic for no apparent reason," fumed Pelé. "Then on St. Louis's first goal Carenza pushed one of our defenders and then was able to put the ball into the goal because someone from St. Louis held our goalie's [Kuykendall's] hands. The referee or the linesman should have called the violation but didn't. Even though it was again only an exhibition game, I don't like to see us lose games that we should have won because of decisions like those. But I still feel the team played well and I am sure that Mifflin and Morais will help us now that we are getting ready for our extended exhibition tour.

"I myself felt no pain at all and the injury appears to have healed completely. I was able to perform all the actions I normally do during a game and I'm happy about that. I missed too many games late in the season, which saddened me."

St. Louis goalie Peter Bonetti, who once wore the colors of his native England in World Cup competition, and American-born Pat McBride lauded Pelé after the match, in which the king played the entire game full steam.

"When the ball goes to Pelé," said Bonetti, "you never know if he's going to shoot or pass the ball off. And the way he was running out there tonight reminded me of the time I played against him four years ago. He's still the greatest."

"I played against Pelé six years ago," remembered McBride, "and he hasn't lost anything in his game. He still is one of the most creative players in the game, and he can execute every move perfectly."

The Cosmos returned home for more practice. After one practice session held at Hofstra, Pelé and Joe Namath got together for a commercial endorsement announcing Pelé's introduction to the staff of Fabergé, a company that also features Namath in some of its commercials. Pelé and Namath joked, but while Pelé was quick to sign autographs, Namath didn't. Pelé seemed concerned when he found that Namath has a history of knee problem and told Joe, "I am lucky. Only a few times I was hurt bad enough to miss some games but never for too long a period of time." Pelé and Namath started throwing around an American football after Broadway Joe showed Pelé how to hold the ball. "I never thought that I'd be playing catch with Pelé one day," Namath said to the amusement of the onlookers, reporters, and photographers. Pelé then tried to bounce the football off his head and did quite well, while Joe wasn't as successful bouncing the soccer ball off his head. A good time was had by all in attendance that day and as Pelé left, Joe headed back to the other end of the Hofstra campus to join the Jets in preseason training.

The Cosmos started their extended trip by playing in San Jose. When the team arrived there, Pelé was kept busy giving interviews to the members of the press who had gathered for the NASL championship game won by Tampa Bay 2–0. Pelé was constantly photographed and queried by reporters and he told them he felt that American soccer was now on the rise. He was one of the guests of honor at the championship game.

The Cosmos played the Earthquakes on August 27. A standing-room-only crowd of 19,338 turned out and Pelé didn't disappoint them. He was all over the field, making his patented moves, leaving enemy defenders bumping into one another. But the Cosmo defense was also loose, giving borrowed goalie Ken Cooper little protection. The Cosmos fell behind with six seconds left in the first half when Ilija Mitic beat Cooper from seven yards out. Early in the second half Pelé set Ord up for the tying goal, but San Jose countered shortly afterward on a goal by Paul Child. Liveric was then fouled inside the penalty area and Pelé converted, tying the score at 2–2. Johnny Moore's goal won the game for the Earthquakes.

Pelé was asked about the American custom of teams hanging signs in their dressing room quoting nasty things other teams have said about them. He revealed that he does not think much of the idea.

"I think that America is the only place I have seen these signs," said Pelé. "And I think it works against your own team because instead of going out there to play your regular game you press too much."

The Cosmos took off for a three-game series in Sweden, and there Pelé was greeted by many who had seen him play in 1958 during his great World Cup performance. Almost every big official in Malmö, Sweden, was on hand as the Cosmos arrived, and although they lost their European opener 5–1 to Malmö, the crowd of 22,000 praised Pelé for his single goal. He started the drive on his goal by getting the ball near the midfield area and then faking out three defenders before scoring from fifteen yards out. The crowd rose to their feet.

Malmö coach Bob Houghton, formerly of England, said, "Pelé is still great. There is no doubt in my mind that at thirty-four he still can play in any competition in the world. He has moves that are amazing, but he can't do it alone. Watching the Cosmos play was like seeing eleven different individuals out there not working together."

"I am not disappointed that we lost," said Pelé who had just suffered his first losing effort in Sweden. "I have known about Swedish soccer for a long time and it is good. I expected this result since it is our first exhibition game in Europe. I expect the boys to learn from their mistakes and get better as the tour progresses."

Next stop on the tour was a game in Göteborg against the Swedish All-Stars. A crowd of 20,448 turned out to see the Cosmos win 3–1, with Pelé getting two goals and assisting on the other New York tally by Ord.

"Pelé! Pelé!" roared the crowd in Göteborg as Pelé leaped into the air, giving his famous goal salute after he had electrified the crowd with his second goal within a five-minute span. Ord, on Pelé's second goal, was seen to jump in perfect harmony as Pelé made his move outdribbling and outfaking three defenders before drawing the goalie out of position and lofting the ball past the outplayed keeper.

"After I scored my second goal," Pelé explained, "I remembered 1958 because it was then that the people in Sweden also stood and shouted my name. I feel good now because many of the people who saw me here now are the same people who saw me back in 1958 and many are children of those who had seen me in the World Cup."

The team went on to Stockholm for a game against the Stockholm All-Stars, which developed into an individual battle between Pelé and Jan Sjostrom. Pelé scored two goals, one on a penalty shot and another as he outdribbled two defenders and then sent a screaming thirty-yarder past the Swedish goalie. But Sjostrom was even more deadly, scoring all three goals in the Swedes' 3–2 victory. The tallies came against Bob Rigby, who was loaned to the Cosmos by the Philadelphia Atoms for the European tour. Pelé was presented to a blond-haired youth named Pelé. His parents had decided to give the youth that name after seeing Pelé play in the 1958 World Cup.

It was on to Oslo, Norway, for an exhibition match against Vaalerengen. Among those who turned out to greet Pelé on a rainy day was King Olaf, who joined the 16,667 fans who saw Pelé score twice and assist on another tally as the Cosmos won 4–2. After his third straight two-goal performance Pelé said, "I am happy with the way I have played on this tour since it shows that the team is adjusting to our new style of play. I am thrilled about the reception I got here and am looking forward to playing our next game in Rome against the strong Roma team. That will be a real test. Meeting the king was great."

Roma was just too strong for the Cosmos, beating the visitors 3–1 before a crowd of more than 60,000, which included many government officials. The loss dejected some of the Cosmos but Pelé tried to comfort them, saying, "Losing 3–1 to a team like Roma is no disgrace. Even we at Santos lost to them a few years ago when we played in Italy. We got experience and it was nice to see John Coyne score his first goal for us."

Four nights later the Cosmos were in Haiti to open the Caribbean phase of their tour and an SRO crowd of 25,000 was on hand to see the Cosmos and the Victory S.C. battle it out in Port-au-Prince. Pelé assisted on a goal by Americo Paredes. The Cosmos won 2–1 when Ord scored the winning goal with seven minutes remaining while Roberto Aquirre, who during the NASL season played for the Miami Toros, scored for the Haitians. But Pelé seemed displeased after the game as he told reporters, "If we had remained tied 1–1, in reality it would have been a defeat for us. We must win games against teams like these without so much difficulty."

The following night the Cosmos, playing before 24,000 who turned out on a rainy, stormy night, lost a 2–1 double overtime decision to the Violette S.C. on a penalty shot by Oscar Montironi, who wound up scoring both goals for the winners. Pelé was held scoreless. The lone Cosmo goal came when Liveric assisted Mifflin, who was now playing without the help he gets from Morais who came up with a knee injury requiring surgery. However, another outstanding Brazilian player, Pitico, from the Portuguese Santista team, was called into service.

"To call a penalty shot was scandalous," screamed coach Bradley after the game. "If we had been awarded penalty shots every time we were fouled inside the area, Pelé alone would have gotten at least three of the calls in his favor."

Pelé and the Cosmos went on to Kingston, Jamaica, to play Santos —not the Brazilian Santos team but the Jamaican Santos club. A crowd of 45,000 turned out while another 25,000 were unable to get into the stadium. Pelé, fouled by a defender, was forced to leave the game with a thigh injury. The opponent who fouled him was jeered loudly by the home fans although the Jamaicans did win 1–0.

Five days later, Pelé and the Cosmos had a field day in San Juan as the Cosmos routed the Puerto Rican National Team 12–1 before a crowd of 11,000. Pelé could have scored many goals but instead spent most of the time directing the flow of play and allowing some of the other boys to get into the goal-producing column. He wound up with one goal and three assists while Ord and Mifflin each had three with Liveric and Maria getting a pair each and Coyne the other goal.

"It wasn't much of a game," said Pelé. "But I understand the crowd was the best they ever had for a soccer game here and that makes me pleased."

Pelé came out of the game with a soreness in his thigh and sat out the scoreless tie the Cosmos then played against Violette S.C., much to the displeasure of the 30,000 who had squeezed into the Haitian stadium. The scheduled tour-closer against the Quebec selection team in Montreal was cancelled because of Pelé's injury.

Thus, in twenty-four games for the Cosmos, Pelé wound up with fifteen goals, bringing his lifetime total to 1235.

He returned to New York, where he signed a lucrative contract for Spalding, which announced that it was going into the soccer market with a new line of balls and shoes and other accessories.

Pelé and Professor Mazzei were then off for a Pepsi instructional tour during which they would attend the opening of the Pan-American Games in Mexico City, as well as the first leg of the South American Copa America championship in Bogotá. There they saw Pedro Zape, who used to cause Pelé all sorts of trouble, blank Peru 1–0 to give Colombia the upper hand in the series between the two nations. Peru, however, won the next two games 2–0 and 1–0 to win the title.

Schoolchildren in Puebla, Mexico, had a holiday when officials gave them the day off to attend a soccer clinic in town run by Pelé and Professor Mazzei for Pepsi. Before the clinic, Puebla Mayor Eduardo cue Merio made Pelé an honorary citizen of the city and then joined the children to see Pelé give his famous soccer demonstration.

When asked to comment anew on the caliber of professional soccer in the United States, Pelé said, "The level of the competition is inferior with the main problem being that the season in the United States lasts only five or six months and that is not enough to prepare and coordinate a team. But," he added, "the possibility of a longer season will change that."

Pelé had a good tour workout for Pepsi and says no matter how tired he gets he always seems to wake up and do his best when he sees the children coming to watch him.

"I love doing these clinics for them," said Pelé. "They love to watch me and then try to duplicate what they have seen. It's great fun for everyone. No matter in what country I go to give these clinics, children are children—the same the world over."

True to his word, Pelé started 1976 off with a clinic tour for Pepsi during which he visited Japan and then traveled all over Africa drawing thousands to see him perform his magic. The last stop on the tour was Nigeria and here Pelé became a victim of the aborted coup against the government. He was stranded in his hotel for a couple of days and then allowed to take brief workouts in the park. But for nine days he was detained in Lagos because the airports were closed to all commercial traffic. Even an appeal by the U.S. State Department and the Brazilian government proved ineffective, although such sports stars as Arthur Ashe and others were flown out to Ghana. Finally Pelé flew home to New York but his original plans to spend three days training with the Cosmos and their new coach Ken Furphy, a former top player and coach in England, had to be scrapped as Pelé had to fulfill obligations for Honda with whom he has an endorsement contract. Honda had flown businessmen in from all over the world for a meeting in Miami from which Pelé would then go to Brazil for a couple of weeks before returning to New York.

Meanwhile the Cosmos had signed a contract to play at Yankee Stadium. Their lineup had changed drastically from the team which played for them in Pelé's initial season. Gone were Maria, Juan Masnic, Julio Correa, Alfredo Lamas, Americo Paredes, Luis de la Fuente, Sam Nusum, Mirko Liveric, Johnny Kerr, Joe Fink and Mordechai Shpigler. Newcomers included former Philadelphia Atom goalie Bob Rigby and his teammate, fullback Bob Smith. They were joined by Dave Clements, a halfback who played with Everton of England and who was also the player-coach of Northern Ireland, and English defender Keith Eddy. The Cosmos hoped that the changes would strengthen their defense.

"I look forward to us not only becoming the championship team in the North American Soccer League but one of the strongest teams in the world," said Toye. Toye's enthusiasm is equalled by that of several other NASL organizations which have strengthened their rosters in the off-season. English star Randy Marsh was signed by Tampa Bay while Geoff Hurst, the hero of England's 1966 World Cup championship over West Germany, was signed by Seattle. The Los Angeles Aztecs were still trying to nail down George Best while Johann Cruyff and Franz Beckenbauer were being chased by several teams.

"I look forward to a great season not only for the Cosmos but for soccer in America," exudes Pelé.

19 THE FUTURE

What does the future hold for Pelé?

Brazilian soccer fans are still hopeful that Pelé will again don the uniform of the National Team and play in another World Cup. The next World Cup is scheduled for 1978, in Argentina, and that would make Pelé almost thirty-eight years old. Pelé does not appear as adamant about not playing in that championship as he was in 1974.

It seems Pelé has a desire to give the Brazilian people something in return for his leaving them as a player and then coming out of retirement to play in the United States.

"I will give it serious thought," Pelé allows. "It's still three years off but if I am in shape and if I feel that I can help the team, then I would consider it. That is all I can say now except that you must remember that I'll be nearing thirty-eight when the World Cup is held again. The competition in the World Cup is rough and unless I feel that I can contribute something concrete I won't consider playing."

Pelé has taken what many feel is one concrete step toward repaying the Brazilian people—not that anyone really feels that he owes them anything. On October 10 while in Guadalajara he revealed that he had been invited by the Brazilian soccer authorities to "play or work in forming Brazil's National Selection. I have gladly accepted the invitation to work in the preparation and selection of the team.

"I feel Brazil can again become world champions. It has many good players but they must be welded into a team and coordinated properly with a lot of hard work. I will do my best to help them accomplish that."

While touring with the Cosmos in Rome, Pelé revealed that he had rejected an offer from Santos to become their player-coach.

"Pelé has often said," explained Professor Mazzei, "that he will never become a coach of a regular team. But I think he wants to one day really become a top junior coach because he works so well and relates so well with the youngsters whom he trains. He has the ideal personality for coaching junior players. He has the knack for working with them closely, not like a professor telling youngsters that this is the way they have to do it, but on a one-to-one basis of relationship which is a credit to his great patience. Watch him conduct a clinic and you'll see that everyone is involved in what is going on. Pelé doesn't stand up there like a god telling everyone that his way is the only way."

Pelé was asked how much longer he expected to play.

"My contract," he said, "calls for me to play with the Cosmos through the 1977 season and then we'll see."

Friends close to Pelé are already insisting that if his health holds out and his desire is as strong as it was during his first year with the Cosmos, contract renewal will be very likely. He has already told some foreign reporters that he expects to be tied up with the Cosmos and Warner Communications for the rest of the decade.

One of Pelé's greatest wishes is to see the United States make the World Cup finals and he has offered his help along those lines.

With the United States having to depend on youngsters now coming out of college and those with only a few years in the professional ranks, wouldn't Pelé be the ideal man to coach the U.S. National Team?

To this, Professor Mazzei replies, "It's an interesting thought."

There is much in Pelé's future other than the regular schedule of games, exhibitions, clinics, endorsements and other business commitments.

"I still want to spend more time with my family," says Pelé. "My daughter is growing up and before too long I'll come home one day and she'll tell me that she's in love and wants to get married and I will have missed seeing her grow up. Now with the contract I have with the Cosmos as well as some of my other business arrangements

I feel I can spend more time with the family and take a regular vacation like everybody else. I haven't done too much of that during my career with Santos."

No matter what the future holds, no matter where Pelé goes he will not be free from the children wanting his autographs. It is also safe to assume that Pelé will take out his pen and write away until someone rescues him. That is Pelé the man.

There has hardly ever been a player who battled against Pelé who did not come away lauding the all-time king of soccer. It would be impossible to enumerate all of the accolades that Pelé has received from friend and foe alike. But three statements about Pelé seem fitting to be recalled here.

The first is from Angelo Asastasio, who was dropped from the Cosmos on the day Pelé signed his contract with the New Yorkers.

"As long as I can remember," said Angelo, "the name Pelé has meant greatness. When I found that he was going to be coming to play for us I was thrilled that I would now fulfill the dream I am sure every soccer player in the world has—that of playing with Pelé. However, circumstances prevented me from being on the same team with him. But I can tell you from my conversations with my former teammates that he has been the most inspiring thing that has ever happened to them. His patience in working with the younger players is something they will never forget. He encourages them to do the right things and if they don't he lets them know how they can improve. He may not be the coach or the manager but he's their inspiration now and always, no matter how long they play soccer. His inspiration is life-giving."

Celeste Nascimento, Pelé's mother, who still calls him Edson as well as her favorite nickname Dico, on the day Pelé announced his decision to end his retirement and play for the Cosmos, said, "As far as I can remember, Edson always wanted to become an idol, to prove himself to the world."

Dr. Athayde Ribeiro, the Brazilian soccer selection's former psychologist, offered his opinion about Pelé on the day he made his historic decision to return to the soccer wars.

"Ever since he was a child," said the good doctor, "Pelé was always seeking perfection, was overdemanding with himself and always unhappy when he did not find himself at the top."

Pelé today is as enthusiastic as he was when he first stepped onto a makeshift soccer field and kicked the stocking stuffed with rags. And although he walks today on the plush carpet of the world as compared to the rocky patches of turf of his poverty-striken youth, he still maintains his sense of perfection, and even more important, his simplicity.